A String of Flowers, Untied . . .

A String of Flowers, Untied . . .

Love Poems from *The Tale of Genji*

MURASAKI SHIKIBU

TRANSLATED BY
JANE REICHHOLD
WITH HATSUE KAWAMURA

Stone Bridge Press • Berkeley, California

Published by
Stone Bridge Press, P. O. Box 8208, Berkeley, CA 94707
TEL 510-524-8732 • sbp@stonebridge.com • www.stonebridge.com

Page design by Linda Ronan.

Front cover design by Peter Goodman using fabric generously loaned by Kasuri Dyeworks, Berkeley, California.

The translators are grateful to Kawade Shobō Shinsha, Publishers, for permission to use its edition of Akiko Yosano's translation of *The Tale of Genji* and her poems.

Printed in the United States of America.

10 9 8 7 6 5 4 3 2 1
2008 2007 2006 2005 2004 2003

LIBRARY OF CONGRESS CATALOGING-IN-PUBLICATION DATA
Murasaki Shikibu, b. 978?
[Genji monogatari. English. Selections]
A string of flowers, untied— : love poems from the Tale of Genji /
Murasaki Shikibu; translated by Jane Reichhold & Hatsue Kawamura.
p. cm.
ISBN 1-880656-62-0
I. Reichhold, Jane. II. Kawamura, Hatsue, 1931– III. Title.
PL788.4.G42 A27 2001
895.6'314—dc21

2002014998

Contents

	Preface	VIII
	Acknowledgments	XIII
	Characters from *The Tale of Genji*	XV
1	Kiritsubo: The Paulownia Court	1
2	Hahakigi: The Broom Tree	7
3	Utsusemi: The Shell of the Cicada	15
4	Yūgao: Evening Faces	17
5	Waka Murasaki: Young Lavender	27
6	Suetsumu Hana: Princess Safflower	39
7	Momiji no Ga: Viewing the Autumn Leaves	46
8	Hana no En: The Flower Festival	55
9	Aoi: Heartvine	60
10	Sakaki: The Sacred Tree	71
11	Hana Chiru Sato: Village of Scattered Blossoms	85
12	Suma	88

13 Akashi 107

14 Mio Tsukushi: Channel Buoys 119

15 Yomogi U: The Wormwood Patch 127

16 Seki Ya: The Gatehouse 131

17 E Awase: A Picture Contest 133

18 Matsu Kaze: Wind in the Pines 138

19 Usugumo: A Rack of Clouds 145

20 Asagao: Morning Glory 150

21 Otome: The Maiden 156

22 Tamakazura: The Jeweled Garland 164

23 Hatsune: The First Song of the Nightingale 172

24 Kochō: The Butterflies 176

25 Hotaru: Fireflies 183

26 Tokonatsu: Wild Carnations 187

27 Kagaribi: Flares 190

28 Nowaki: The Typhoon 192

29 Miyuki: The Royal Outing 195

30 Fujibakama: Purple Skirts 200

31 Makibashira: The Black Pine Pillar 204

32 Ume ga E: A Branch of Plum 214

33 Fuji no Uraha: Wisteria Leaves 219

Afterword: *The Tale of Genji* as a Book 228

For my first Japanese teacher, Sensei,
whose work remains written
with each of the poems

Preface

Without question, *Genji Monogatari*, brushed by a woman known as Murasaki Shikibu just 1,000 years ago, is the greatest romance novel ever written. It is certainly the oldest and, until only recently, was the longest novel the world had known. Easily the greatest literary work in the Japanese language, *Genji Monogatari* has delighted readers, flummoxed scholars, influenced and inspired writers ever since.

Only in this century has the story been available to English readers. *Genji Monogatari* has become *monogatari* (the telling of things), or, as the work is commonly known, *The Tale of Genji*. Genji (rhymes with "Glen G.") is "the Shining Prince," the main character of the book.

The first English translation was by Arthur Waley, done in the years 1923–33. Because Waley's work was breaking so much new ground, and was such an immense undertaking, later translators found much that was felt to need correcting. In 1976, Professor Edward G. Seidensticker published his 1,090-page version, again with the title *The Tale of Genji*. In addition, portions of the tale have been translated by Amy Heinrich (one chapter) and Professor Helen Craig McCullough (who published ten chapters under the title *Genji and Heike*). The most recent translation is that of Royall Tyler, which appeared in 2001.

Embedded in the story of *The Tale of Genji* are over 800 poems, which many people feel are the true gems of the work. These poems were called *waka* when the story was written. But that was so long ago that the word *waka*, which came to mean poetry, has been replaced with a new term, *tanka*. Both terms are currently used in Japan, but in English, and when referring to modern poems, tanka is the customary expression.

When referring to the poems written and added by Akiko Yosano, which open each chapter in this book, the correct term is tanka; tanka is used for both the plural and singular cases.

When Seidensticker made his translation, he was careful to make the *waka* in the story stand out, as they deserved to, and not be simply set into the story as statements in quotes as if they were dialogue, as was often the case in Waley's translation. However, Seidensticker evidently felt English readers would not understand or accept tanka-like poems as poetry, so he chose a conventional English poetry form, the couplet.

William J. Puette, author of *The Tale of Genji: A Reader's Guide,* puts it mildly: "His [Seidensticker's] regular couplet formula for all the poems may be doing injustice to the original five-line, asymmetrical waka."[1]

Helen Craig McCullough, in her version of ten of the fifty-four chapters, does use the five-line format for the poems, but unfortunately she bends each poem into a complete English sentence.[2]

As English readers became acquainted with newer translations of tanka in other Japanese literary works, it was obvious that the poems in *The Tale of Genji* also needed a new investigation and a translation that worked with the techniques as well as the spirit of tanka composition.

As Donald Keene writes in *Seeds in the Heart,* "Closer reading of the poems, however, makes it evident that they contribute not only to the beauty of the style but also to the creation of a lyrical mode of narration."[3] Thus, it seems very necessary to offer English readers a more accurate and adequate translation of the poems.

For *A String of Flowers, Untied . . . ,* not only the poems have been redone, but additional notations and clarification of the story have been supplemented. It is possible to obtain a condensed version of the whole story of these thirty-three chapters by reading just the poems and the headings that set the scene for the poem. In this way, the reader is taken directly to the heart of the most exciting situations: the highest romantic moments and the deepest experiences of grief and woe that surround the poetry.

The poems also operate as windows into the very being of the characters. While the reader is carried by Shikibu through the story by the prose, the poems stop the action, then advance it as it is perceived by the individual. In this way the story is taken to another level that has never been equaled in any other novel of this scope.

Even when a poem is written in response to a previous poem, and therefore is bound thematically, the change of character and his or her perception of a shared experience or similar situation brings a dramatically varied handling. It is hard to remember as one reads the poetry of *The Tale of Genji* that Murasaki Shikibu wrote all the poems from the

[1] William J. Puette, *The Tale of Genji: A Reader's Guide* (Rutland, Vt.: Charles E. Tuttle, 1983), p. 57.

[2] Helen Craig McCullough, *Genji and Heike: Selections from the Tale of Genji and the Tale of Heike* (Stanford, Calif.: Stanford University Press, 1994).

[3] Donald Keene, *Seeds in the Heart: Japanese Literature from Earliest Times to the Late Sixteenth Century* (New York: Henry Holt, 1993), p. 479.

perspective of such various personalities.

When one reads only the tanka in sequence, there is a strong current or theme or word choice that surfaces again and again. It is as if Shikibu was toying with themes and wordplays that she ingeniously bent to suit the various voices and situations of the story line.

In Donald Keene's notes to *The Tale of Genji* in *Seeds in the Heart* he quotes the eminent scholar Esperanza Ramirez-Christensen, who wrote in "The Operation of the Lyrical Mode in the *Genji Monogatari*" of the "paradigmatic transparencies of meaning. The paradigm, by reiterating the same message in various reifications, endows the narrative with a certain permanence, and at the same time a certain ambiguity and richness."[4]

By adding the headings, a conventional tanka technique, it is possible to give the reader enough of the story to clearly see and feel the situation surrounding and inspiring each of the poems. With the addition of notes on the story, the customs of Japan, and sidelights on the language, the reader is given a solid, basic grounding to this very valuable part of the novel.

Faced with the plethora of books and essays written on the subject of translating poetry and from the numerous examples (thankfully growing every day), the reader still might ask, "But what was the original author writing?" or "How can several translators come up with such widely divergent versions of the same poem?"

One has to realize that words are actually rather crude symbols to carry feelings and ideas. As anyone who writes knows, finding the right words or even enough words to express an idea often seems nearly impossible.

Part of a writer's job is finding new words, or at least words new to him or her. One word is never enough. The words are juxtaposed, piled up, and spread out so that the flavors of each mingle and combine, making a bouquet of images for the mind. Each word adds its own little tug and pull of meaning to create a room in which the reader spins to absorb the influences. It is in this process, I believe, that poetry takes its place. In the whirl, when the mind can no longer travel in a straight line, poetry is created.

When trying to exchange the words of one language for the words of another, one is thrown again and again into a deep pool where there seem to be no words designed to carry the thought. Impressions and ideas float tantalizingly just out of the reach of cognizance. The task of words carrying thoughts and ideas from and to such different languages as Japanese and English creates its own special pitfalls. Increasingly the translator finds that it is impossible to create the same experience of reading even one line in both languages. Grammar and syntax not needed in one language often have to be added in the other or the images fall into an indecipherable jumble that leaves the reader's mind flail-

4 Ibid., p. 510.

ing uselessly. And, in the case of translating Japanese, adding in English the pronouns and objects of sentences mars the ambiguity on which the poetry rests and functions.

It has been my experience that Japanese translators, in their eagerness to explain their complex poetry to us, in their desire to make it understandable to us, are willing to say or do anything to the lines to create a false feeling that they are English poetry. Instead of letting the author's words stand as way markers to a new understanding of the relationship between ideas or emotions, they try to explain away this process so the English reader does not have to think or feel while swimming across the deep waters where there is no toehold.

I have chosen a middle way for these poems from *The Tale of Genji.* Instead of making complete little English poems or sentences in the translations, I have tried to use the words as signposts. In other words, my goal has been to recreate the experience of perceiving, understanding, and illumination. I have not tried to make English poetry out of these poems because they are not English poetry. They are Japanese poems. And Japanese poetry works with poetic techniques and symbols, in some cases, very differently from what we are accustomed to in our Euro-American literature. One of the reasons it is important for us to have translations of Japanese literature is to discover these new ideas and methods. The reader cannot do this when the poetry is packaged in the couplets or quatrains of our literary history, or when the lines roll into the mind on the wheels of perfect sentence structure.

Yet, because the poems of *The Tale of Genji* are also carriers of information about the emotional states of the characters and in many cases are relied upon to elaborate or further the story, the reader needs more than simple posts stuck in the wide sands of an ebbing tide. Sometimes there is the feeling that Shikibu herself shifted between creating poems and giving information. In these latter instances, the translated words automatically fell into a sentence structure—actually asking to be made into English sense. In other poems one could almost feel her delight in playing with the language, playing with ideas and images. Even to the Japanese reader comes the knowledge that she has abandoned strict sense and literal meaning for the pure joy of creating emotion from words.

It was at these times the native speaker would wave her hands helplessly in the air, saying the words meant neither this nor that but something deeper and more emotional than any of the possible English words. Thus, the English reader must either experience this helplessness or be guided by words that resonate slowly and come only with practice.

I assume English readers are capable of launching their minds, hearts, and intellects out across space to discover where the mind of Murasaki Shikibu has gone on before us. We may not place our feet in the tiny shuffling steps of one wearing a kimono, so there may be times when our leaps heap us in piles of misunderstanding, but I have tried to give the English reader a sense of feeling of where her poetry has led the readers of the last millennium instead of pushing them in wheelchairs of our literary heritage.

Nearly every essay on translation repeats Robert Frost's remark that "poetry is what gets lost in translation." He would not have made this statement if there was not a degree of truth in it. But I am just bold and foolhardy enough to challenge the concept. It seems to me that, given the images, concepts, and techniques of another culture's poetry, added to similar words in the target language, one can recreate the journey the mind makes across the landscape of the poem. It is on this passage that the poetry is discovered. And this is where I would like to lead you.

And please understand that no one person can produce the definitive translation, because it does not exist. Poetry is alive—living and breathing in the chest of every reader. Because we are each created differently and have grown up in different neighborhoods, our own inner poetry is different. That there are differences in individuals extends in greater degree into differences in cultures. But as we get to know each other, as we exchange our thoughts, feelings, and literature, the differences between individuals is paved over with understanding. In the same way, with practice the variances between cultures recede so that the words pass more easily into the comprehension of each other's deeper understanding. It is this process that unlocks the doors to poetry.

See a row of houses all containing families—fulfilling the same goal of shelter. Yet how different each one is. Translation builds various houses to give a home to a written work. Thanks to the efforts of many persons, but especially to my teacher, Sensei, and Hatsue Kawamura, I can show you what kind of a house I have attempted to give Murasaki Shikibu's poetry. Please enter these rooms with a glad heart.

For our translation of the poems from Shikibu's masterpiece *The Tale of Genji,* we have used Akiko Yosano's modern Japanese translation of the archaic version. And as Yosano did in her book, we have included, at the beginning of each chapter, her own modern tanka as overture.

As a woman and as a poet, I decided that one could better trust the feelings and abilities of a woman poet to say what another woman and poet had written. Shikibu's work is, in many places, very sensual, so it seemed that only another woman could acknowledge, appreciate, and reflect the nuances that might be smoothed over or ignored by someone less acquainted with speaking openly of feelings and facts.

Acknowledgments

My first and deepest thanks go to Their Majesties, Emperor Akihito and Empress Michiko of Japan. If they had not invited my husband, Werner, and me to be honored guests at the Utakai Hijime (The New Year's Poetry Party) at the Imperial Court in January 1998, I never would have had the courage to attempt to fulfill my dream of giving Murasaki Shikibu's poetry a new life. It was through the experience of attending this famous tanka poetry event that I glimpsed the importance of tanka in Japanese life and the history of the country.

This trip was made possible through the kindnesses and donations of Mr. Hojo Nakajima, Vice Grand Master of the Ceremonies of the Imperial Household; Mr. Kazuo Ito of Star in the Forest Publishing Company (Hoshi to Mori); Professor Takashi Aoyagi, the Japanese voice of Mickey Mouse; Mr. Etsuo Yamamoto, Mr. Shinsuke Arai, Mr. Michiro Ohbayashi, and Fr. Neal Henry Lawrence, OSB, the American tanka poet at St. Anselm's Priory. Special thanks go to the translators during the trip, Mr. Misao Okimoto and Michiko Kōga, who not only helped us across cultural barriers of words but also gave us so much delight while at the same time educating us. A special thanks belongs to Takuro Ajiki and Sei'ichirō Nakagae, who made the day in Atami so magical. The greatest burden of the work organizing the trip and our days fell to Mr. Matsuo Shukuya, member of the Society of the Reizei Family, to whom we continually give our thanks and our wonder for all he accomplished.

If this trip had not been possible, I never would have met Professor Hatsue Kawamura, editor of *The Tanka Journal*, and her husband, Yasuhiro, that snowy night at the Garden Palace Hotel, where we first talked about this project. It was only through her most patient and kind way of showing me how to translate the Japanese poems that our work on this book and the other two, *White Letter Poems* by Fumi Saito and *Heavenly Maiden Tanka* by Akiko Baba, has been realized. No one has been as good to work with as Hatsue is and I have only endless praise for her as a person and her abilities in both English and poetry.

My thanks to Leza Lowitz for her encouragement and for suggesting that her Japanese translator, Miyuki Aoyama, be the one more pair of eyes to go over the *rōmaji.* Miyuki Aoyama took time she did not have to willingly give so much help. My gratitude goes to Dr. Amy Vladeck Heinrich for her expertise on so many questions and her patience in reading the first thirteen chapters before her own important work called her back to Japan. Help was also given by correspondence with Aya Yuhki, Sumiko Koganei, Janine Beichman, and Sanford Goldstein. D. S. Lliteras also gave continual encouragement for the work, up to and including today, through so many long phone calls.

I gratefully acknowledge the foresight and forbearance Peter Goodman showed through the many necessary revisions of the manuscript. The staff at Stone Bridge Press has been marvelously kind and efficient through every phase of getting the poems into a book. Michael Ashby did a yeoman's job of copyediting, for which I am extremely grateful.

I am also grateful to the spirits of Murasaki Shikibu and Akiko Yosano, who I always felt were guiding the sometimes rocky course of the translations. I cannot relate how often I came to the place of not knowing how to state a line until, in a quietness of waiting, the words would form themselves with a clarity greater than my own understanding.

Last, but surely never least, my thanks to Werner, my husband, who gave me the life, peace, and companionship that nourished each day.

J.R.

Characters from *The Tale of Genji*

The names of the characters in the story are rarely designated absolutely, so they have been assigned names and titles, often taken from one of the poems or from their position at court or even place of residence. The fictional names in the story have been translated into English, leaving in Japanese the historical names of the emperors, Genji, and the lead female character, who bears Murasaki Shikibu's own name.

Akashi Empress. The daughter of Genji by the Akashi Lady. She is also called the Akashi Girl or Akashi Princess.

Akashi Lady. The daughter of a retired governor. She bears Genji's daughter at Akashi but moves with her mother to Oi before moving to Genji's Sixth Ward palace.

Akashi Monk. The former governor of the province of Harima. He has become a lay monk and retired to the coast of Akashi. He is the father of the Akashi lady.

Black Beard (Higekuro). The son of the Minister of the Right. He is the husband of the sister of Murasaki. After leaving Murasaki's sister, he becomes the husband of Lady Jeweled Garland.

Concubine of the Paulownia Court. The consort of the Paulownia Court (Kiritsubo) Emperor and the mother of Genji.

Emperor of the Paulownia Court. Genji's father and the reigning emperor at the start of the tale.

First Secretary's Captain (Tō no Chūjō). The son of the Minister of the Left and the Great Princess. He is the brother of Lady Heartvine, and thus brother-in-law of Genji, with whom he becomes best friend and rival. He is also the father of Lord Oak Tree, Lord Rose Plum, Lady Jeweled Garland, and the Lady Wild Goose in the Clouds, Miss of Ōmi.

Genji (the Shining Prince). The son of the Paulownia Court Emperor and his favorite consort, Concubine of the Paulownia Court. He fathers three children: the Reizei Emperor, the Akashi Empress, and Lord Evening Mist.

Gosechi Dancer. The daughter of Genji's servant Sir Reflected Brilliance. She becomes one of Lord Evening Mist's wives and bears him six children.

Great Princess (Ōmiya). The sister of the Paulownia Court Emperor . She is the mother of the First Secretary's Captain and of Lady Heartvine, making her Genji's mother-in-law. She also raises Lord Evening Mist and Lady Wild Goose in the Clouds in her palace on Third Avenue.

Handmaiden (Ukon). The lady-in-waiting to Lady Evening Faces. After the death of Lady Evening Faces, Genji takes her into his service. When she is reunited with the child of Lady Evening Faces, she becomes the gentlewoman to Lady Jeweled Garland.

Lady Evening Faces (Yūgao). The mother of Lady Jeweled Garland. She is loved successively by the First Secretary's Captain and Genji.

Lady Heartvine (Aoi). The daughter of the Great Princess and the Minister of the Left. She is Genji's first wife and the mother of Lord Evening Mist.

Lady Jeweled Garland (Tamakazura). The daughter of the First Secretary's Captain and Lady Evening Faces. She is adopted by Genji and marries Black Beard and bears him three children.

Lady of the Beautiful Hall (Kokiden). The daughter of the Minister of the Right. She is the first wife of Genji's father, sister of Princess of the Night of the Misty Moon, and mother of the Suzaku Emperor. She is chief rival to Genji's mother and later is the main reason Genji goes into exile.

Lady of the Beautiful View (Reikeiden). A concubine of Genji's father and the sister of Lady Scattered Blossoms. After the death of Genji's father, Genji takes her into his care.

Lady of the Cicada Shell. The wife of the vice-governor of Iyo. After one night of passion, Genji continues to attempt to woo her without success.

Lady of the Sixth Ward (Rokujō). The widow of the former crown prince and mother of Lady Who Loves Autumn. She becomes Genji's mistress and later accompanies her daughter to Ise Shrine when Genji goes into exile.

Lady of the Wisteria Apartment (Fujitsubo). The wife and empress of the Paulownia Court Emperor. She is the stepmother of Genji and the mother of Genji's child who becomes the Reizei Emperor. She is also the aunt of Murasaki, Genji's second and principal wife.

Lady Reeds Under the Eaves. The stepdaughter of Lady of the Cicada Shell. She accidentally becomes the object of Genji's lust.

Lady Scattered Blossoms. The sister of Lady of the Beautiful View. Genji admires her cultured ways and installs her in his palace, where she and her sister rear Genji's son Lord Evening Mist and later Lady Jeweled Garland.

Lady Who Loves Autumn (Akikonomu). The daughter of the former crown prince and Lady of the Sixth Ward. She is a first cousin of Genji and Princess Morning Glory. After being the high priestess at Ise Shrine, she becomes a consort and then empress of the Reizei Emperor.

Left Palace Guard (Sahyōe). The brother of Murasaki and a suitor of Lady Jeweled Garland.

Little One (Kogimi). The younger brother of Lady of the Cicada Shell. He aids Genji in Genji's pursuit of Lady of the Cicada Shell.

Lord Oak Tree (Kashiwagi). The son of the First Secretary's Captain. He is a friend and later brother-in-law of Lord Evening Mist. He is also the brother of Lord Rose Plum and half brother of both Lady Jeweled Garland and the Miss of Ōmi.

Lord Rose Plum (Kōbai). The son of the First Secretary's Captain. He is the brother of Lord Oak Tree, half brother of Lady Jeweled Garland and the Miss of Ōmi, and brother-in-law of Lord Evening Mist.

Minister of the Left. The patriarchal head of the Fujiwara Clan. He is the husband of the Great Princess, father of the First Secretary's Captain and of Lady Heartvine, making him Genji's father-in-law.

Miss of Ōmi. The long-lost daughter of the First Secretary's Captain. He later claims her and sends her to court with one of his other daughters.

Miss of the Captaincy (Chūjō no Kimi). The head serving woman of Lady of the Sixth Ward. She becomes the object of Genji's attentions, but she wisely resists his attempts to flatter her into having an affair with him.

Murasaki. The daughter of Prince Director of Military Affairs. She is the niece of Lady of the Wisteria Apartment, and granddaughter of a previous emperor. She is raised by her grandmother and the bishop of a temple in the hills north of Kyoto and later becomes Genji's principal wife. She remains childless but acts as surrogate mother to the Akashi Empress.

Prince Director of Military Affairs (Hyōbu). The brother of Lady of the Wisteria Apartment. He is the father of Murasaki and of the mad wife of Black Beard.

Prince Firefly (Hotaru). Genji's brother and a suitor of Lady Jeweled Garland.

Princess Morning Glory (Asagao). Genji's first cousin and high priestess of Kamo Shrine. She is another woman who successfully repulses Genji's amorous advances.

Princess of the Night of the Misty Moon (Oborozukiyo). The sister of Lady of the Beautiful Hall. She becomes Genji's mistress and later the consort of the Suzaku Emperor.

Princess Safflower. The impoverished daughter of a prince. She is an occasional mistress of Genji, who takes care of her and her mansion in her old age.

Reizei (Cool Fountain) Emperor. The son of Genji and Lady of the Wisteria Apartment. He believes his father is the Paulownia Court Emperor.

Sir Reflected Brilliance (Koremitsu). Genji's servant and the father of the Gosechi Dancer, whom Genji sponsors in the Reizei Court.

Suzaku (Red Sparrow) Emperor. The son of the Paulownia Court Emperor and Lady of the Beautiful Hall. He is thus Genji's half brother. His empress is Princess of the Night of the Misty Moon. He leaves the throne while Genji is in exile, making way for Genji's son, who becomes the Reizei Emperor.

Woman of the Bedchamber (Naishi). A concubine of Genji's father who is also visited by Genji.

KIRITSUBO
THE PAULOWNIA COURT

Genji's birth to his twelfth year

The story of Genji begins with his mother, Concubine of the Paulownia Court, who is a favorite of the Emperor but who lacks strong family backing. Thus, the lady is often reviled and gossiped about by the other women of the court, causing her much grief and shame. When she bears the Emperor's son, who turns out to be a dazzling child, she comes under increased attack by the Emperor's first wife, Lady of the Beautiful Hall, who is not only jealous but afraid that the son of the Emperor's consort will be made the next emperor instead of her own older son. When the son of Concubine of the Paulownia Court is about three years old, the lady falls deeper into her anxiety-caused illness and dies. The scene of her parting from the Emperor at the palace just hours before she dies brings the first poem in the tale, creating an unforgettable moment. After having the lumps on the child's head "read" by a Korean physiognomist who predicts that the child will never rule but that all of his children will, the Emperor makes him a commoner with the surname of Genji and picks the son of Lady of the Beautiful Hall to be the Crown Prince.

The Emperor takes a new mistress, Lady of the Wisteria Apartment, who greatly resembles Genji's dead mother but who has better family connections and thus enjoys a more secure position at court. At the end of the chapter, Genji is initiated into adulthood in a ritual of tying up and cutting his hair. In the same ceremony, at twelve years old, he is married off to Lady Heartvine, a woman several years older than he.

---

1 - A

murasaki no	the royal purple
kagayaku hana to	of the shining flower
hi no hikari	is the sun's light
omoi awazaru	there are no reasons
kotowari mo nashi	this wish cannot be so

---

1 - 1

As in a story, there is a lady, not of the first rank, whom the Emperor loves more than any other. When she bears the Emperor a son, he becomes even more enamored of her. When the child is around three years old, his mother becomes ill. As was the custom, she wants to return to her parent's home before she dies. The Emperor orders a hand-drawn carriage for her journey—a high honor. Still he cannot let her go. She is breathless in her agony and very near death, yet her words for him are:

kagiri tote	whatever the end
wakaruru michi no ni	parting for separate ways
kanashiki ni	is sad—however
ikama hoshiki wa	the way I would want
inochi nari keri	would be to go on living

1-1. In Heian Japan, it was customary for persons living in the Imperial Palace to return to their homes or the homes of their parents when ill. The action was even more necessary if death was thought to be imminent. The many ceremonial taboos surrounding death would have thrown the court into dysfunction, and this had to be avoided at all costs. No matter how hard it was for the persons involved to be parted at this moment, it was accepted that this custom had to be observed. This poem hinges on the two meanings of the word for "way," as it does in English, also. "Way" can mean the road or path that is physically traveled and the illusionary way one goes into the unknown territory of death.

---

1 - 2

After the death of his beloved, in the chilly winds of autumn, the Emperor feels even more sad and alone. Also, he is missing his woman's child, who has been taken to live at the home of her mother. He decides to send one of his women, the Royal Command Woman, to the grandmother's house with a message asking her to send the boy to him. At the end of his request he brushes this poem.

miyagino no	the sound of wind
tsuyu fuki musubu	brings the dew to the fields
kaze no oto	of Miyagino
ko hagi ga ue wo	to the tiny bush clover
omoi koso yare	I do send my thoughts

1-3

The Royal Command Woman is very moved by the desolate autumn scene around this house of bereavement. When she sees how deeply grieved the woman's mother still is and how painful it is for her, as grandmother, to now think of giving up the grandson, her only tie with the dead daughter, the lady-in-waiting cannot keep from weeping. The Emperor has invited the grandmother to come to court with the child, but the old woman feels her age will make her repugnant to the fine ladies and gentlemen. Thus, if she is to obey the Emperor's request, she will have to give up her last living relative. The Royal Command Woman sympathizes with her completely and wishes to stay longer to comfort her, but is aware of the lateness of the hour and knows she should be returning to the Emperor. The Royal Command Woman's heartfelt farewell poem is:

suzumushi no	there is no end
koe no kagiri wo	to falling tears or the chirping
tsukushi temo	of the bell cricket
nagaki yo akazu	both use up the long night
furu namida kana	without growing weary

1-4

At this farewell, the grandmother realizes that soon she will be forced to part with her grandson because of the Emperor's command. This is what happens when a commoner's wishes are in conflict with imperial will: tears fall upon tears.

itodoshiku	it's bad enough
mushi no ne shigeki	the incessant cry of insects
asajiu ni	where thatch reeds grow

1-2. The wordplay in this poem depends on the word *Miyagino,* which refers to the fields of Miyagi, a place in northern Japan famous for bush clover, and *miya,* meaning imperial palace. *Ko* (child) with *hagi* (bush clover) implies "the bush clover child," the imperial prince, or the woman's grandson. *Hagi* is *lespedeza,* or bush clover. It grows low to the ground and blooms with purple or white pealike blossoms in the autumn months. In classical Japanese poetry bush clover carries the emotional message of sadness or regrets in the same way roses are used to express love.

1-4. The phrase *kumo no uebito* literally means "a person on a cloud," but it is used to refer to persons of the high court or nobility. The higher the person's standing at court, the higher they are in the clouds. Thus, the emperor is of the nine-fold cloud.

One of the oldest poetical clichés in Japan is the connection between tears and dew. The idea that clouds bring dews and sadness clouds one's heart, bringing tears, is completely natural.

tsuyu oki souru now tears as dew are falling
kumo no uebito from the noble clouds

1-5

When the Royal Command Woman returns to the palace, she is moved to find the Emperor still awake and waiting for her report. From this action the lady-in-waiting knows how important the message she is bringing is to him. The Emperor listens attentively to her describing the desolate autumn surroundings of the grandmother's house and her own impressions of her sadness. Again and again the Emperor reads the grandmother's message and the poem. He is made uneasy by her poetic style as well as her implication that he can be no help at all for the child.

araki kaze	such a wild wind
fusegishi kage no	since the tree that gave shelter
kareshi yori	has withered away
ko hagi ga ue zo	things concerning the bush clover
shizu kokoro naki	do not leave my mind at ease

1-5. The first line of the poem is a rather startling way to begin a poem to an emperor, but very true to the depth of the lady's feelings. The grandmother must have felt her life was being ripped up by very strong winds; still this was no way to speak to the emperor. The lines "since the tree that gave shelter / has withered away" is a poetic reference to her daughter and her death. It would have been culturally incorrect for her to refer directly to her own daughter, so she uses this image. In the same way, she cannot mention her grandchild, so she calls him *ko hagi*, "tiny bush clover," or "the child of regrets or sadness," as did the emperor in poem 1-2.

1-6

Along with her note to the Emperor, the grandmother also sends a memento of her daughter, a set of robes with some of the dead woman's combs and hair ornaments. As the Emperor sadly fondles these relics, he recalls an old Chinese tale about the wizard who was capable of bringing the comb of a lover back from beyond the grave. The Emperor, with a twist on the tale, wishes there might be another wizard who could, by touching the woman's combs, bring his own beloved back from death.

tazune yuku	how I wish
maboroshi mo gana	for a magic wizard to go
tsute nite mo	for a message
tama no arika wo	from the place of spirits
sokoto shiru beku	where I may find her

1-7

The departed lady's keenest rival for the love of the Emperor was his first wife, Lady of the Beautiful Hall. Not in mourning herself, and eager for the return of the Emperor's attentions, she heedlessly orders to have music played late into the bright moon night, in complete disregard for his grief. Refusing to go to bed even though the lamps are trimmed more than once and now the oil burned down to nothing, the Emperor sees that even the moonlight becomes dimmer while his mind dwells on his lost lady and her child and the grandmother who wanted to keep him. In this darkness he jots down a verse.

kumo no ue mo	here above the clouds
namida ni kururu	tears from overwhelming grief
aki no tsuki	dim the autumn moon
ikade sumu ran	how is it for those who live
asajiu no yado	in the lodge on thatch reeds plain

1-8

Finally the grandmother is able to let the child go to court, where he is named Genji, the Shining Prince. When he is twelve years old, the Emperor grandly holds the ceremonies in which the child receives the cap of adulthood. As the boy's long locks are tied up and ritually cut away, the Emperor is close to tears as he thinks of how alone the child is without a mother, and even more so since the grandmother died six years ago. Later, while the Minister of the Left is being entertained by the Emperor, the Emperor surprises him with a poem as he pours wine for him. The Minister of the Left had suggested his daughter as bride for Genji, and now the Emperor seems to be accepting the offer.

itoki naki	now that the young child's
hatsu motoyui ni	hair has been bound up
nagaki yo wo	insuring a long life
chigiru kokoro wa	is it not time to tie up
musubi kometsu ya	his heart with marriage vows?

1-8. The English expression "tying the knot," meaning marriage, works also for this poem. To speak of the boy at the entrance of adulthood as a "a young child" shows how hard it was for the emperor to see him growing up and leaving him.

The Minister of the Left conveys his approval for the match of his daughter, Lady Heartvine, in his poem to the Emperor. After receiving a horse from the imperial stables and a falcon in splendid and impressive ceremonies, the Minister of the Left takes Genji home with him that night, where the nuptial observances are conducted with due solemnity.

musubi tsuru	may the knot tied
kokoro mo fukaki	with the thin thread of troth
motoyui ni	and these pledged hearts
koki murasaki no	be dyed the deepest purple
iro shi asezu ba	be as fast—never fading

1-9. The grass *murasaki,* from which the author of *The Tale of Genji* takes her name, was a tall plant of limber stems with purple flowers dispersed among the lanceolate leaves. From its roots was extracted a fluid used for dyeing fabric lavender or purple. As in other cultures, this purplish color was the indication of royalty. The color was also esteemed as the color of alliance. The wordplay works with the idea of a knot holding "fast" as well as a dye being "fast," in that it does not fade.

HAHAKIGI
THE BROOM TREE

Summer of Genji's seventeenth year

While visiting at his new wife's estate, Genji makes the acquaintance of her brother, The First Secretary's Captain, who becomes Genji's lifelong friend and closest rival. One rainy evening while the two are comparing notes on life and love, they are joined by a group of young gallants. Each relates the story of an affair, with discussion on the various types of women and which woman is the best sort to have. The chapter closes with Genji going to Third Avenue, where he visits his wife, who responds to him so coldly he sets out again unsatisfied. Unable to go back to his home because it lies in an unlucky direction, he is invited to stay overnight in another friend's home. There, through the thin wall, he overhears a young woman talking about him. She turns out to be Lady of the Cicada Shell, who is Genji's friend's stepmother. After everyone is asleep, Genji breaks into her apartment to carry her off to his room for what is called "a dreamlike encounter." Leaving the next day, Genji takes the brother of Lady of the Cicada Shell into his services as a page, making him the carrier of messages to his newest ladylove. When Genji tries to visit her again, she refuses to see him by quickly disappearing from the room. Genji compares her to the legendary broom tree, which seems to have the magical ability to change its shape and location. Outmaneuvered, Genji spends the night instead with the young page.

Some commentaries see this chapter as an example of how male relationships were forged and functioned in Heian Japan. The chapter begins with Genji's wife's coldness and his growing relationship with her brother, the First Secretary's Captain. After the brilliant and now famous "In Study of Women on a Rainy Night," the scene shifts to another romantic misadventure by Genji, which results in his spending the night with the page instead of the desired woman.

---

2 - A

nakagawa no	the Naka River—
satsuki no mizuni	a river of relationships
hito nitari	with the waters of May
katare ba musebi	like one who talks while sobbing
yore ba wana naku	then trembles when one nears

---

2 - 1

One rainy night as Genji and his young male friends are discussing various women they have known, a guardsman tells a story in which he tries to cure his girlfriend of jealous nagging. Instead of changing her ways, she suggests they part and then bites his little finger deeply. Terribly insulted, the man feels he cannot show up at court so mutilated and will have to become a monk. As he departs, flexing his wounded finger and saying they must part forever, the guardsman's poem to his toothsome lover is:

te wo orite	bending each finger
ai mishi koto wo	I can count the many times
kazoure ba	we have met in love
kore hitotsu ya wa	but on this one I ask you
kimi ga ukifushi	doesn't it show our misery?

---

2 - 2

The guardsman's girlfriend's tearful reply:

2-A. The Naka River flows into Naka Harbor on the coast of Sanuki, which is in modern Kagawa Prefecture.

2-1. In opposition to our way of counting by extending a finger out of a fist, the Japanese most often start with an open hand and then bend down each finger, starting with the thumb. It makes a lovely fanlike movement as the counted-off fingers are then again extended. A romantic idea was for women to prove their faithfulness to a lover by cutting off the little finger at the first joint. In this case, it was the man who had a wounded finger.

ukifushi wo	yes our miseries
kokoro hitotsu ni	I continue to count them
kazoe kite	only in my heart
ko ya kimi ga te wo	is this a reason for you
wakaru beki ori	to withdraw your hand from me?

2-3

The young guardsman continues his stories of his women by telling of one who played the Japanese harp quite well, wrote beautifully, and was very clever. Yet, he often felt uneasy with her and so did not visit her often. One night, after being at court, he was accompanied by a young man who asked him to wait while he checked in at a house where he felt he was expected. The guardsman, who seemed to be well acquainted with the place, went into the courtyard, sat down on the verandah, inspected the chrysanthemums and moonlight, and began to play his flute. The lady instantly responded with accompanying melodies on a ready-tuned harp. Delighted with the music, but suspicious of the guardsman's prior connection to this very lady, the guardsman's companion sarcastically says, "I see no one has yet broken a path through your fallen leaves." He breaks off a chrysanthemum to attach this poem to it, and to slip it under the blinds to her.

koto no ne mo	the harp's chill tone
kiku mo enaranu	splendid as the chrysanthemums
yado nagara	in these lodgings, yet
tsurenaki hito wo	could the coldness of someone
hiki ya tome keru	be enough to make one stay?

or

the harp's cold sound
so splendid to listen to
in this dwelling, yet
could it be someone's coldness
that forces me to linger?

2-3. The *koto,* or *sō no koto,* was a thirteen-string zitherlike instrument about six feet long that was played with removable bridges, as is the modern *koto.* It was a development from the seven-string *koto,* which was borrowed from the Chinese *cheng* in the Nara period. The word *koto* was often used in poems because of the possible wordplay in which one can either mean the musical instrument or "things" or "affairs."

The word *kiku* can refer either to "chrysanthemum" or "to listen."

2-4

She picked up on his playful manner to suggestively reply:

kogarashi ni
fuki awasu meru
fue no ne wo
hiki todomu beki
koto no ha zo naki

a cold withering wind
seems to play together with
the tone of the flute
reason enough to restrain
leaving one at the harp?

or

in trees withered by cold
wind seems to play along with
the notes of the flute
should you be detained
by the language of leaves?

2-5

The First Secretary's Captain (Genji's brother-in-law) then relates of an affair of his in which he admits he treated a woman badly. He had promised to take care of her, yet he abandoned her when she bore him a daughter. Being an orphan herself, and now unsupported with a young child, the woman sent him a note attached to a wild carnation.

yamagatsu no
kaki ho aru tomo
oriori ni
aware wa kake yo
nadeshiko no tsuyu

a rustic's hedge
fencing in an area of ruin
is also a place
for showing mercy to dew
on the pink carnation

or

a rustic's hedge
fences in an area of ruin
is also a place
for giving love to the short
life of the love child

2-4. The words *koto no ha* can also be understood as *koto*, "words," *no*, "of," and *ha*, "leaves" or "language."

2-5. *Yamagatsu* is "hunter," "woodcutter," or "rustic mountain dweller"; *kaki* means "hedge" or "fence" or the kind of fence such an uncultivated mountain person would have made. *Nadeshiko* is the name for the wild carnation, and it can also be heard as *nadeshi*, "stroked" and *ko*, "child," or "love child." The woman chose this flower because its name is a reminder of his own "wildflower love child."

2-6

As a result of the refined tone of this poem, the First Secretary's Captain was drawn to visit her. Because she was not wild with jealousy and incriminations, but only stared pensively into the autumn garden, he felt she had forgiven him. When her quiet weeping joined the sound of the insects in the grass, he became very aroused. The scene was as if one from an old romance, and he admits he felt very romantic as he whispered to her:

saki majiru	I can't distinguish
hana wa izure to	one flower from another
wakane domo	in this wild array
nao tokonatsu ni	but the bed of summer pinks
shiku mono zo naki	is surpassed by no one else.

2-7

Her answer shows she was aware of the drift of his thinking and the results it could bring her again. Thus the mother of one of the First Secretary's Captain's unrecognized children answered him with:

uchiharau	brushing off
sode mo tsuyukeki	sleeves wet with dew
tokonatsu ni	from wild carnations
arashi fuki sou	gale storms add to the ruin
aki mo kini keri	that also comes in autumn

2-8

Another friend of Genji and the First Secretary's Captain tells his story. He had a relationship with his Chinese teacher's daughter. Oh, he learned a lot from her, but he could not commit to her because her superior knowledge made him feel inadequate. Still, after not seeing her for a very long time, he casually dropped in for a visit. He was upset that she stayed behind a heavy screen and thought she was only being coy and thus, he thought, he finally had a good reason for leaving her. But she was too wise for him. She tells him, with malodorous

2-6. In her poem, she had used the word *nadeshiko* for the love child and wild carnation, which is sometimes simply called a "pink," but he picked the synonymous *tokonatsu*, which can also mean bed of summer (*toko*, "bed," and *natsu*, "summer"), another, more suggestive, name for the same flower. However, *tokonatsu* can also mean everlasting or perpetual summer, in reference to the fact the plants stay in bloom from spring through autumn.

2-7. The abandoned mother has several double-meaning words in her poem to give it a wider latitude. *Arashi* , "gale" or "storm," also means "destroy," "ruin" or "damage," and *aki* means "autumn" or "to be bored with, get tired of," so the poem can also be understood to mean that she is bored with being ruined by having a child out of wedlock that he has not officially accepted as his own. She also feels she has been "brushed off" of an attachment to him.

breath, that she has been taking garlic for a condition of her health. Disgusted that he was being denied access to her, he stayed only long enough to write this note:

sasagani no	surely a spider's action
furumai shiruki	made it clear I would be here
yūgure ni	by twilight
hiru ma suguse to	that spending the day with garlic
iu ga aya naki	makes no sense for both of us

2-9

But she surprised him by quickly sizing up the real crux of the situation and writing it in her poem:

au koto no	if our conduct
yo wo shi hedate nu	was like man and wife each night
naka nara ba	we wouldn't be separated
hiru ma mo nani ka	by the embarrassment
mabayukara mashi	of garlic in the daytime

2-10

Genji, while visiting the house of a friend—the governor of Kii—discovers that the governor's very young and attractive stepmother is sleeping in the very room next to his. With the help of the woman's younger brother, Genji sneaks into her room. Surprising her, he grabs up the tiny figure to carry her off to his bed. Sweating in her distress, the woman tries to talk him out of his plans. But all of her arguments are so sweetly given that his passions are merely inflamed. His very splendor makes her more resistive, which makes her even more attractive to him. When she begins weeping, he truly has his hands full, but he will not miss this experience for the world. Added to these stimuli, this household is strange to him, and the fact that it is in a lower class section of the city than Genji is used to unsettles the young lover. In the morning he hears a cock crowing nearby. The other strange predawn noises from her close neighbors' morning routines startle as they awaken Genji. Deeply impressed by this experience, his

2-8. Instead of blaming himself for not letting her know he was still interested in her, and because he cannot fault her for treating her illness, he blames a spider, or indirectly does blame her for not paying attention to the omen of his coming. According to folklore, spiders spun their webs to announce the coming of a lover. *Furumai* can mean "act" or "action" or "treat, entertainment." *Hiru* refers to "noon" or "garlic," and *hiru ma* is "daytime." It is interesting to note that garlic was seen as a health herb 1,000 years ago and now suddenly again it is popular.

2-9. *Ou* is "go after" or "chase" and sounds very close to *au,* "to meet as man and wife." Also she uses *wo,* objective case indication, with *shi,* for emphasis, which, when combined in *woshi* (modern *oshi*), means "dear," "value," "regret."

farewell message to her combines a mixture of his feelings about the woman and about the morning.

tsurenasa wo	such coldheartedness
urami mo hate nu	does someone else bear a grudge
shinonome ni	at dawn?
toriae nu made	I guess I am startled because
odorokasu ran	I am not ready for this bird

---

2 - 11

The woman, thinking of her older husband, the vice-governor of Iyo, whom she considered a boorish dolt, yet who she was very afraid might hear of how she had spent the night, replies:

mi no usa wo	grieving over
nageku ni akade	hardships unsatisfied
akuru yo wa	then night is broken
torikasanete zo	adding to my woes
ne mo nakare keru	by the cries of the cock

---

2 - 12

Although he now spends more time at the villa on Third Avenue, the estate of his wife, Genji's thoughts remain with the unwilling lady he has met in the night at his friend's house. In an effort to meet this reluctant lady again, Genji makes friends with her brother, a very young boy whom he questions deeply. Genji shocks the boy by informing him by hints of what has happened with his sister. Thus, Genji is able to use him as a secret courier to send the lady a message with a long letter and a poem.

mishi yume wo	yearning for that time
au yo ari ya to	once seen in a dream
nageku ma ni	when we met
me sae awade zo	yet my eyes never closing
koro mo he ni keru	as the night flies by

2-10. Often in tanka there are phrases, such as in the first line, that can be arbitrarily assigned to various persons in the poem. Such undesignated phrases can apply to the uncaring persons next to the woman's room, surely to the rooster making such a noise, and perhaps to the woman herself, who may not be completely trained in all the customs of entertaining men such as Genji. It could even be Genji himself (or any man who must, according to the custom, get up at the crack of dawn when the cock crows and leave a warm bed to make his way homeward) who felt the custom to be coldhearted.

2-12. This poem takes inspiration from one by Minamoto Shitagō published in the *Shūishū:* "where / shall comfort be found / in my longing / there are no dreams / for night brings no sleep."

2 - 13

Still, the reluctant lady tries to avoid a tryst with Genji. When she finds out her own brother knows of Genji's action that night, she is horrified. Thus, when Genji tries to force her to meet him, she conceals herself in another part of the house. Genji sends her little brother off to find where she is hidden. Even though found, she refuses to see Genji. So he sends her a note relying on the metaphor of a broom-shaped tree of Sonohara ("that plain") in Shinano Province that would seem to offer shade but then disappear as soon as one approached it.

hahakigi no	legendary broom tree
kokoro wo shira de	unable to know your heart and
sonohara no	on that plain
michi ni aya naku	I have strayed from the path
madoi nuru kana	and lost my way

2 - 14

Tempted, and therefore sleepless, the lady, lying in the dark, is afraid to give in to Genji's pleas for a tryst. She picks up on the broom tree image to wish she too could vanish if anyone drew near to her.

kazu nara nu	it doesn't matter
fuseya ni ouru	that I grew up in a lowly house
mi no usa ni	such are one's hardships
aru ni mo ara zu	since I don't exist
kiyuru hahakigi	I'll vanish like a broom tree

2-14. By referring to a *waka* by Sakanoe Korenori (997) in the *Shin Kokinshū*, "O broom tree / of Fuseya / in Sonohara / you seem to be there / yet I cannot find you," she builds on the word *fuseya* (hut or a place name) to emphasize her station in society, which is lower than Genji's, and indirectly indicates her only reason for not meeting him again.

UTSUSEMI

THE SHELL OF THE CICADA

Summer of Genji's seventeenth year

This chapter continues Genji's attempts to again meet the reluctant woman now known as Lady of the Cicada Shell. Her younger brother, Little One, sympathizes with Genji so completely that he leads him one sultry night into her apartment, where she is playing a game of Go with her stepdaughter. Genji spies on the women until the lights are extinguished. As he creeps toward them in the dark, Lady of the Cicada Shell detects the aroma of his robes and, leaping up without her own robe, slips out of the room. Gleefully Genji discovers only one woman on the sleeping mats. As he pulls aside the sleeping woman's clothing, one feature after another seems strange to him. With a jolt he realizes this is not the woman he was expecting it to be! The girl awakes and is also surprised to find the very Genji she had admired leaning over her! Inexperienced, the girl has no idea of Genji's error. As Genji thinks, though, on the woman who has avoided him, who is surely off in the dark gloating over her victory, he finds her hostility strangely exciting. And finding that the girl before him has her own charms, he is soon deep in the vows of love to her.

Afterwards, Genji warns the stepdaughter not to tell her mother of what has passed between them. When Genji finds that the pair were lying on the pale amber robe of the lady he had first sought, he takes the robe home with him. Fondling the robe, Genji sees how similar it is to the shell of the cicada that has flown, leaving only the perfect imprint of its body.

3-A

utsusemi no	empty cicada shell
waga usugoromo	my thin robe was familiar with
miyabio ni	an elegant man
nare te nuru ya to	was the reason then
ajiki naki koro	for an unpleasant dampness

3-1

When back home, Genji reflects on his amorous events of the evening. His thoughts about the reluctant woman he was unable to have arouse him, and he is unable to forget her. He compares, in his mind, the woman with whom he had sex and the one who got away. Her thin summer sleeping robe seems to suggest that she is like those insects one only hears on a hot night but does not see. He decides to send her a note telling her he has her robe and a poem to let her know that he still desires her in spite of having satisfied himself with the other woman.

utsusemi no	empty cicada shell
mi wo kae te keru	how different from the body
ki no moto ni	beneath the tree's root
nao hitogara no	more and more I'm longing for
natsukashiki kana	the one it personifies

3-2

Now both Lady of the Cicada Shell and her stepdaughter are in love with Genji, but the mother feels even more strongly that Genji should stop trying to see her. Unwilling to even write a poem to him, she simply jots down a well-known one, from an anthology by Lady Ise, that expresses her feelings.

utsusemi no	in this world
ha ni oku tsuyu no	dew falls on the cicada's wings
kogakure te	hidden by a tree
shinobi shinobi ni	to avoid public notice
nururu sode kana	sleeves wet with tears

3-1. From this poem the reluctant woman is given the name Lady of the Cicada Shell, *Utsusemi*. *Utsusemi*, "cicada shell," from *utsu*, "empty" with *semi*, "cicada." *Utsusemino* is a conventional modifier used in tanka for the idea of the empty shell of the world, of reality, of life, or of a person. The reference to "the tree's root" can apply to the place where the shells of cicadas are usually found and to the part of Genji's body where he found her robe.

3-2. It was very rare for Murasaki Shikibu to include a poem in her novel that was written by someone else. However, in this case, wishing to show how reluctant the woman was even to write to Genji, the idea to have Lady of the Cicada Shell merely quote a well-known poem from the anthologies was the best possible thing to do, and so she did it.

YŪGAO
EVENING FACES

Summer to Tenth Month of Genji's seventeenth year

Yūgao ("evening faces") flowers appear on a vine, the bottle gourd, that grows in the summer and reaches a height of six to nine feet. It is usually trained to grow on a trellis. The flower is also called moonflower, because the flowers begin opening at four or five o'clock in the afternoon, so they are at their best during the evening. The showy, pure white flowers actually seem to glow at dusk as earthly, round moons in the dark. Then in the night, the fragile flowers close and wither away. One cannot imagine a better flower to personify Genji's lady in this chapter.

On his way to visit Lady of the Sixth Ward, the widow of the previous crown prince and with whom he is also having a sporadic affair, Genji hears that an old nursemaid of his has taken her vows as a nun and is now lying near death. Spontaneously he decides to visit her with her natural son Sir Reflected Brilliance, who has become Genji's most trusted retainer. As they enter an area of Kyoto that is unknown to Genji, he sees growing over a rustic fence a profusion of evening faces flowers, and over the screens facing the verandah he sees the foreheads of women peeking at him. As an excuse to dally, he sends one of his men to pick a flower for him, but, before he can break one off, a little girl comes running out with a scented white fan for him to carry it on. After his visit to the nun, who seems to prefer Genji to her own son, Genji begins to speculate on the woman he spied behind the evening faces flowers. When Sir Reflected Brilliance investigates, he finds that the First Secretary's Captain has already visited the house. After Genji hears this, he decides that he, too, must meet Lady Evening Faces.

She is a frail, submissive beauty who Genji suspects is the mysterious lady in the First Secretary's Captain's rainy night story about the carnation love child. Genji, however, is charmed by her gentility, especially when finding her in such unaccustomed humble circumstances. He decides to abduct her, taking also Handmaiden, her lady-in-waiting, to a deserted villa hideaway. After spending a night and a day together, Genji dreams of a beautiful, but very angry, woman bending over him whom he recognizes as Lady of the Sixth Ward. She castigates him for having this new affair, and at that point he wakes and sees the apparition next to Lady Evening Faces. Lady Evening Faces is sweating and trembling and, within a few minutes, she is dead. The retainer, Sir Reflected Brilliance, takes over by sending Genji to his home on Second Avenue and secretly taking the girl's body to a temple for burial. Frightened and unhappy, Genji feels he must see the body once more, so he gets on a horse to race to the temple. He becomes ill on the journey, falling from his horse in a faint, and it is several months before he is himself again. He summons the maid who witnessed the tragic affair, and together they share memories of the deceased lady.

At the end of the chapter, Genji again tries to contact Lady of the Cicada Shell, but, though she and now her stepdaughter are deeply in love him, they break off all contact with him.

In this chapter Shikibu introduces again the figure of a jealous woman who can cause death; this archetype in Japanese literature is known as *hannya* and was later a popular feature of Noh plays. It was Lady of the Beautiful Hall whose jealousy was responsible for Genji's mother's death, and now Lady of the Sixth Ward is another of these dangerous women figures who prove that hate can kill.

---

4 - A

uki yowa no	bitterness of midnight
akumu to tomo ni	bad dreams come together with
natsukashiki	the dear ones of yore

yume mo ato naku	but dreams also disappear
kie ni keru kana	without a trace as the past

4 - 1

While waiting to be admitted to the compound to visit his old nurse, the mother of his retainer Sir Reflected Brilliance, Genji finds next door an extraordinary display of moonflowers twining over a rustic fence newly made of woven cypress strips. In this neighborhood of small, run-down houses, the genteel atmosphere makes him feel that the occupants are in a temporary shelter. What really attracts him, however, are the several foreheads of women that can be seen above the edge of a screen, also new and clean. As an excuse to linger while he figures out this unusual situation, Genji tells one of his men to pluck a flower for him. Before the man can do that, a small girl runs out with a fan on which to lay the flower. Much later Genji sees that on the fan is written a poem by someone who has been observing him admire the flowers.

kokoroate ni	by just guessing
sore ka to zo miru	who was that one I saw
shiratsuyu no	the visiting dew
hikari soe taru	adding its own radiance to
yūgao no hana	the face of the evening flowers

4 - 2

Genji asks his retainer, Sir Reflected Brilliance, to inquire about the residents dwelling next door. He learns that it is the home of the wife of an honorary vice-governor who has several sisters who stay with her when they are out of service. Thinking that it would be a lark to meet the sister whose charming poem had graced the fan, Genji makes his move. He disguises his handwriting and writes on a scrap of paper the following poem, which extends his challenge and invitation. It is delivered by the man who picked the flower.

yori te koso	if you'd come closer
sore ka tomo mime	you might find out more about

tasogare ni	something at twilight
honobono mi tsuru	the vague face in the evening
hana no yūgao	is more than a moonflower

4-3

In the meantime Genji continues his affair with the stern, hard Lady of the Sixth Ward. One morning of heavy mists, she refuses to get up to say farewell to him, so her serving woman, Miss of the Captaincy, escorts Genji out onto the verandah. There he asks her to sit with him. He is attracted to her long hair and flowing robes, so, while preparing to depart, he takes her hand and says:

saku hana ni	each opened flower
utsuru chō na wa	changed by love is named hearsay
tsutsume domo	though I want to hide
ora de sugi uki	it's hard to pass without picking
kesa no asagao	this morning glory today

4-4

In responding, the Miss of the Captaincy speaks from the awareness of a lady-in-waiting who does not want to compete with her lady by becoming another one of the many conquests of Genji. She makes her poem sound as if it was not from herself but from her lady.

asagiri no	so unable to wait
hare ma mo mata nu	for a clearing in morning mists
keshiki nite	the view seems to be
hana ni kokoro wo	a flower you cannot love
tome nu tozo miru	that's what I think they will say

4-4. To complete the scene, a small boy runs into the garden and picks a morning glory flower for Genji. The scene seems like a picture painted long ago. *Keshiki* has two meanings: "look, attitude, intention" and "scenery" or "view."

4-5

Genji continues to question Sir Reflected Brilliance about his neighbor known as Lady Evening Faces, the writer of the poem on the fan. Finally, going in disguise, and without Sir Reflected Brilliance, Genji is able to spend the night with her.

She is eager to know the identity of her charming visitor, so she sends out persons to follow him home, but Genji is able to dodge them. All of this only makes his visits to Lady Evening Faces more exciting. He is astonished at himself as he finds he can hardly wait through a day so he might go in the evening to her. Very early one morning, before leaving her residence, they overhear, in an adjoining room, a person saying his prayers. Genji tries to get her to accompany him to another place where they can enjoy the remaining hours alone. Her timid resistance brings Genji to the point of making vows.

ubasoku ga	the lay priest
okonau michi wo	learning Buddhist teachings
shirube nite	becomes a guidepost
ko n yo mo fukaki	on our way to the other world
chigiri tagau na	so we can never break our vows

---

4 - 6

Then, fearing such an oath could bode ill for him, Genji alters his vow.

saki no yo no	previous lives
chigiri shiraruru	know so well other vows
mi no usa ni	thus it's much harder
yukusue kakete	to depend on the future
tanomi gatasa yo	hardly something we should do

---

4 - 7

Suddenly, when the setting moon sinks into a bank of clouds, Genji picks up Lady Evening Faces, thrusts her into his carriage, and drives off with her to an abandoned villa. While he waits for someone to unlock the gate, he tries to comfort the woman, who is feeling uneasy and frightened, with these words:

inishie mo	in olden times
kakuya wa hito no	people just like us
madoi ken	were confused

waga mada shiranu	why can I not discover
shinonome no michi	the early morning way?

4 - 8

Still waiting to be admitted to this strange place, Genji finally coaxes a few words from Lady Evening Faces as she tells him only how afraid she is. She turns away shyly as she answers.

yama no ha no	the unsure heart
kokoro mo shira zu	at the mountain's edge
yuku tsuki wa	the moon proceeds
uwa no sora nite	lightly into the heavens
kage ya kie nan	vanishes without a shadow

4 - 9

After spending the rest of the night together in the deserted villa, and when the sun has risen high, Lady Evening Faces wants to know who this man is who has carried her off in the night. All this time, Genji has carefully kept her unaware of his identity, and she feels the affair has come to the point where he should show his face to her in the daylight and reveal his identity.

yū tsuyu ni	in evening dew
himo toku hana wa	strings of flowers were untied
tamaboko no	in this way
tayori ni mie shi	thus by chance our destinies
e ni koso ari kere	have a reason to exist

4 - 10

"And how do you view it?" Genji asks her. Lady Evening Faces gives this reply as she turns away and speaks in a whisper. She finds him even more handsome than when she saw him stop to admire her moonflowers.

hikari ari to	seeing an evening face
mishi yūgao no	in the dewy radiance shining

4-8. In the light of the rest of her story, this poem becomes an eerie omen and prophecy.

4-9. Taken together, the words *himo* (string, cord) and *toku* (untie, take off, thaw) comprise a euphemistic expression for sleeping together.

uwatsuyu wa	from trees and grasses
tasogare doki no	now at twilight it is clear
sorame nari keri	someone has been mistaken

---

4 - 11

Both refuse to reveal their names to each other, but this does not stop Genji and Lady Evening Faces from spending an affectionate day together. Then, in the night, about midnight, Genji wakes to the feeling that a beautiful woman is by his pillow. She berates him for abandoning her for this new girl and seems about to shake her, when Genji wakes to a darkened room. Lady Evening Faces is moaning and trembling. Genji tries to rally his bodyguards, but by the time some begin twanging their bows to frighten away evil spirits and others are sent to get a light, Genji realizes the girl has died. His situation becomes desperate, so he turns to his retainer, asking him to arrange a secret funeral at an obscure temple in the hills. Genji takes with him the serving lady, Handmaiden, home to the palace at Second Avenue. Later, on quiet evenings, Handmaiden is able to tell Genji the story of the life of Lady Evening Faces. He learns she has left a child of two years whom he wishes to have brought to him, but he realizes her presence would raise too many questions he did not want to answer. The skies cloud over and a chilly wind springs up from the withered flowers about the verandah. Gazing into the distance, Genji speaks softly.

mishi hito no	seeing a loved one
kemuri wo kumo to	in the crematory smoke
nagamure ba	rising as a cloud
yūbe no sora mo	the evening skies then look
mutsumajiki kana	surprisingly familiar

---

4 - 12

Genji is so shaken by the experience of the woman's death that he seems to be ill for several weeks afterwards. Lady of the Cicada Shell is sorry to know he is confined to his home, as well as being worried about her husband taking her off to a dreary distant province, and thus sends her little brother again to Genji with a note to keep alive their connection.

towanu wo mo
nadoka to towade
hodo furu ni
ikabakari ka wa
omoi midaruru

not asking you why
you no longer ask for me
time goes by slowly
still I want you to be sure
I am worried about you

---

4 - 13

Surprised and delighted that she has not forgotten him though they have never met again, Genji writes, in a hand still shaky, to Lady of the Cicada Shell of his aimless life.

utsusemino
yo wa uki mono to
shiri ni shi wo
mata kotonoha ni
kakaru inochi yo

empty as it is
this worldly shell full of pain
so it seems to me
that having your poem-note
gives me the strength to go on

---

4 - 14

Genji's thinking about Lady of the Cicada Shell reminds him of her stepdaughter (who from this point on has the name Lady Reeds Under the Eaves) with whom he had "accidentally" spent the night when his intended woman, her stepmother, had slipped away. Genji knows that Lady Reeds Under the Eaves has since married a guards lieutenant and he is curious about how she finds her new situation, so he sends her this provocative note tied to a long, slender reed.

honoka nimo
nokiba no ogi wo
musuba zu ba
tsuyu no kagoto wo
nani ni kake mashi

however loosely
this one reed under the eaves
if it is so bound
complaining with dewlike tears
then I wish to untie it

4-13. After experiencing the death of his lover, Genji now shows a new awareness of the meaning of the shell of the cicada. The poem shows us how our lives are merely animated shells or husks and how easily life can be extinguished.

4-14. Similar to the English "tying the knot," the reference here is to marriage, and also to the method of thatching a roof with reeds tied together in bundles.

4 - 15

With her husband away, Lady Reeds Under the Eaves is delighted and confused about what she should do. Yet she cannot keep herself from responding to Genji's poem.

honomekasu	the wind hints
kaze ni tsuke temo	no matter how much in love
shita ogi no	the heart of reed
nakaba wa shimo ni	the half exposed to frosts
musuboore tsutsu	is the most firmly fastened

4 - 16

When the forty-ninth-day funeral services for Lady Evening Faces are held, Genji writes a memorial petition that deeply touches his mentor and tutor in Chinese poetry. Genji does not reveal the name of the deceased, so his teacher only wonders the more who has played such an important part in Genji's young life. Among the secret offerings Genji sends to the service is this poem tied to an item of a lady's intimate apparel.

naku naku mo	weeping and weeping
kyō wa waga yū	even today as I tie up
shitahimo wo	these familiar cords
izure no yo ni ka	are loosened only in that world
toke te miru beki	where we are again joined

4 - 17

When the husband of Lady of the Cicada Shell has to return to his provincial outpost, taking her with him, Genji makes many gifts to her of fans, combs with beautiful workmanship, and fabric he has dyed especially for her. He also returns to her the robe—the shell of the cicada—that he took from her bed. Only someone who could see it would know whether the sleeves were still attached to the gown and whether he had forgotten her or not.

4-16. To continue the connections in this chapter on ties and binding, the poem refers to the cord that secured the underskirt worn beneath the outer costume; this underskirt was the last garment removed when disrobing.

au made no
katami bakari to
mishi hodo ni
hitasura sode no
kuchi ni keru kana

hoping to meet you
I've held this as a keepsake
yet as time goes by
the sleeves have rotted away
complete with my memories

4 - 18

Lady of the Cicada Shell, using the analogy of wings and the wide sleeves of a kimono, lets Genji know she thinks the sleeves have been cast away, as she has been cast out of his memory, and so feels remorse.

semi no ha mo
tachikae te keru
natsugoromo
kaesu wo mi temo
ne wa naka re keri

cast off in the past
as wings of the cicada
summer robes
I see have returned to me
I become the crying voice

4 - 19

The reply from Lady of the Cicada Shell causes Genji to have many sad thoughts, so he stays in bed during the dark day of the first winter showers and writes the following:

sugi ni shi mo
kyō wakaruru mo
futa michi ni
yukukata shira nu
aki no kure kana

one has gone away
today I part from the other
two ways
which I cannot understand
the departing of autumn

4-17. The word *au*, "meeting," can also, like the English expression "to know," mean the act of knowing as man and wife. The sleeves of a kimono would not really "rot away," but the threads holding the sleeves to the body of the garment would be the weakest point. When these threads pulled loose, the sleeves would fall away.

4-19. *Sugi*, "to pass or exceed," can refer to either time passing or persons passing away.

5

WAKA MURASAKI
YOUNG LAVENDER

Third to Tenth Month of Genji's eighteenth year

Feeling ill from the several disappointments he has suffered in his love life, Genji travels to visit with a holy man living in a cave in the hills north of Kyoto in an attempt to be cured of his mysterious malady, which seems unaffected by the regular religious services. Before returning home, he glimpses a beautiful young girl who reminds him very strongly of Lady of the Wisteria Apartment. When the priest from the villa where Genji glimpsed the girl invites Genji for a visit, Genji learns the child's name is Murasaki (Lavender) and that she is a niece of Lady of the Wisteria Apartment, the woman he secretly loves. He decides to adopt the child, but her grandmother nun and the Bishop, her uncle, believe Genji does not understand how young she is, and think that he only wants her as a mistress. When Genji recovers completely from his illness and is ready to leave the area, he asks again to adopt Murasaki, but they tell him "perhaps in a few years." At home Genji is again repulsed by his coldhearted wife, Lady Heartvine. This makes him press his plans to adopt Murasaki and strengthens her custodians' refusal.

Lady of the Wisteria Apartment, Genji's stepmother, becomes ill and leaves the court. Genji uses this opportunity to go to her secretly for a nighttime tryst. From this encounter, Lady of the Wisteria Apartment becomes pregnant. The excitement of this, and his courtly duties, makes Genji forget about Murasaki, until he accidentally learns that the grandmother nun has died. While the family is still deciding what to do with Murasaki, her father, Prince Director of Military Affairs, concludes that he will take her into his home. When Genji hears of this, he races off to Murasaki and lies to her nurse in order to abduct both of them to his home on Second Avenue. Genji begins Murasaki's education by grooming her to be the perfect wife for him.

5-A

haru no no no	spring fields
ura wakakusa ni	with tender grasses
shitashimi te	as to young girls
ito ōdoka ni	love comes true
koi mo nari nuru	very easily

5-1

While at a temple deep in the northern hills, Genji climbs even higher to visit an old monk living in a cave who makes a secret drink for him and prepares spells and incantations for his healing. While waiting for the next concoction, Genji sees a fence of slats and brushwood that intrigues him. That evening, after sending most of his retinue away, Genji peeks through a screen at the women enclosed within and observes an old nun weeping over a young girl child and he hears the nun recite:

oitata n	growing up
arika mo shiranu	here the young grass
wakakusa wo	doesn't know
okurasu tsuyu zo	she's left behind by dews
kie n sora naki	not yet vanished in the sky

5-A. The word *wakakusa,* "young grass," is used in poetry as a metaphor for young girls. Akiko Yosano, in her poem, effects both meanings of the word at once.

5-2

A woman with the nun recites a poem to comfort the older woman, who fears both that she will die before the girl grows up and that she cannot give up and die or become a good nun because of her obligation to care for the child:

hatsukusa no	spring grass
oiyuku sue mo	grows up not knowing
shiranu ma ni	how short life is
ikadeka tsuyu no	how can it be that
kie n to su ran	the dew would vanish?

5-3

While visiting with the temple bishop, Genji learns the story of Murasaki's life: The bishop's sister had a daughter who had a relationship with Prince Director of Military Affairs (the brother of Lady of the Wisteria Apartment), which explains the resemblance Genji saw in her. Abandoned by the prince, the mother went into a decline and died, leaving the child to be raised by the bishop and his sister, the grandmotherly nun. Genji offers to adopt the girl, but the first reaction of her caretakers is to say no. Later that evening, after a chilly shower, Genji hears the voice of an old woman in the room behind a screen. Unable to sleep, he attempts to make contact with the nun. A woman comes to the screen and is naturally confused about who this person with the aristocratic voice is and what he wants with her or anyone else. Genji whispers his poem to her and asks her to give it to her lady.

hatsukusa no	since first seeing
wakaba no ue wo	the leaves of spring grass
mi tsuru yori	this noble girl
tabine no sode mo	the sleeves of the wanderer
tsuyu zo kawaka nu	know no respite from the dew

5-4

The serving woman relays Genji's message to the nun, the child's grandmother, who wonders if Genji really knows that the child is about ten years old. She hesitates answering for so long that others with her fear she will seem rude, so she

5-2. Because the name Murasaki refers to the color lavender and an autumn grass, these poems are especially apt. This motif is used throughout the whole book.

writes a quick reply, thus revealing deep feelings she might otherwise have left hidden had she taken more time for a more careful answer.

makura yū	don't even compare
koyoi bakari no	your pillow while traveling
tsuyuke sa wo	only slightly damp
miyama no koke ni	with the dews which soak
kurabe zara nan	the moss in the mountains

5-5

By now, the grandmother nun finds Genji's behavior completely outrageous. After sitting in the Lotus Hall listening to voices raised in contrition mingling with the roar of the waterfall and the wild winds, Genji appeals to the bishop for his help in obtaining custody of Murasaki. In his poem Genji shows how distraught he is due to his feelings that he must have this child.

fukimayou	tossed about by
miyama oroshi ni	winds blowing from the mountain
yume same te	I wake from dreams
namida moyoosu	my many tears are the cause
taki no oto kana	of the waterfall's loud sound

5-6

The Bishop dryly answers:

sashigumi ni	being moved to tears
sode nurashi keru	too quickly dampens your sleeves?
yama mizu ni	our mountain waters
sumeru kokoro wa	are noisy yet clearly
sawagi yawa suru	they calm our hearts the most

5-7

Now that he is cured of his indisposition, Genji prepares to leave the temple. The First Secretary's Captain and his other friends arrive to escort him home. Wishing to show his goodwill, the Bishop sends Genji off with a round of wine and good wishes. With his promises to return before the cherry petals fall, Genji replies:

miyabito ni	I suppose my escorts
yuki te kataran	will hasten to go and tell others
yama zakura	to see the mountain
kaze yori saki ni	cherry blossoms or the wind
ki temo miru beku	will certainly see them first

5-8

The Bishop's reply is:

udonge no	having waited for
hana machi etaru	the three-thousand-year flower
kokochi shi te	I feel inclined
miyama zakura ni	never to move my eyes toward
me koso utsura ne	the mountain cherry blossoms

5-9

To the farewell event has been invited the ancient sage who had come down from his hermitage cave in the mountains to pray for Genji's cure. As Genji fills the guest's wine cup, the sage recites his pleasure at having met Genji with tears of appreciation in his eyes.

okuyama no	here in these mountains
matsu no toboso wo	my rustic door made of pine
mare ni ake te	is rarely open
mada minu hana no	I've yet to know the flower
kao wo miru kana	which was never seen before

5 - 10

As Genji prepares to depart, the bishop tries to get the nun to let Murasaki go with Genji, but she is steadfast in her refusal. She says that perhaps in three or four years Murasaki can go to him. The bishop disagrees with her but passes her decision to Genji without comment. Very disappointed, Genji sends a message back by an acolyte to the grandmother nun:

yūmagure	in evening dusk
honoka ni hana no	the flower seen so faintly
iro wo mi te	shows its beauty
kesa wa kasumi no	thus this morning's mist is
tachi zo wazurau	loath to rise for leaving

5 - 11

The grandmother nun's reply recognizes Genji's sadness about leaving Murasaki, similar to her own feelings that when she dies—becomes smoke in the skies—the lingering haziness of the sky will show her own regret about leaving the child.

makaoto ni ya	isn't it really true
hana no atari wa	the one who's near the flower
tachi uki to	is loath to leave also?
kasumuru sora no	the haziness of the skies
keshiki wo mo min	is a sign we wait to see

5 - 12

Back home in the city, Genji is met and then taken by his father-in-law to see his wife, Lady Heartvine, who is not very sympathetic with him about his illness nor his trip. Feeling rebuffed, Genji thinks longingly of the child Murasaki. He decides to write to the grandmother nun and encloses this poem in a tightly folded note for Murasaki.

omokage wa	the image
mi wo mo hanare zu	of mountain cherry flowers
yamazakura	remains with me

5-11. Genji views himself and his sadness as lingering morning mist, whereas she views herself as being closer to a cloud of smoke, a good indication of the differences in their ages.

kokoro no kagiri	however my serenity
tomete koshikado	is unable to come or go

5 - 13

The grandmother nun writes back that Murasaki cannot yet manage the brush well enough to send him a reply to his note. She is deeply troubled by Genji writing again so soon after his leaving and is at a loss as to know how she should reply to this impetuous but very wealthy and influential man.

arashi fuku	from the mountaintop
onoe no sakura	storms blow the cherry flowers
chira nu ma wo	so quickly scattered
kokoro tome keru	your own fickle affections
hodo no hakanasa	are just as vain and fleeting

5 - 14

Undaunted, Genji sends his steward Sir Reflected Brilliance to make contact with Murasaki's nurse. He is persuasive, being a ladies' man himself, but the bishop and the nun now seem united in feeling that Genji is being too capricious. Genji nonetheless takes the opportunity of sending another note with his retainer to Murasaki under the thin guise of it being a calligraphy lesson.

asakayama	Mount Asaka
asaku mo hito wo	is known for its shallow springs
omowanu ni	shallow I am not
nado yamanoi no	then why is the mountain spring
kake hanaru ran	I long for so distant from me?

5 - 15

Again, it is the grandmother nun who writes a reply, expressing her opinion of his behavior. Sir Reflected Brilliance reports back that the nun will bring the child to the city as soon as she is a little stronger and will answer him then.

5-14. Mount Asaka was known for having shallow springs in the already-famous poems in the *Manyōshū* and *Kokinshū*, imperial anthologies of poetry.

kumi some te
kuyashi to kiki shi
yamanoi no
asaki nagara ya
kage wo misu beki

beginning to scoop
you sully the little water
from this mountain spring
isn't it your shallowness that
shows in a shadowy image?

---

5 - 16

Genji turns his romantic attentions to Lady of the Wisteria Apartment, his stepmother, who is ill and has gone to her parent's home to recover. Through her nurse, Genji arranges a meeting with Lady of the Wisteria Apartment in her bedroom and manages to get her to let him spend the night. Genji weeps as he leaves her this poem in the morning at their parting.

mi temo mata
au yo marenaru
yume no naka ni
yagate magiruru
wagami tomogana

seeing you once more
tonight again entering
this exquisite dream
I wish only that someday
my complete being joins it

---

5 - 17

Lady of the Wisteria Apartment feels sorry for him, but she is very aware of her compromised position and how his dream could affect her.

yogatari ni
hito ya tsutaen
tagui naku
ukimi wo same nu
yume ni nashi temo

a source of gossip
for people to pass around
nothing equals
to one's woes when not waking
to a dream of being bedded

---

5 - 18

Genji later learns Lady of the Wisteria Apartment is pregnant, and although he suspects her condition is the result of their night together, he continues to pursue Murasaki. When he accidentally hears that the grandmother nun, who now dwells at the edge of the city, is near death, he impulsively stops to visit her. Just as he asks to see Murasaki and the grandmother nun tells him she is asleep, Murasaki comes into the room, saying she heard that "the gentleman from the temple" is here. Genji is charmed that she remembers him, so the next day, while sending a note to the grandmother nun, he again includes a tightly folded one for Murasaki.

iwakenaki	since hearing the cry
tazu no hitokoe	of the nestling crane
kiki shi yori	one so innocent
ashima ni nazumu	in the place where reeds grow
fune zo enaranu	this little boat is sadly lost

---

5 - 19

In a note from Murasaki's nurse, Genji learns the grandmother nun is not expected to live out the day. On an autumn evening, he recalls the nun describing herself as smoke holding back from the heavens because of the girl child. Genji also thinks of his attraction for Lady of the Wisteria Apartment, which is now bringing them so much sadness he has been banned from her side. As he wonders if bringing Murasaki to his home will truly bring him the happiness he seeks, he writes into a poem these thoughts.

te ni tsumi te	taking it in hand
itsushikamo mi n	may I soon take care of
murasaki no	Murasaki
ne ni kayoi keru	the root of royal purple
nobe no wakakusa	still in the field of young grasses

---

5 - 20

In the rush and excitement of autumnal court festivities, Genji forgets about the grandmother nun's health and her little charge. When he finally does inquire about her, the Bishop replies that she died at the end of the previous month. Genji goes off to see Murasaki, but first must visit with her nurse, from whom he learns there are plans to send Murasaki to live

5-18. Genji's use of the phrase "this little boat" can be in reference to himself or a part of his body seeking a grassy place.

with her father, Prince Director of Military Affairs. Genji asks to speak to Murasaki with this double-entendre poem.

ashi waka no	concealed sea grasses
ura ni mirume wa	in the reeds of Wakanoura
kataku tomo	even if severe
kowa tachi nagara	this resistance is enough
kaeru nami kawa	to turn aside such a wave?
	or
	a chance to meet
	in the rushes of Poetry Bay
	though it's difficult
	for the rising wave as it is
	there's no returning is there?

5 - 21

The nurse's skillful reply makes him almost forget the poem's lack of encouragement for his cause.

yoru nami no	coming closer but
kokoro mo shira de	unable to know the wave's heart
wakanoura ni	at Poetry Bay
tamamo nabika n	the sea grass bends so deeply
hodo zo uki taru	it consents to just drifting

5 - 22

The night becomes so dark and stormy that the nurse and ladies-in-waiting for Murasaki are grateful when Genji decides to spend the night with them. Instead of it being an amorous meeting, Genji and Murasaki's lady-in-waiting sit by Murasaki, telling her stories and promising her dolls and pictures if she will come to live with him. When the storm abates, he leaves feeling slightly depressed. As he passes the house of a woman he has seen in secret previously, he has someone knock on the gate. When there is no response, he has another man from his retinue recite twice this poem to attract attention.

5-20. Wakanoura, the name of a famous place in Japan, can be understood as: *waka,* "poetry," *no,* "of," and *ura,* referring to an inlet, bay, gulf, creek, seashore, or beach. *Kataku* has two meanings, "severe" or "difficult." *Kaeru* can mean either "turn" or "return." All of these possibilities add to the depth and ambiguity of the poem.

asaborake	misty skies of dawn
kiritatsu sora no	and lost as I seem to be
mayoi nimo	my dearest woman
yukisugi gataki	it is hard to just go on
imo ga kado kana	when I find your gate like this

5 - 23

The woman sends out an ordinary maid with this written answer:

tachi tomari	the fog is not stopped
kiri no magaki no	by the strongest bamboo fence
sugi uku ba	is it hard to pass
kusa no tozashi ni	this gate of mine that is barred
sawari shimo seji	with nothing more than grasses?

5 - 24

The thought that people could accuse him of a perversion if he abducted the child only makes Genji more eager to have her. In a secret mission in the night, and among the great confusion by her ladies and tears and sobbing by Murasaki, Genji carries her to a deserted wing of the palace on Second Avenue. In the following days, Genji begins lessons for Murasaki in poetry and calligraphy. He writes out for her the old poems from the anthologies for her to copy. One day, choosing lavender paper, he writes the following *waka* from an unknown author in the *Kokin Rokujō*.

shira ne domo	though I cannot see it
musashino to ieba	when one speaks of Musashino
kakota re nu	I sigh so deeply
yoshiya sakoso wa	the reason for this are thoughts
murasaki no yue	of those grasses of lavender

5-24. *Musashino*, "the fields of Musashi," which, at the time of the story, spread over Tokyo, Saitama, and part of Kanagawa, were famous for the huge stands of *murasaki* grass. Because this was many miles from Kyoto, most people only had heard of the great grassy plains but never seen them. But just the name of the plain brought to mind Murasaki's name. This is a skillful application of an old poem to a new use.

5 - 25

When Murasaki reads the poem, she sees that Genji has written his own poem in very small characters beside it just for her.

ne wa mi ne do	not to see the roots
aware tozo omou	though said to be impressive
musashino no	in Musashi Plain
tsuyu wake waburu	tearfully I try to proceed
kusa no yukari wo	through the tightly bound grass

or

though so very dear
not to know the origin
of dew in Musashi
I worry about finding
the relationship of this grass

5 - 26

Genji tells Murasaki she must write a response, but she claims she cannot. He tells her she must think of him as her teacher. So she writes a response, but out of fear she has made an error, she hides it. He takes the poem from her and reads it:

kakotsu beki	I do not know what
yue wo shiraneba	causes you to sigh so much
obotsukana	I wonder
ikanaru kusa no	what kind of grass am I
yukari naruran	that you fear a relationship

5-25. Very artful, the poem can be read two ways to show Genji's feelings about Murasaki's parentage. The word *wake* can mean either "distinguish" or "divide, clear the way."

SUETSUMU HANA
PRINCESS SAFFLOWER

Genji's eighteenth year

While still embroiled in his many affairs, Genji learns of an orphaned princess who has a reputation for playing the harp. Genji arranges to go to her secretly to hear her play. Once there, he discovers the First Secretary's Captain has the same objective. They agree to become friendly rivals. Genji successfully influences the lady-in-waiting of Princess Safflower to allow him admittance to the princess's quarters, but the princess is so flustered by Genji's appearance that she is incapable of formulating any responses to his poems—a job left to her ladies. Genji does sneak a look at her and is not impressed. The lady-in-waiting presses Genji to try again, and he finally does spend a night with her. In the light of the morning snow he gets a good look at her nose, which is unusually large and very red, as if it had rouge on it. In his parting poem he compares her nose to a dripping icicle, red with morning light. Out of pity he sends her gifts, and she responds with a poorly made jacket and the first of a collection of her stilted poems about clothes. Genji returns to Murasaki and playfully paints his own nose red, wondering why a red nose is ugly but rosy cheeks, like Murasaki's, so delightful.

6 - A

kawagoromo	as my darling
ue ni ki tare ba	is clad in nothing more than

wagimoko wa	clothes of skin
kiku koto no mina	I'm sure she hears everything
mi ni shima nu rashi	even if her body isn't touched

---

6 - 1

With the child Murasaki living in his palace, Genji nonetheless continues his affairs with other women. The next encounter starts when a court serving woman tells of a princess, the daughter of a late prince, who is very cultured but destitute, having no supporters or friends. The court serving woman uses her connection to Princess Safflower—they played the harp together—to bring Genji to secretly hear the musical duet. Afterwards Genji is ready to leave without trying to visit the princess, when he stops in the main hall to see if there is anything of interest for him there. While hidden behind a leaning section of moldy bamboo fence, he is surprised by his best friend, the First Secretary's Captain, who speaks:

morotomoni	leaving together
ōuchiyama wa	the mountain of the high court
ide tsure do	but with secret ways
iru kata mise nu	it comes in this direction
izayoi no tsuki	moon of the sixteenth night

---

6 - 2

Genji is at once surprised and annoyed that his friend has followed him on a night it is rather clear he is out to meet a woman. Thus he responds with:

sato waka nu	not caring
kage wo mire domo	if its rays are seen or not
yuku tsuki no	the moon
irusa no yama wo	enters any mountain pass
tare ka tazunuru	who cares who is watching?

or

6-1. In Japan, until the reformation in the nineteenth century, months were calculated by the moon. The night of the dark of the moon was the first night. The fifteenth night of the moon was when it was full. Thus, on the sixteenth night the moon was just past full and beginning to wane.

6-2. Though the kanji character used is for "village," *sato*, it makes more sense to read *sa* as the pronoun "it" and *to* as "such as, like."

indistinguishable
the village from its light
even if the moon goes
to the entrance of the mountain
who would ask such a question?

6 - 3

Enjoying the feeling of being in competition, both Genji and the First Secretary's Captain start sending notes to the princess, known later in the chapter as Princess Safflower, but neither one receives a response. Genji's ambitious spirit, as well as the challenge to get a response from her, make him repeatedly ask the court serving woman about her. Finally the court serving woman helps to sneak Genji into her rooms. Princess Safflower is so shy and inexperienced with gentlemen from the high court, she can neither speak nor write a word. Most eloquently Genji pleads his case:

ikusotabi	untold are the times
kimi ga shijima ni	your silence has silenced me
make nu ran	that doesn't mean
mono na ii so to	we cannot love one another
iwa nu tanomini	even if I'm asked not to speak

6 - 4

Since Princess Safflower is too shy to answer, one of her nursemaids speaks from behind the screen.

kane tsuki te	to ring a bell
tojime n koto wa	would not end the affair
sasugani te	even so
kotae mauki zo	with no desire to answer
katsu wa ayanaki	it all becomes meaningless

6 - 5

Genji is puzzled at the garrulity of the sudden answer and the voice. Thinking the response not appropriate for one of the princess's rank—as it was too coquettish—he himself feels speechless.

iwa nu wo mo	silence I know
iu ni masaru to	far surpasses speaking out
shiri nagara	however I feel
oshikome taru wa	to choke down one's words
kurushi kari keri	seems to be the most painful

6 - 6

Although not particularly excited by Princess Safflower, Genji does spend the night with her. The next morning, when it is time to send the customary "lover's morning-after" note, Genji is forced by the First Secretary's Captain to hurry to the palace to work together on the arrangements for an outing for the emperor. It is not until evening that he has time to send his messenger with this, the obligatory poem.

yūgiri no	at dusk the thick fog
haruru keshiki mo	clears away from the scene
mada mi nu ni	yet one cannot see
ibusesa souru	how early evening rains
yoi no ame kana	only increase my gloom

6 - 7

Princess Safflower is dismayed that the note did not come in the morning, and that now, instead of Genji coming for the customary second night with her, he sends only a messenger. She hardly knows how to answer but does finally write on paper that once had been purple but now has faded to gray.

hare nu yo no	nothing is cleared up
tsuki matsu sato wo	the village awaits tonight's moon
omoi yare	the disregard
onaji kokoro ni	seems the same as in your heart
nagame se zu tomo	thus long rains aren't my view

6-7. The practice in courting was that if a man spent three nights in a row with a woman, the action signified their marriage. When a woman assented (if she did) to spending one night with a man, it was vital to her to know if this was merely a dalliance or a real marriage. For a woman without other financial and emotional support, it was absolutely crucial to, not only the woman but the rest of her retinue or her whole village, that a rich man like Genji, who would insure her future security, appear for his second and third visits.

6-8

Occasionally Genji calls on Princess Safflower for his nightly visits. One early morning, when the winter cold is at its worst, he is preparing to leave. As the lady comes to the verandah to see him off, he finally gets a good look at her in the light off the snow. Now he sees that she not only has a large nose, but that it is very red. She is so thin and poor, Genji feels she truly needs a lover to support her. And yet Genji remembers how she was so cold and unresponsive to him in the night.

asahi sasu	in the morning sun
noki no tarui wa	icicles underneath the eaves
toke nagara	begin to melt
nadoka tsurara no	why is it that the ice here
musubōru ran	remains so firmly frozen?

6-9

As Genji prepares to leave the courtyard of her mansion, he finds the outer gate still locked, so he sends for someone to unlock it. It is as if her servants are not prepared to be letting men out of the compound so early in the morning. It is snowing heavily and as the old, poorly dressed man comes out to open the gate against the drifts, he struggles in vain. He is joined by a young woman wearing very dirty clothes carrying embers in a pot, who also tries feebly to help him. Finally one of Genji's men has to push the gate open against the deep snow. As Genji waits and watches the scene with interest, he recites:

furi ni keru	look at him
atama no yuki wo	with snow which has fallen
miru hito mo	on his head
otora zu nurasu	is no less wet than tears
asa no sode kana	on my morning sleeves

6-10

Now clearly aware of the poverty in which the princess and her retinue live, Genji, in his celebrated generosity, sends many garments to her. However, because he is not greatly enam-

6-8. There is speculation that the poem is also drawing a comparison between Princess Safflower's cold (perhaps) dripping nose and the morning sun shining through an icicle dripping as it begins to melt.

ored with the princess, he does not enclose a note with the gifts professing his love. So Princess Safflower sends a thank-you note through her serving woman, saying:

karagoromo	an imported robe
kimi ga kokoro no	from the heart of a husband
tsurakere ba	filled with such a cold
tamoto wa kaku zo	that is the reason these sleeves
sobochi tsutsu nomi	are continually wet

6-10. *Karagoromo* refers to a short coat worn by women in Heian times. *Kara* originally meant "Korean" and later, "Chinese," and still later it stood for something that was imported or from a foreign culture. At the time of Shikibu, things brought from China were precious and considered to be of a very high quality.

6-11. It is from this poem of Genji's that the princess is given her name.

6-12. The serving woman immediately saw Genji's joke in the pun on *hana*, which can mean either "flower" or "nose." There is also an allusion to safflower, or *benibana*, the rouge-plant flower. The Latin name is *Carthamus tinctorius*, referring to its use for making rouge and for dyeing food a warm yellow-orange or reddish color. She thought Genji should be ashamed of his wicked pun and therefore red faced, while she only felt sorry for the princess.

6 - 11

Making fun of her large, red nose, which he has had a clear view of, Genji wonders if the sleeves in the poem are wet from tears or from her dripping nose. Along with the thank-you note is an old hamper containing a set of very old-fashioned robes in an impossible color for Genji to wear on New Year's Day. Seeing these, the serving woman and Genji are both embarrassed for the lady. To lighten the mood, Genji jots this poem beside her note, which he lets only the serving woman read.

natsukashiki	the color red
iro tomo nashi ni	is not dear to my heart
nani ni kono	why therefore
suetsumu hana wo	was the safflower
sode ni fure ken	touched by my sleeve?

6 - 12

Although the serving woman is not someone Genji is interested in, he is impressed with her poem, which she recites in quick response.

kurenai no	dyed a vivid red
hito hanagoromo	is a person with flowery clothes
usuku tomo	even if shallow
hitasura kutasu	do not entirely stain the name
na wo shi tate zu ba	if you can save her honor

6 - 13

Genji therefore takes a whole day to create his carefully considered response, which he shows the serving woman beforehand, saying how hard he has worked on it. When it is delivered to Princess Safflower, her women gather around to admire it.

awa nu yo wo	the nights we don't meet
hedatsuru naka no	adding layers of separation
koromode ni	are not dyed garments
kasanete itodo	layers even thicker between
mi mo shimi yo toya	the touch of our bodies?

6 - 14

Genji seems genuinely puzzled as to why red on the nose of Princess Safflower disturbs him so much, whereas the red cheeks of his girl-child Murasaki seem as attractive as the red plum that was about to bloom.

kurenai no	the rouge plant's
hana zo aya naku	red flower was not without reason
utoma ruru	to be slighted
ume no tachie wa	a branch of red plum blossoms
natsukashi kere do	however is what one longs for

7

MOMIJI NO GA
VIEWING THE AUTUMN LEAVES

Autumn of Genji's eighteenth year to autumn of his nineteenth year

The Emperor, Genji's father, arranges a royal excursion to the nearby hills to admire the autumn leaves. The ladies of the court, and Lady of the Wisteria Apartment, who is in advanced pregnancy, lament that they will miss the concert that will be a part of the event. Thus, the Emperor orders that a rehearsal first be held at the palace. Genji and the First Secretary's Captain dance to the ceremonial music so magnificently that Lady of the Beautiful Hall only increases her jealousy of Genji, whom she still sees as a threat to her son, the Crown Prince.

Genji is occupied with his education of Murasaki, who grows in grace and maturity. The sweetness of his relationship with her only makes more uncomfortable the one with his wife, Lady Heartvine. As he tries to spend less time with his wife, her own father does his best, with gifts and kind words, to draw Genji into the family.

About the time of the New Year, Lady of the Wisteria Apartment, who has grown very feeble in her pregnancy, is delivered of a male child. Everyone notices that it has a strong resemblance to Genji, which makes him try to avoid appearing in public. However, the Emperor is so pleased with his new child, he makes Lady of the Wisteria Apartment empress.

Though delighted with Murasaki, Genji is drawn into an encounter with an older woman, in her fifties, Woman of the Bedchamber, who served his father and who remembers Genji as a child. It seems he is eager not to just know this woman, but to experience various possible romantic attachments. It seems the First Secretary's Captain has similar aims, because while Genji is dozing beside her, he hears someone coming to her rooms. Genji fails to gather up his clothes as he tries to hide behind a screen. The First Secretary's Captain bursts in threatening them both with his sword. The two men begin to tussle and the wrestling escalates so that clothes are torn, while the poems fly back and forth. Laughing, the two young men go off arm in arm, leaving the old woman alone and outraged.

---

7 - A

seigai no	classical music
nami shizuka naru	the waves of the blue ocean
sama wo mau	yet the scene is quiet
wakaki kokoro wa	the dance of a young heart
shita ni nare domo	pounds inside of the sound

---

7 - 1

While preparing for an autumn excursion for viewing the colored leaves and a musical concert, the Emperor holds a rehearsal at his residence so Lady of the Wisteria Apartment can at least enjoy the musical numbers. Everyone in attendance is greatly impressed by Genji's dancing of the classical number, "Waves of the Blue Ocean." Knowing that Lady of the Wisteria Apartment has been watching him stimulates him in trying even harder. Eager to know her feelings, Genji sends her this verse in a note afterwards.

mono omou ni	beside the waving
tachimau beku mo	of the traditional sleeves
ara nu mi no	could you see a heart
sode uchi furi shi	worried with the many thoughts
kokoro shiri ki ya	how did you view the dancer?

7-A. The word *seigai* can mean either "blue ocean" or "classical music" used for dances. This is interesting if one thinks of the sound of the ocean as being the most traditional, or classical, "music" we know.

7-2

Lady of the Wisteria Apartment replies to Genji with the following poem.

karahito no	a foreigner's sleeves
sode furu koto wa	waved by a person of this world
tōkere do	seemed vague and distant
tachii ni tsuke te	yet my heart was drawn to each
aware to wa mi ki	motion and touched me deeply

7-3

After the birth of the child, Genji is even more eager to see Lady of the Wisteria Apartment and the baby, so he goes repeatedly to her quarters but is always turned away by her lady-in-waiting. The lady-in-waiting is secretly pleased by Genji's attentions to her mistress and by her own role in bringing the two together. During one of their conversations, Genji asks the lady-in-waiting:

ikasama ni	what far legacy
mukashi musuberu	do we bring from other lives
chigiri nite	that our lot is
kono yo ni kakaru	connected to this child
naka no hedate zo	the middle of our distances

7-4

Seeing Genji's tears brings the lady-in-waiting almost to the point of crying herself. Sad about being unable to show him his child and sad for the two people who are in such pain, she sends him off with this poem:

mi temo omou	sad to see the child
mi nu hata ikani	yet sadder not to see it
nageku ran	one must grieve it seems
ko ya yo no hito no	in a world of ordinary persons
madou chō yami	puzzled by worldly passions

7-2. *Karahito,* meaning a Chinese or Korean person can also refer generally to a foreigner.

7-4. One of the traditions of Japanese poetry, still used today, is a practice called *honka dori,* the clever references, parodies, and changes to well-known poems in the literature. Thus, the above poem brings to mind *hito no oya no kokoro wa yami ni aranedomo ko wo omou michi ni madoi nuru kana,* by Fujiwara Kanesuke, poem 1103 in the *Gosenshū,* translated as "in people's hearts is no darkness, but when they have children and think of them, they suffer and are in distress due to them." Having just the bald translations, we non-Japanese can hardly find the points of similarity that add such richness to the poem for native speakers.

7-5

Then one day, while Genji is at his father's palace and enjoying music near Lady of the Wisteria Apartment's quarters, the Emperor comes through carrying the four-month-old child. Genji flushes crimson and is shocked at the similarity between the child's looks and his own. He is frightened, pleased, and awed as he becomes quite uncomfortable. He decides to visit his own wife, but before he does so, he stops to admire some wild carnations growing in the garden by his verandah. He sends a long letter to Lady of the Wisteria Apartment's lady-in-waiting and includes this note for the lady.

yosoe tsutsu	while resembling you
miru ni kokoro mo	looking at it with my heart
nagusama de	I'm discomforted
tsuyukesa masaru	by the weight of tear-like dew
nadeshiko no hana	on wild carnation flowers

7-6

The lady-in-waiting shows the note to her mistress, pleading with her to answer him "if with something of no more weight than the dust on these petals." Lady of the Wisteria Apartment is beset by violent emotions, so her reply is very brief and written in a faint hand.

sode nururu	sleeves have been wetted
tsuyu no yukari to	by dewlike tears on its behalf
omou nimo	but do not worry
nao utomare nu	the dislike has disappeared
yamatonadeshiko	for this native wild carnation

7-7

Seeing that his desires for Lady of the Wisteria Apartment only bring grief to himself and a widening circle of others, Genji tries to sublimate his feelings as he spends more time with Murasaki. But since he still treats her as a child, he strikes up a relationship with Woman of the Bedchamber, the older woman who served his father the Emperor. Although Genji thinks of

7-5. Again, "wild carnation" was a euphemism for a love child. Another reading is that Lady of the Wisteria Apartment's face resembles the dewy carnation flower with her weeping.

her as old and wanton, he is surprised how warmly she seems to welcome his advances. Genji continually thinks of her in critical ways, even finding fault with the poem on her fan. He thinks that her writing "withered is the grass of Oaraki" was a rather blatant reference to her most private parts. Genji begins to talk to her about poetry and the poem she has on her fan. She shocks Genji by reciting:

kimi shi ko ba	if the master comes
tenare no koma ni	to manage the pony well
kari kawan	maybe it will rear
sakari sugi taru	up and over past-their-prime
shitaba nari tomo	leaves though on low branches

7-8

Genji has some apprehension about Woman of the Bedchamber's coquettish mood, so he replies:

sasa wake ba	if I were the man
hito ya togame n	to part the bamboo grasses
itsutonaku	there would be the fear
koma narasu meru	all the ponies you have tamed
mori no kogakure	would be hiding in the trees

7-9

While Woman of the Bedchamber and Genji are still talking, the Emperor looks in on them and seems amused at the odd couple but pleased to find that his son has "his ways with women." Soon the situation becomes palace rumor, so that even Genji's friend the First Secretary's Captain hears of it. Thinking that Genji is having an experience that he has so far missed out on, the First Secretary's Captain also begins seeing Woman of the Bedchamber secretly. One evening, Genji hears Woman of the Bedchamber playing on the lute a ribald folk song about a melon farmer who wants to marry. Genji begins to hum the tune of "The Eastern Cottage," with the words "I am wet from the rain from the eaves of the Eastern Cottage, will you open the door and let me in?" and she joins him by singing,

7-7. "Pony" was a euphemism for the male organ, and the connection between "grasses" and "hair" is easily understood.

"Open my door and come in. I am your wife." She reinforces the invitation with her own readiness for him in her poem:

tachi nururu	standing in the rain
hito shimo ara ji	there's no one like that at
azumaya ni	my summer cottage
utate mo kakaru	just when the touch increases
ame sosogi kana	the rain comes falling down!

---

7 - 10

Genji replies to Woman of the Bedchamber:

hitozuma wa	a married woman
ana wazurawashi	oh! ah! how very annoying
azumaya no	in the garden house
maya no amari mo	making friends would be reckless
nare ji to zo omou	with the room under the eaves

---

7 - 11

Nonetheless, Genji does decide to spend the night with Woman of the Bedchamber. Later, while Genji lightly sleeps, the First Secretary's Captain creeps into the room. Genji grabs up his scattered clothing as he scrambles behind a screen. With a furious crash, the First Secretary's Captain folds back the screen. Genji leaps up, wondering how to escape with his dignity. Then he sees before him a person brandishing a long sword. Genji gives him a pinch in the arm, and the two men share a good laugh together. The First Secretary's Captain refuses to give Genji the rest of his clothes back, so Genji begins to pull off the other's robes. In the tussle, Genji tears a seam in the captain's undergarment, who chides him with:

tsutsumu meru	as if it's hidden
na ya mori ide n	I think your fame will leak out
hiki kawashi	pulling on each other
kaku hokoroburu	like this loosens the knot
naka no koromo ni	to reveal a garment of friends

7-9. *Azumaya,* "eastern cottage," could also refer to a garden- or summer-house. Houses of the wealthy were roofed with tiles, but poor people used reeds to make thatched roofs. A small garden house was given a rustic look by thatching the roof. Entering the low doorway under thickly thatched eaves is the perfect metaphor for what the woman desires.

7-10. *Azumaya no maya no* can mean either "the edge of the eaves of a house" or "recklessly."

7 - 12

Genji replies:

kakure naki	it is obvious
mono to shiru shiru	you are well-known for
natsugoromo	summer robes
kitaru wo usuki	wearing your shallowness
kokoro to zo miru	of heart is easy to observe

or

it is obvious
you are well-known for
summer robes
the coming out of your shallow
heart is easy to observe

7 - 13

Genji and the First Secretary's Captain then leave Woman of the Bedchamber to go off together. The next morning, Woman of the Bedchamber finds among her bedclothes an indigo strip of woven cloth, the belt used to close a robe. She assumes it is Genji's, because he spent the first part of the night with her. So she sends the belt and a set of trousers to him with this note.

urami temo	when bearing a grudge
ii kai zo naki	it is no use speaking of it
tachikasane	some robes are cut out
hiki te kaeri shi	to be and cannot be returned
nami no nagori ni	as when the wave has passed

or

the bow-shaped coast
one does not talk about
yet at the same time
the tide ebbs and the waves
both left together

7-12. *Ki taru* can express either "put on" or the perfect tense of "to come." In the thrill of the sham fight Genji's poem allows the impression that his friend's excitement has shown itself in another way.

7-13. The note of Woman of the Bedchamber was craftily filled with double meanings based on *urami,* which can mean either "bear a grudge" or "a seacoast bay shaped like a bow." Also, *kasane* indicates a robe and under robe, or "things happen at the same time."

7 - 14

Genji's reply to Woman of the Bedchamber:

are dachi shi	surging high
nami ni kokoro wa	the wave with my heart in it
sawaga ne do	was not dashed even
yose ken iso wo	beating on a rocky seashore
ikaga urami nu	of the bow-shaped coastline

or

surging high
the wave with my heart in it
was not dashed even
beating on a rocky seashore
how should I complain?

7 - 15

Thus, the next day Genji ends up having the First Secretary's Captain's belt, while the First Secretary's Captain finds among his clothes a section of sleeve that is missing from Genji's robe. Genji feels he lost the fight because his sleeve was torn off, while the First Secretary's Captain only neglected to gather up his belt, and is concerned that this defeat will affect his connection to Woman of the Bedchamber. Genji sends the belt to the First Secretary's Captain with this note.

naka tae ba	taking the blame
kagoto ya ou to	lest the friendship be cut off
ayausa ni	dangerous as
hanada no obi wa	an indigo belt band is
tori te dani mi zu	I didn't even touch it

7 - 16

The First Secretary's Captain answers Genji:

7-15. In a *saibara*, a folk song, is the story of a hero who was broken-hearted when his belt was taken away—in the same way Samson lost his strength when his hair was cut. In Japan, the belt was also a sign of ownership. A man could legitimize a child by giving the pregnant woman his belt.

kimi ni kaku
hiki to rare nuru
obi nare ba
kakute tae nuru
naka to kakotan

in the same way
you yanked on it to steal
the belt
so my love affair is ruined
no wonder I am complaining

---

7 - 17

As reward for bearing him such a beautiful child, the Emperor makes Lady of the Wisteria Apartment his empress. She is thus removed even farther from contact with Genji. As he watches the ceremonies installing her as empress, he thinks these sad thoughts:

tsuki mo se nu
kokoro no yami ni
kururu kana
kumoi ni hito wo
miru ni tsuke temo

endlessly unending
a heart with earthly passions
is crushed with grief
even if I could see my love
in the sky-touching palace

7-17. Notice what a wise author Murasaki Shikibu was. She does not end the chapter with the end of the event but, as usual, adds a hook to keep the reader wanting to read more.

HANA NO EN
THE FLOWER FESTIVAL

Spring of Genji's twentieth year

Again a chapter opens with an imperial festival, this one to honor the new Empress, Lady of the Wisteria Apartment, and the baby. There is a poetry contest in which Genji performs admirably. Afterwards, he goes prowling around trying to find access to the Empress. Failing this, he goes by his stepmother's apartments. There he hears a soft voice singing the song "Oborozukiyo" (night of the misty moon). Although the woman is very easily seduced, she refuses to reveal her identity, so she is known only by the title of the song: Princess of the Night of the Misty Moon. As he is leaving her, they exchange fans. Genji suspects she is one of the many sisters of Lady of the Beautiful Hall, and it turns out he is right. She is the sixth princess and has been promised to the Crown Prince.

Later that same spring, the father of Princess of the Night of the Misty Moon invites Genji to a party celebrating his wisteria flowers. While creeping about by the women's rooms, Genji sings a song about a fan, enabling him to find and be with Princess of the Night of the Misty Moon again. Genji seems to be not only gathering experiences with women but courting disaster. With the Empress, Lady of the Wisteria Apartment, he had cuckolded the Emperor, and now with Princess of the Night of the Misty Moon he defiles the wife of the future Emperor and sister of his arch-enemy, Lady of the Beautiful Hall. One wonders how long it will be before his time of retribution arrives.

8 - A

haru no yo no
moya ni soi taru
tsuki nara n
tamakura kashi nu
waga kari bushi ni

on a spring night
it was the haze accompanying
the moon I guess
that loaned me for a short nap
someone's arm for my pillow

8 - 1

In spring the Cherry Blossom Festival is held for the court. Again Genji dances and again the Empress of the Wisteria Apartment is touched by seeing his performance. She thinks about her relationship with him as she whispers to herself:

ōkata ni
hana no sugata wo
mi mashika ba
tsuyu mo kokoro no
oka re mashi yawa

generally
if one could see flowers
as just an image
there would be less dew
or tears to cloud the heart

8 - 2

After the festival ends and everyone has left or gone to bed, Genji is still looking for someone with whom to spend the night. While checking to see if the person he once visited has left her door ajar, he hears a young woman's voice reciting a bit of a poem from an anthology, "What can compare with a misty moon of spring?" Genji is surprised when the woman comes closer to the door to view the moon. He reaches out and grabs her sleeve. She is frightened and asks who he is. Genji recites this poem to reassure her.

fukaki yo no
aware wo shiru mo
iru tsuki no

deep in the night
it's a joy to see the moon
enter the mists

8-2. *Oboroge* can mean either "misty moon" or "vague, not clear."

oborоge nara nu	I think nothing is misty
chigiri tozo omou	about the plight we share

8-3

Genji expertly lifts the girl into his arms and carries her down the gallery to another room, where he closes the door. Her surprise is so delightful he cannot resist adding to it by touching her body, which pleases him very much. The girl tries to call for help, but Genji tells her that he always gets his way. Being young and inexperienced, she does not know how to stop him. He is thrilled with her naive but heartfelt responses, but becomes very nervous as it is almost dawn—the time when he could be discovered. When he asks her name, she responds in a soft, unsure voice.

uki mi yo ni	useless worldly self
yagate kie naba	which will vanish soon enough
tazune temo	if you look for it
kusa no hara oba	within the fields of grass
towa ji toya omou	would you think to ask for me?

8-4

Genji tries again to find out to whom he should address his customary morning-after note by pointing out to her what can happen if she doesn't tell him.

izure zo to	I wish to know
tsuyu no yadori wo	whose dewy lodge it is
waka mu ma ni	before harsh winds
kozasa ga hara ni	blow across the fields of
kaze mo koso fuke	the tiny bamboo grasses

8-4. The implication of "harsh winds" is that gossip or rumors (the winds from the mouths of others) about their affair will at once inform him of the woman's identity and probably then cause his interest in her tender grasses to wither away.

8-5

The princess gives him her fan with a picture on it of a misty moon reflected on water. Later, unable to sleep, Genji looks at it closely, and seeing it is a "three-fold cherry," he muses on its owner. He writes his own poem on the corner of the fan.

yo ni shira nu	incomparable
kokochi koso sure	to have a feeling that shows
ariake no	in the sky at dawn
tsuki no yukue wo	yet I'm unable to find the
sora ni magae te	whereabouts of the wan moon

8-6

The Minister of the Right, who is rearing the princesses, has invited Genji to attend an archery meet he has sponsored, as well as a wisteria-viewing banquet, in addition to seeing two late-blooming cherry trees. When Genji does not show up, the minister sends his son to Genji with this message:

waga yado no	as if at my lodgings
hana shi nabete no	flowers were a common sort
iro nara ba	for such beauties
nanikawa sarani	why should I have to repeat
kimi wo mata mashi	that I am waiting for you?

8-7

Genji decides to attend the minister's party. Later, pretending to be drunk and sick, he excuses himself in order to seek out Princess of the Night of the Misty Moon. In the dark, while he talks to a woman who does not catch his references to a fan, he hears another one sighing softly. He moves to her to take her hand with these words.

azusayumi	from a birchwood bow
irusa no yama ni	the moon shoots behind
madou kana	the mountain
honomi shi tsuki no	where I am so lost
kage ya miyuru to	will I get a glimpse of the moon
	I saw only in a reflection?

8-7. Beginning with this poem is a series of wordplays based on archery terms that are brilliantly used. The normal way to express line two would be "the moon sets," but for this situation it "shoots."

8-8

Princess of the Night of the Misty Moon continues the archery motif in her reply:

kokoro iru
kata nari mase ba
yumihari no
tsuki naki sora ni
mayowa mashi yawa

if you were the one
who pulled on my heart
the bow string
of a moon hidden in the sky
wouldn't anyone lose their way?

8-8. *Iru* is "enter" or "shoot," or in archery terms, "to pull or span the bow." *Yumihari* refers to the bow-shaped, or crescent, moon.

AOI
HEARTVINE

Fourth Month of Genji's twenty-second year to New Year's of his twenty-third year

The Kamo Festival is also known as the Heartvine or Hollyhock Festival *(Aoi Matsuri)*. The flower of the *aoi* has been designated by some, for convenience, as a hollyhock *(Althaea rosea)*, but hollyhocks do not grow as a vine. The *aoi* is *Asarum caulescens*, which is a form of the snakeweed or bistort. Although the flower has a shape similar to that of hollyhock flowers—bell-like and fairly large—the color is described as flesh colored. The vine's leaves are clearly heart shaped, and for this reason it was customary to make garlands to be worn in the hair for the Kamo Festival, as well as to attach them to pillars, screens, and blinds. The Kamo Festival is thus often called the Hollyhock Festival. Edward Seidensticker first gave the plant the English name "heartvine," which is an admirable and more accurate term to describe the plant, the character of Genji's first wife, as well as the festival. Because the Kamo Festival was one dedicated to fertility rites, occurred in the spring (now celebrated in the middle of May), and was a time to dress up, a time to see and be seen, the *aoi* vine became a symbol, since the blossoms appear side by side on the stem, for a couple meeting or having an affair. This practice of being allowed a time in the spring for illicit relationships coincides with European spring rites, with their same objective and result.

Genji's father has, as was often the custom then, abdicated his position as emperor to enjoy his old age. The new Suzaku Emperor is Genji's half brother, son of Lady of the Beautiful Hall. With more time on his hands, Genji's father counsels him that he should spend more time with Lady of the Sixth Ward, whose daughter is going to be installed as the new high priestess of the shrine at Ise and who therefore needs Genji's support. Before Genji can act on the good advice, he finds out that his own wife, Lady Heartvine, is pregnant, and in his excitement he forgets about everything else.

At the lustration ceremony at the river before the Kamo Festival, there are great crowds come to see the parade of nobility. Women are brought in palanquins, which are set up on blocks so they may view the festivities and still remain hidden from common view. Lady Heartvine, not feeling she wanted to go, is persuaded by her women at the last moment, and thus arrives very late. The other palanquins are already in place, but her men, feeling secure in her high rank, roughly push aside another carriage, even breaking part of it, to give Lady Heartvine a good place. It turns out the damaged carriage belongs to Lady of the Sixth Ward, who is very angry over the insult. She is also bothered by her knowledge that, without Genji and as a widow, she has no backing.

As Lady Heartvine's pregnancy advances, her health declines. As she weakens, Genji finds her more attractive and, for the first time, begins to truly love her. Slowly it also becomes clear that she is ill due to spirit possession, and in the end it is known to all that the evil force is coming from Lady of the Sixth Ward! This woman's uncontrollable spirit has already killed one of Genji's lovers, but still he cannot believe this, even though he hears her voice while attending Lady Heartvine. Soon Lady Heartvine's baby is born, a son, who will be called Lord Evening Mist (Yūgiri). Just when everyone believes the priestly exorcists have succeeded in ridding her of the possession, the spirit returns with a vengeance and Lady Heartvine dies. The whole court mourns her death.

In his grief, Genji decides it is time to make Murasaki his wife. (She is now nearly fifteen years old.) Without consulting her, he suddenly forces himself on her in the night, which is a great shock to the coddled young girl and leaves her very unhappy and bewildered about this man who had seemed more like a father to her.

9 - A

urameshi to	the resentfulness
hito wo me ni oku	of the person's eye which ignores
koto mo koso	fear-causing matters
mi no otoroe ni	thus the body declines and
hoka nara nu kana	never becomes a whole being

9 - 1

With the change of emperors, a new priestess is to be installed at Ise Shrine. First, however, an elaborate ceremony of purification is held at the river, which is attended by a great crowd dressed in their best holiday finery. The mother of the priestess-to-be is a former lover of Genji's, Lady of the Sixth Ward. She has arrived early at the river for the best viewing position for the ceremony. At the last moment, carriages arrive bringing Genji's wife, Lady Heartvine, who is now pregnant. There is some dispute between the attendants of both women, with the result that Lady of the Sixth Ward's carriage is displaced, and Genji's wife receives the advantageous position. When she sees Genji passing by in the procession, Lady of the Sixth Ward feels alone and defeated and recites to herself:

kage wo nomi	only the image
mitarashigawa no	in the purification waters
tsurenasa ni	is heartless—cold
mi no uki hodo zo	when one's lot in life is bitter
itodo shiraruru	it becomes increasingly so

9-1. Remember that Lady of the Sixth Ward was married to the former crown prince, who has died. Thus, she was a widow as well as an older woman without a larger family to support her—emotionally as well as in other ways. As she aged, she knew she would not be able to count on this charming young man, Genji, who had so many romantic interests.

9 - 2

On the actual day of the priestess's installation festivities, Genji is preparing to set out from his own mansion, when he notices Murazaki's hair, which he feels should be trimmed. He decides to trim it himself, but when he tries to do this simple act, his fingers become entangled in the long strands. He stops cutting to say a blessing: "may it grow to be a thousand fathoms." Her nurse watches with awe and gratitude.

hakari naki	beyond measuring
chihiro no soko no	the thousand fathoms depth
mirubusa no	may the sea weeds
oiyuku sue wa	keep growing to be so deep
ware nomi zo mi n	I'll be merely a caretaker

9-3

Murasaki takes up her brush to write her response, one that surprises Genji with her ability to gently chide him:

chihiro tomo	if a thousand fathoms
ikadeka shira n	how can I know when
sadamenaku	the restless
michi hiru shio no	flow of the ebbing tide
nodokekara nu ni	leaves no calm?

9-4

When Genji arrives at the ceremony for the installation of the high priestess of Ise, at the Kamo Festival, he is too late to get a good place for his carriage. An unknown lady offers him her place and this poem written on her fan.

hakanashi ya	how hopeless!
hito no kazase ru	a lover wearing flowers
aoi yue	for a meeting
kami no shirushi no	with the god's permission
kyō wo machi keru	I'm waiting for you today

9-5

Genji recognizes the handwriting of the old Woman of the Bedchamber, so he sends his pert reply, in which he lightly refers to her long life and the number of men with whom she has had "a day of meeting":

9-2. It was common at this time for women of the nobility to have hair longer than they were tall. Naturally their hair was a thing of pride and a lot of work to maintain. Still, then like now, the ends needed to be trimmed occasionally.

Miru can refer either to the name of a sea kelp or to "look after" or "take care of." The twist in the poem hinges on the long hair, which looks like dark sea kelp and also needs to be cared for.

9-4. The symbol for the Kamo Festival was the *aoi*. *Aoi* could also be associated with *au hi*, "a day of meeting," an expression often used in poetry to designate a rendezvous of lovers.

kazashi keru
kokoro zo adani
omōyuru
yaso uji bito ni
nabete aoi wo

the vine of meeting
commonly worn in the hair
by the fickle heart
is available to everyone
in the eighty clan family

9-6

Deeply abashed, Woman of the Bedchamber writes back:

kuyashiku mo
kazashi keru kana
na nomi shite
hitodanomenaru
kusaba bakari wo

it's regrettable
flowers worn in the hair are known
by their name only
one cannot depend on persons
with merely the leaves of grass

9-7

Genji's wife, Lady Heartvine, continues to suffer very much with her pregnancy. The exorcists fear it is a jealous lover of Genji's who is causing her to weep, so much so she is tormented with nausea and shortness of breath. So Genji goes to Lady of the Sixth Ward to discuss this distressing matter, but when he finds she also is not well, he ends up spending the night with her. The next evening he excuses himself from meeting with her by naming his concern for his wife's health. Lady of the Sixth Ward, who always displayed a certain harshness but is now crushed, answers his note with her poem:

sode nururu
koiji to katsuwa
shiri nagara
oritatsu tago no
mizukara zo uki

staining one's sleeves
with burning love on one hand
as we so well know
how the peasant wallows in it
for myself I find it deplorable

9-8

Later that same night Genji sends another note to Lady of the Sixth Ward. He feels she thought he was using his wife's

9-6. Some commentators view the character of Woman of the Bedchamber as a comic element in the story. However, it is possible to see her as an example of a woman who rises to her position at the court purely through her "use" of being a sexual object. This is how she got to be where she is and it is how she reacts to any man, offering herself even when it is no longer necessary. Men may see her situation as funny, but women would understand the sadness she portrays.

9-7. Koiji can mean "mud" or the state of "burning with love." An additional factor in the lady's references could be to the fever she has because of her illness, which is surely due to her own mixed feelings about her love for Genji.

Sometimes the poems of Murasaki Shikibu are so faithful to the feelings of her characters, she even allows them to admit to practices that are normally not spoken about in mixed company. Remember, Genji's wife is experiencing a difficult pregnancy, which causes him his own discomfort.

health as an excuse and that she was not truly as ill as she is. With this poem he accuses her of having feelings that are not deep.

asami niya
hito wa oritatsu
waga kata wa
mi mo sobotsu made
fukaki koiji wo

you only dip
into shallow waters
in my morass
my body is totally submerged
in the ways of burning love

---

9 - 9

When Lady Heartvine goes into premature labor, she has Genji called to her bedside. Thinking she is dying, he finds her more lovely than ever. Then when she speaks, Genji notices it is not Lady Heartvine's voice but that of Lady of the Sixth Ward.

nagekiwabi
sora ni midaruru
waga tama wo
musubi tomete yo
shimogai no tsuma

disturbed by grief
the soul departs from a body
into the skies
please bind it fast by
tying up the robe's hem

---

9 - 10

Lady Heartvine finally is delivered of the baby. Later, however, when it seems the danger is past, she suddenly dies. At the crematorium at dawn, Genji sees her father, faltering with grief, stumble. Genji whispers to himself as he gazes at the morning sky.

nobori nuru
kemuri wa sore to
waka ne domo
nabete kumoi no
aware naru kana

ascending
crematory smoke
cannot be told
from the rest of clouds
yet there is mourning

9-9. The idea existed that one could be kept from dying if the person's spirit could be kept within the robe.

9-10. In the customs of Heian Japan, it was considered a sin for a woman to die in childbirth (a device to give women the will to live in this most dangerous and painful situation?). Thus, to avoid casting doubt on Genji's wife's ability to avoid sin, she seems to recover from the birth but dies shortly afterwards.

9 - 11

As Genji puts on his robes of mourning, he realizes that had he died instead, Lady Heartvine's robes, as widow, would have been dyed a darker gray.

kagiri are ba	restricted
usuzumigoromo	the shallow black of my robes
asakere do	is lacking depth and yet
namida zo sode wo	the many tears on my sleeves
fuchi to nashi keru	are creating deep dark pools

9 - 12

In late autumn, while Genji is still in deep mourning for the death of his wife, a letter on dark green-gray paper attached to a sprig with an opening chrysanthemum is delivered with a poem from Lady of the Sixth Ward.

hito no yo wo	it's sad to learn
aware to kiku mo	one's destiny in this world
tsuyukeki ni	is dewlike and yet
okururu tsuyu wo	I worry about the fleeting life
omoi koso yare	of the one who is left behind

9 - 13

When Genji sees who sent the note, he wants to fling the paper away, but her handwriting is so beautiful that he cannot. He debates for a long time what his relationship should be with her. In the end, he sends his reply on a soft, purple paper, because he does not want to seem to be cold and insensitive.

tomaru mi mo	those who remain
kie shi mo onaji	as well as those who vanish
tsuyu no yo ni	are fleeting as dew
kokoro oku ran	yet the heart left behind is
hodo zo hakanaki	in a helpless condition

9-11. Alert to every subtlety, the Japanese picked various shades of gray for mourning. The darker the robe, the deeper the mourning. Because a man was expected to show less grief than a woman, male mourning clothes were less dark, being a purplish gray instead of coal black. As patriarchal as one might see this custom, Murasaki Shikibu makes the reader have only sympathy with Genji, who is "prevented" by custom from wearing sleeves as dark as his sorrow. All he can do is to deepen their color by wetting them with tears.

9 - 14

During an autumn rainstorm, Genji is visited by the First Secretary's Captain, who, looking up into the skies, speaks of Lady Heartvine, his sister.

ame to nari	changing into rain
shigururu sora no	autumn showers fall from skies
ukigumo wo	full of brooding clouds
izure no kata to	in which direction will I
waki te nagame n	be told to look up for her?

9 - 15

Unable to answer the First Secretary's Captain's question, Genji replies:

mi shi hito no	when we were lovers
ame to nari ni shi	rains in those days used to be
kumoi sae	only clouds in the sky
itodo shigure ni	all the more autumn showers
kakikurasu koro	darken the season this year

9 - 16

Seeing some wild pink carnations and gentians tangled in the frost-covered grasses, Genji thinks about his motherless son. He gathers a small bouquet to send with a poem to the mother of Lady Heartvine, the Great Princess, who is still caring for the boy.

kusagare no	in withered grasses
magaki ni nokoru	left behind the bamboo fence
nadeshiko wo	a carnation child
wakare shi aki no	I take for a keepsake
katami tozo miru	of our parting in autumn

9-16. Again, pinks, or carnations, remind him of a love child, even though he was married to Lady Heartvine. He is sensitive to the fact that the child is an "orphan," without one parent, so the reference is apt.

9 - 17

The Great Princess, who is less resistant to tears than the autumn leaves are to winds, responds to Genji:

ima mo mi te	now that I see it
nakanaka sode wo	my sleeves are even wetter
nurasu kana	as if I'm weeping
kakio are ni shi	that plain fence is now torn down
yamatonadeshiko	where the wild carnations grew

9 - 18

Bored and lonely in the sadness of the coming winter, Genji attempts to establish a correspondence with his cousin, Princess Morning Glory, with a note on sky-blue Chinese paper.

wakite kono	especially now
kure koso sode wa	at the dark end of the year
tsuyuke kere	sleeves are dampened
mono omou aki wa	thus I have spent my autumn
amata he nure do	being lost in many thoughts

9 - 19

Carefully, and with a certain coolness, Princess Morning Glory replies in a delicate handwriting that she understands his grief.

akigiri ni	within autumn mists
tachiokure nu to	the one who's been left behind
kiki shi yori	now only listens
shigururu sora mo	to cold rains fall from the sky
ikaga tozo omou	do you think I should worry?

9 - 20

After a year, with the mourning period completed, Genji moves his things from his wife's home. When Lady Heartvine's father, the Minister of the Left, visits the deserted rooms, he finds Genji has written a poem, jotted down on a scrap of paper, in response to a verse by Po Chū-i, the famous Chinese poet, and left it by the pillow of the couple's bed.

9-17. Part of the modesty and reticence of the Japanese people is expressed in their unwillingness to name names. Thus, in the poetry as well as in the prose of *The Tale of Genji*, persons are designated by some aspect of their lives or even, as we have seen, a poem associated with the person. Here, the Great Princess refers to her dead daughter as "that plain fence . . . now torn down." Although Lady Heartvine was an exalted person of the times from her position from birth and marriage, the mother refers to her in this acceptable manner.

nakitama zo	the departed one's soul
itodo kanashiki	by the bed where we slept
ine shi toko no	all the more sorrowful
akugare gataki	that I cannot depart also
kokoro narai ni	as is my heart's desire

---

9 - 21

Also, next to the phrase "the flower is white with frost," in Po Chū-i's poem "The Song of Everlasting Sorrow," the Minister of the Left finds that Genji had written:

kimi naku te	now that you are gone
chiri tsumori nuru	how the dust has piled up
tokonatsu no	on our flowery bed
tsuyu uchiharai	I've only brushed away tears
ikuyo inu ran	the many nights I've slept here

---

9 - 22

Now back home in his father's palace on Second Avenue, where he is still keeping the girl, Murasaki, Genji quickly begins to desire to have her as his wife. He makes several amorous overtures, but she seems not to understand his method of courting. They play games of Go, and her many delicate ways please him enormously. Suddenly he can no longer restrain himself. The next morning he rises early, but the girl uncharacteristically stays in bed. When he leaves the room, he pushes a writing box to her pillow. In it she finds his "morning after" poem:

ayanaku mo	almost meaningless
hedate keru kana	how we were once kept apart
yo wo kasane	nights we had together
sasugani nare shi	yet we became acquainted
naka no koromo wo	with all the robes between us

---

9 - 23

For days afterwards, Murasaki is so outraged by Genji's behavior that she hides from him in a sullen silence. He

9-21. Here is a wordplay based on *tokonatsu*, "wild carnation": *toko* can mean "bed" and *natsu* "summer," which helps explain how the poem could transpose "frost" into "dust" on a flower and a bed.

finds the change both sad and interesting. He murmurs to himself that his efforts to make her more affectionate toward him seem to have been wasted. On New Year's Day, Genji makes the traditional visit to his former parents-in-law. The mother-in-law, the Great Princess, gives Genji a set of robes that she has made for him. As he puts them on, he recites:

amata toshi
kyō aratame shi
irogoromo
ki te wa namida zo
furu kokochi suru

again a new year
and today as in the past
the beautiful robes
yet I am wearing tears
that fall in sadness

---

9 - 24

The Great Princess replies:

atarashiki
toshi tomo iwa zu
furu mono wa
furi nuru hito no
namida nari keri

even for New Year's
they are much too precious
these old things
from a person of advanced age
are simply tears of the past

SAKAKI
THE SACRED TREE

Ninth Month of Genji's twenty-third year to summer of his twenty-fifth year

Sakaki presently corresponds to the *cleyera,* but in earlier times referred to the anise tree. With its waxy evergreen leaves, similar to the camellia, it was commonly considered as a manifestation of the divine presence. It has always been sacred to the Shinto religion and plays an important part in dances and official observances. It is still planted in areas that have or are intended to have a holy atmosphere.

Lady of the Sixth Ward, who is very distracted by her jealous feelings about Genji and her realization that he is an impetuous young man, decides to leave the city by accompanying her daughter to the Shinto shrine at Ise on the eastern seacoast, where the daughter is the new high priestess. Genji tries very hard to dissuade her from going by begging her to stay closer to him, but when his father dies, he forgets about her, as he again tries to resume a relationship with the empress, Lady of the Wisteria Apartment. She rejects Genji totally due to her fears of what this could mean for her son, the crown prince. As a result of her delicate health, coupled with the recent death of her husband, she decides to become a nun. Thus, these two women in Genji's life surround themselves with religious atmospheres—acts that only excite Genji's passions all the more.

As he sees these women retreating from his possible sexual

escapades, he redoubles his activities by renewing his acquaintance with Princess Morning Glory, the daughter of Genji's uncle. She is the high priestess at Kamo Shrine, so she continues this connection to his affairs with women in religion. Even though Princess of the Night of the Misty Moon is now the wife of the emperor, Genji insists on gaining access to her. This time he is caught in the act by the Minister of the Right, her father. This gives Lady of the Beautiful Hall another reason for wishing to be rid of Genji.

10-A

isuzugawa	the Isuzu River
kami no sakai e	a boundary to the gods
nogare ki nu	so there's no escape
omoiagari shi	for the egotistical one
hito no mi no hate	this is the end of her

10-1

After the strange circumstances surrounding Lady Heartvine's death, which implicated Lady of the Sixth Ward, the latter decides to leave the court and retire with her daughter, who will be the high priestess of the shrine at Ise. Before Lady of the Sixth Ward departs, Genji insists on seeing her once more. Because meeting her at the temporary shrine is not proper, Genji is very moved by having a rendezvous in this setting. He plucks a branch from the sacred bush and pushes it under the curtains to announce his arrival. Lady of the Sixth Ward replies:

kamigaki wa	this is not
shirushi no sugi mo	a shrine with a boundary
naki mono wo	marked by cedars
ikani magae te	how could you mistake
oreru sakaki zo	this sprig with the sacred tree?

10-A. The Isuzu River, then in the province of Ise, is now in Mie Prefecture. The river forms one of the barriers to Ise Shrine. Pilgrims believed that crossing over the river, aided by the cypress and cedarwood bridge, initiated their lustration rites even before reaching the purification hall or the stone steps leading down to the river for further cleansing.

10-1. When the Japanese read this upper part of the poem (the *kami no ku*), they remember the verse *waga iho wa / miwa no yamamoto / koishikuba / toburai kimase / sugi tateru kado,* which means "my house lies / at the foot of Mount Miwa / seeking the sacred place / you need only to look for / the tall cedars at the gate." The cedars in Miwa Shrine are a symbol for lovers' visiting. This is the meaning, but there is such a legendary tree in Miwa. Noh plays and other dramas often alluded to this anonymous poet's tanka in the *Kokinshū.*

Shirushi no sugi refers to the tree where the god dwelt on the boundary of Miwa Shrine in Yamato. *Sugi,* Japanese cedar, has a very straight growth habit and lives to over 2,000 years; its straight trunk and longevity make it an

10 - 2

Made bolder by Lady of the Sixth Ward's reciting of a verse that implied he was a lover who had erred in his search for her, Genji replies with his poem as he leans farther inside the curtains surrounding and protecting her.

otomego ga	thinking the maiden
atari to omoe ba	was somewhere hereabouts
sakakiba no	leaves of the sacred tree
ka wo natsukashimi	broken off by my desire
tome te koso ore	for the beloved fragrance

10 - 3

All night Genji and Lady of the Sixth Ward discuss their sorrows and frustrations. The gamut of their feelings for each other ranges from sadness to irritation. At dawn, as he is leaving, Genji takes her hand and says:

akatsuki no	lovers parting
wakare wa itsu mo	at dawn are usually
tsuyukeki wo	rather damp
kowa yo ni shira nu	I know nothing in this world
aki no sora kana	as bitter as today's autumn sky!

10 - 4

A cold wind is blowing and the couple seem to have nothing more to say. Only a pine cricket in the grass makes a sound. At long last, Lady of the Sixth Ward replies:

ōkata no	ordinarily
aki no wakare mo	partings in autumn are sad
kanashiki ni	don't add chirping
naku ne na soe so	to the endless sadness
nobe no matsumushi	oh, cricket in the field

important source of pillars for temples.

For the purification ceremonies at the river, a temporary shrine was customarily erected, called "the palace-in-the-fields." Later the high priestess and her retinue would journey to the actual shrine at Ise, located on a peninsula on the Pacific coast. The origins of the shrine are shrouded in mystery and legends, but from the beginning, it was associated with the imperial family. Amaterasu Ōmikami, Goddess of the Sun, was enshrined, originally, on the palace grounds of each new emperor. Under the legendary Emperor Sujin, ca. 100 B.C., the shrine was established at the foot of Mount Miwa near Nara, and in the fourth century A.D., it was moved to its present site at Ise. Earlier, with each change of emperors, the shrine was torn down and rebuilt completely. Now, as a tradition, this is done every twenty years. The Ceremony of Renewal will be performed again in 2013.

10-2. The sacredness of the *sakaki* tree came about through the legend of Amaterasu, the Sun Goddess, who was offended by the amorous and incestuous actions of her brother,

10-5

On the day the high priestess and her mother, Lady of the Sixth Ward, leave the temporary shrine for the one at Ise, the ceremonies are especially grand because the old emperor is so fond of the high priestess. Genji wants to say many things to her, but instead he sends her a ritual cord made of twisted mulberry paper. On the wrapping he writes, "To the one it would be blasphemy to address in person." The poem he includes reads:

yashima moru	guarding eight islands
kunitsumikami mo	protector of our country
kokoro ara ba	take thought of how
aka nu wakare no	partings never satisfy
naka wo kotoware	when judging this affair

10-6

In spite of the many activities involved in moving, the note is answered by the priestess's lady of honor.

kunitsukami	our land's guardians
sora ni kotowaru	ruling from the empty sky
naka nara ba	if the relationship
naozari goto wo	has any indecorum
mazu ya tadasa n	may it soon be cleared up

10-7

Genji greatly enjoys this exchange with the high priestess, taking a new interest in her. He is sorry he had not met her sooner, but imagines they will perhaps meet again. As the many carriages prepare to leave for the shrine, Lady of the Sixth Ward has to pass through the palace once more in a procession. This causes her to think of how she came to serve the crown prince when she was sixteen, how he died when she was twenty. Now at thirty years of age, she is in the palace—but only so briefly as she passes through again.

sonokami wo	the former days
kyō wa kake ji to	may not be compared to this

Susa-no-O, so she hid in the Celestial Cave, which turned the whole world's day into night. As the land suffered in the continual darkness, various methods were tried to lure her out. One was the installation of an eight-foot-wide mirror (still one of the Three Sacred Treasures of Japan), hoping with this that she would come out to see herself. In the *sakaki* tree was hung an eight-foot strand of curved beads (blue glass beads in the shape of commas) as decoration and enticement. This strand of beads is supposedly still enshrined there as the second of Japan's Sacred Treasures.

10-4. Remember that Lady of the Sixth Ward, who was used to living in the palace or the city, was now, due to the custom of the installation of the high priestess, having to spend the night out in a field. It was very different having an insect chirp in one's garden and being out in a field filled with the sound of their shrill cries. The poem is skillfully constructed so that the lady's comments demanding quiet could be directed to Genji. It is only in the very last line that she turns her remark to the cricket.

10-5. While dipping their hands into the river for

omoe domo	whatever one thinks
kokoro no uchi ni	still deep within the heart
mono zo kanashiki	is something full of sorrow

10 - 8

Although it is evening before the high priestess's procession passes his area of the palace, Genji cannot help sending out one last poem to Lady of the Sixth Ward. He attaches it to a branch of the sacred *sakaki* tree.

furisute te	as you go away
kyō wa yuku tomo	today you have cast me aside
suzukagawa	but won't your sleeves
yasose no nami ni	be wetted by the waves of
sode wa nure ji ya	the Suzuka's many shoals?

10 - 9

The last reply from Lady of the Sixth Ward to Genji comes from beyond Osaka's gate:

suzukagawa	Suzuka River
yasose no nami ni	with waves of many crossings
nure nure zu	whether wet or not
ise made tare ka	I am sent as far away as Ise
omoi okose n	who there will think of me?

10 - 10

The next morning, heavy with mist, seems sad and forlorn. Genji is too distracted to even visit Murasaki. As he mopes around, he wonders how it is for the lady on the road, and murmurs to himself:

yukukata wo	so lost in thought
nagame mo yara n	I don't know where she's going
kono aki wa	oh mists of autumn
ōsakayama wo	on the Mountain of Meetings
kiri na hedate so	please do not separate us

the purification rites, cords made of paper, which were tightly twisted, were used to tie up the long, wide sleeves of the participants. As late as this century, poor people, unable to obtain string, used twisted paper as cordage.

10-6. At this time the high priestess was only fourteen. Not only Genji was impressed by her, but the emperor was reported to be near tears as he put the comb in her hair that confirmed her position of high priestess. When in office, the high priestess had to remain celibate.

10-8. The Suzuka River flowed from Kyoto to Ise, forming the border between Mie and Ise provinces (modern Shiga and Mie prefectures). The Suzuka Mountain area was famous for its showers and autumn leaves.

10 - 11

Soon thereafter Genji's father, the retired emperor, dies. This means that the emperor's wife, Lady of the Wisteria Apartment, has to leave the palace to move back with her family. On a day with snow flurries driven by a sharp wind, when her brother, Prince Director of Military Affairs, comes for her, he has a sad talk with Genji about the changes in their lives. The Prince's poem, though not thought to be that good or suitable, brings tears to Genji's eyes, as he misses his father.

kage hiromi	the spreading pine
tanomi shi matsu ya	whose shadow sheltered us
kare ni ken	withered away
shitaba chiri yuku	now at the end of the year
toshi no kure kana	needles fall from low branches

10 - 12

Standing in the courtyard near a frozen pond, the tearful Genji manages to murmur:

saewataru	now frozen over
ike no kagami no	the clear mirror of the pond
sayakesa ni	while bright and pure
minare shi kage wo	was accustomed to seeing
mi nu zo kanashiki	a figure sadly seen no more

10 - 13

The maid of Lady of the Wisteria Apartment, who had facilitated her lady's affair with Genji, offers:

toshi kure te	as this year ends
iwai no mizu mo	water from the rocky springs
kōri toji	freezes over
mi shi hitokage no	the figure seen in the past
ase mo yuku kana	is fading more and more

10-12. The word *saewataru*, "freeze over" or "clear, become clear," is meant to express the idea that when the ice formed it acted as a mirror. Although this might seem illogical (water reflects more than ice), the idea of a piece of ice resembling a piece of mirror prevailed.

10 - 14

The new Suzaku Emperor brings a change of power and persons. Now Princess of the Night of the Misty Moon is living in the palace as the emperor's wardrobe mistress and consort. Although it is very risky, Genji resumes his relations with her and stays the night when he visits her. Not only Genji visits, but one of his men has availed himself of the company of one of her women. Another guardsman, wanting to tease his fellow worker who is absent from his "job," announces loudly the coming of the dawn. It happens that Genji and Princess of the Night of the Misty Moon, though hidden by screens, are very near the shouting guardsman. The princess very softly recites this poem:

kokoro kara	it's my feeling
katagata sode wo	one way or other everyone's sleeves
nurasu kana	are made moist
aku to oshiuru	it is dawn that informs us
koe ni tsuke temo	as if responding to a voice

10 - 15

Genji answers with:

nageki tsutsu	continually grieving
waga yo wa kakute	is it my destiny to spend
suguse toya	my life this way?
mune no aku beki	if only daybreak broke
toki zo tomo naku	this grievous situation

10 - 16

With the former emperor now dead, Genji again comes secretly into the quarters of the widowed empress, Lady of the Wisteria Apartment. Even though Genji tries to convince her they are doing the right thing to continue their affair, she repulses him vigorously. When he insists on having his way with her, she becomes so upset with him that she begins having severe chest pains. He reels from her repulsion of him and the fear of what these pains mean. He decides to remain with her even though the day is breaking. When Prince Firefly and his chamberlain are sent for by Lady of the Wisteria Apartment, two women shove the half-conscious Genji and his clothes into a cupboard. Near evening Lady of the Wisteria Apartment begins to feel better, and Genji creeps out and continues his pleas for her affection. Again he stays the night, threatening to die if she does not accept him. He tells her, though she is barely conscious, that if he dies out of his rejected love for her, she will be his obstacle to salvation and he will continue suffering in uncounted lives to come.

au koto no	becoming man and wife
kataki wo kyō ni	is not easy in these times
kagira zu ba	now without limits
nao ikuyo wo ka	how many more generations
nageki tsutsu he n	will we live weeping in grief?

10 - 17

Genji has added to his poem "and the sin yours also." One can almost hear the heavy sigh accompanying Lady of the Wisteria Apartment's reply:

nagaki yo no	in a long life
urami wo hito ni	even if a grudge is borne
nokoshi temo	I want you
katsuwa kokoro o	to know this one thing—
ada to shira nan	feelings are transitory

10 - 18

The encounter with Genji leaves Lady of the Wisteria Apartment an invalid, and she knows that if the affair continues, it will place their son, the crown prince, in a precarious position. She talks with Genji about becoming a nun. Genji thinks this to be a terribly cruel move on her part, so he decides that autumn to make a retreat at a temple in Uji. There the atmosphere is so attractive that he himself is very tempted to become a monk. However, he knows he is still very attached to and concerned with the several women in his life, chief among them Murasaki. He writes many letters to her, wanting to know if she misses him. He sends her this poem on heavy handmade paper in a casual, but distinguished, hand.

asajiu no	you have been left
tsuyu no yadori ni	fragile as dew on a house
kimi wo oki te	in a field of reeds
yomo no arashi zo	where wind blows four ways
shizugokoro naki	this does not calm my heart

10 - 19

With tears in her eyes, Murasaki sends her poem to Genji at the temple at Uji on a small piece of very thin, white paper.

kaze fuke ba	because the wind blows
mazu zo midaruru	at first there is disorder
iro kawaru	yet colors change
asaji ga tsuyu ni	in the reeds a drop of dew
kakaru sasagani	hanging on a spider's web

10 - 20

While at the temple at Uji, Genji is close to Kamo Shrine, so he sends a message to his cousin, the new high priestess, Princess Morning Glory. His note is attached to a branch from the sacred tree with streamers of ritual cords.

kakemakumo	tied to the idea
kashikokere domo	how very awesome you are
sonokami no	yet long ago
aki omooyuru	in autumn I only thought
yūdasuki kana	of white cotton ritual cords

10-18. The word *tsuyu* means "dew" and can also refer to the tip of a hanging thread. This begins a string of poems based on wordplays with threads and cords

10-19. Iro can mean "color" or "love." In this way Murasaki is making a veiled threat that her feelings might change if he leaves her.

10-20. Kamo Shrine was dedicated to peace, fertility, and the ruling class under the tutelage of the Thunder God. This strange combination was arrived at through the legend that the Thunder God had impregnated the woman who bore the first son of the Hata Clan when she picked up and saved a white arrow she found floating on the river. This legend is celebrated in Noh plays performed often in the New Year's holidays. Kamo festivities celebrate Japan's many and beautiful rivers, as well as encouraging the fertilization and fruition of the spring fields. Now these ceremonies are held around the fifteenth of May.

10 - 21

Princess Morning Glory sends her message to Genji, also tied up by a ritual cord.

sonokami ya	only in those days?
ikagawa ari shi	in what way was it only then
yūdasuki	the ritual cords
kokoro ni kake te	brought to mind the reasons
shinobu ran yue	of what I must endure now

10 - 22

When Genji returns home from the temple visit, he attempts to resume a correspondence with Lady of the Wisteria Apartment by sending her a handsome branch of autumn leaves. Afterwards he is delayed at court by the new emperor, his own half brother, so he sends a note that he has been detained. Lady of the Wisteria Apartment sends a poem as a thank-you note with her lady-in-waiting.

kokonoe ni	have mists arisen
kiri ya hedatsuru	at the Imperial Palace
kumo no ue no	enough to separate
tsuki wo harukani	the moon from the far sky?
omoiyaru kana	I can imagine the distance

10 - 23

Lady of the Wisteria Apartment is so near and yet, for him, so far, that the bitterness he has felt toward her completely melts. Genji has tears in his eyes as he answers:

tsukikage wa	the moonlight we saw
mi shi yo no aki ni	in the autumn of olden times
kawara ne do	has not changed
hedatsuru kiri no	but the separating mists
tsuraku mo aru kana	seem more cold and bitter

10 - 24

Since Genji is no longer very welcome in the court of the new emperor, his interest in Princess of the Night of the Misty Moon wanes. Already autumn is turning to winter and he has not written to her. As she has missed getting any messages from Genji, she takes the initiative and writes to him.

kogarashi no	a cold wind
fuku ni tsuke tsutsu	keeps on blowing while
machi shi ma ni	I wait for you
obotsukanasa no	the long-awaited season
koro mo he ni keri	has now come and gone

10 - 25

As the messenger waits for an answer, Genji seems to take a long time choosing a paper from the large supply kept in a cabinet. Then he turns to selecting a brush and ink. His women attendants wonder who the mysterious lady is to make him so melancholy.

aimi zu te	to not meet while
shinoburu koro no	having to endure this season
namida wo mo	causes me to weep
nabete no aki no	in general don't you think
shigure toya miru	it's like seeing autumn showers?

10 - 26

For the anniversary of her husband's death, Lady of the Wisteria Apartment commissions special religious memorial services. Upon the occasion, a day of heavy snow, Genji sends this poem to her:

wakare ni shi	parting from the past
kyō wa kure domo	today comes to remind us
mi shi hito ni	of our beloved
yukiau hodo wo	in the snowy future
itsu to tanoma n	will we be united?

10 - 27

Out of the sadness of the day, Lady of the Wisteria Apartment responds to Genji's continued pleas to meet again.

nagarauru	to live so long
hodo wa ukere do	without him has been
yukimeguri	bitter yet today
kyō wa sono yo ni	it feels as if those times
au kokochi shi te	have returned
	and I have a feeling we may
	meet again

10 - 28

Without warning, at the end of the memorial services, Lady of the Wisteria Apartment announces her decision to become a nun. Everyone is stunned and deeply saddened, yet she retains her composure, and is able to do so even when Genji comes to her rooms. Still, when a message from her son, the Crown Prince, arrives, she breaks down with weeping and is unable to write a response. Genji sends their son a poem with two distinct messages within it.

tsuki no sumu	the moon's clear shining
kumoi wo kakete	covered by the highest cloud
shitau tomo	that for which one yearns
konoyo no yami ni	within this world of darkness
nao ya madowan	will be more and more missed
	or
	the moon's clear shining
	brings to mind the Imperial Palace
	the one for whom I yearn
	within this world of darkness
	is the one who has been lost

10 - 29

A note is sent out from the quarters of Lady of the Wisteria Apartment, but Genji feels it is the work of her women.

10-27. This poem and that immediately preceding have a subtle play on words containing *yuki*, meaning "snow" or "to go."

10-28. The act of a woman becoming a Buddhist nun, very often done at the funeral of her husband, involved, in addition to vows, the cutting off of her long hair. A woman with her beautiful hair cut was a signal to men, day or night, that she had "given up the world," meaning all ties to the physical plane, including sex. Nun's heads were and still are shaven, but often a woman's first step was to have her hair cut to shoulder length, or at least part of it, depending on her determination.

ōkata no	generally
uki ni tsuke te wa	it's useless to respond to
itoe domo	that which one hates yet
itsuka konoyo wo	I am looking forward to
somukihatsu beki	wholly leaving this world

---

10 - 30

Now that Lady of the Wisteria Apartment has become a nun, she commissions a chapel built and has her residence moved to be near it. At New Year's, instead of attending the festivities of the court, Genji goes to visit her and finds the atmosphere subdued and so religious that he is deeply impressed. He whispers, as if to himself, "an uncommonly elegant nun":

nagame karu	at the mere sight
ama no sumika to	of fisherfolk by the sea
miru karani	singing as they reap
mazu shiotaruru	briny water drips from sleeves
matsu ga urashima	as from the pines of Bay Island

or

it has been said
that nuns living in shrines
reap only
briny sleeves like the pines
on the beaches of Bay Island

---

10 - 31

Because the chapel is small and crowded with holy objects, Genji can barely hear the faint voice of Lady of the Wisteria Apartment, which seems lost in the religious atmosphere.

ari shi yo no	the passing world
nagori dani naki	does not even leave tide pools
urashima ni	on Bay Island
tachiyoru nami no	where waves rise and surge
mezurashiki kana	in all their splendor

or

10-30. Genji uses a classic pun on *ama,* which can refer either to fisherfolk, a woman diver, or to a nun. Urashima can be a place name or indicate "beach" or "bay" *(ura)* "island" *(shima).*

10-31. Lady of the Wisteria Apartment responds with a pun on *nagori,* which can mean either a tide pool or the regret after parting.

how marvelous
that waves rise to surge
on Bay Island
when all the regrets of old
have finally passed away

10 - 32

At a party given by the First Secretary's Captain, his son sings an old song, "I May Have Met the First Lily of Spring," which touches Genji so deeply he stands up and removes his robe to give it to the boy. A slight flush from the drink has made Genji's skin glow under his thin summer robe. In response as a thank-you, the First Secretary's Captain offers Genji a cup of wine with a poem.

sore moga to	longing to see
kesa hirake taru	the first flower of the season
hatsu hana ni	that which opens
otora nu kimi ga	today is not inferior to
nioi wo zo miru	an exquisite fragrance

10 - 33

Smiling at the compliment from his old friend, the First Secretary's Captain, Genji receives the cup with the words:

toki narade	today's flower
kesa saku hana wa	has bloomed out of season
natsu no ame ni	in summer rains
shiore ni kerashi	it has withered away with
niou hodo naku	its brief sweet fragrance

10-33. The last lines of these two poems, with a reference to fragrance, makes a bridge to the orange blossom fragrances in the next chapter. You will see how Yosano applauds this by using her poem to reinforce the device.

11

HANA CHIRU SATO
VILLAGE OF SCATTERED BLOSSOMS

Fifth Month, twentieth day of Genji's twenty-fifth year

Almost as if wishing to seem a better person, Genji decides to visit Lady of the Beautiful View, who had been a consort of his father's. He realizes that she and her sister have now been abandoned and removed from the high court by the change of emperors, so he decides to go out to their remote villa to cheer them up. On the way, he is briefly distracted by passing by another house, wherein someone is playing a harp. The music, the plantings, the small house, even the call of a cuckoo, seem to invite him in. Genji sends a poem, but the women turn out to either not know him or not want to know him, and the situation passes—to Genji's regret.

Genji finds his father's consort to be a refined woman, with admirable awareness and sensitivity. Though she was not one of his favorites, Genji finds her to be the kind of woman who is attractive to him. Her sister, Lady Scattered Blossoms, also seems gentle and persuasive. How different these women are from the others in his life, he thinks.

11 - A

tachibana mo	orange blossoms too
koi no urei mo	seem to be feeling lovesick
chirikae ba	when they scatter

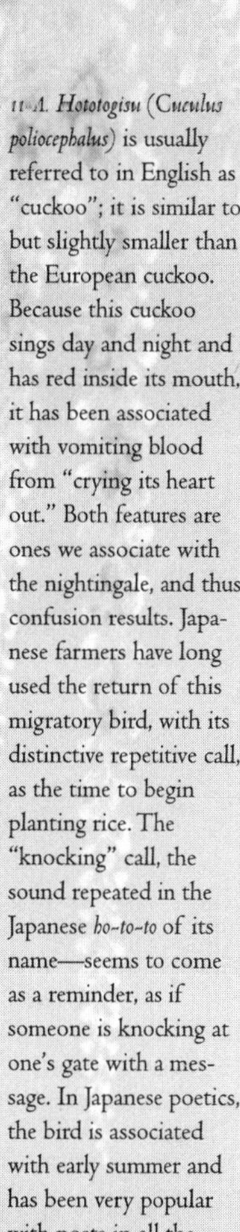

11-A. Hototogisu (*Cuculus poliocephalus*) is usually referred to in English as "cuckoo"; it is similar to but slightly smaller than the European cuckoo. Because this cuckoo sings day and night and has red inside its mouth, it has been associated with vomiting blood from "crying its heart out." Both features are ones we associate with the nightingale, and thus confusion results. Japanese farmers have long used the return of this migratory bird, with its distinctive repetitive call, as the time to begin planting rice. The "knocking" call, the sound repeated in the Japanese *ho-to-to* of its name—seems to come as a reminder, as if someone is knocking at one's gate with a message. In Japanese poetics, the bird is associated with early summer and has been very popular with poets in all the

ka wo natsukashimi	with their beloved fragrance
hototogisu naku	a cuckoo bird cries out

11 - 1

One night, while passing by a house Genji remembers once visiting, he hears a person playing a Chinese harp and another one playing on a Japanese harp. He has the carriage turn so he can alight to listen. Just then a cuckoo sings out clearly. He sends his messenger to the house with this poem.

ochikaeri	returning to
e zo shinoba re nu	its favorite place where
hototogisu	the cuckoo
hono katarai shi	was friends with the hedge
yado no kakine ni	surrounding your lodgings

11 - 2

The women inside seem unsure about who is sending the note, but when the messenger Genji has sent to the verandah comes back with their poem, he thinks they are only feigning bewilderment.

hototogisu	it seems the cuckoo
katarau koe wa	whose voice kept us company
sore nagara	once so long ago
ana obotsukana	but alas we can't be sure
samidare no sora	under rainy-season skies

11 - 3

Genji continues on his way to visit one of his father's ladies, Lady of the Beautiful View, who is now living quite simply at her home since being turned out of the palace after the emperor's death. Genji feels sorry for her, and, when he arrives at the intended woman's house, he finds her lonely and quiet. In her garden, scented with orange blossoms, he again hears a cuckoo call.

imperial anthologies. When the name of the bird is used in the long line (using seven sound units) of the poem, it is often called a *yamahototogisu*, or mountain cuckoo, but the mountain cuckoo is a rarer bird, whereas the *hototogisu* is commonly heard.

tachibana no	longing for
ka wo natsukashi mi	the fragrance of orange blossoms
hototogisu	the cuckoo bird
hana chiru sato wo	stops in for a call at the village
tazune te zo tou	where blossoms have scattered

11 - 4

Genji apologizes for neglecting Lady of the Beautiful View for so long, but charms her and her sister with his memories of them and the times spent at the palace. Lady of the Beautiful View is touched by his attention and responds with the grace and modesty of her refined life.

hitome naku	deserted by all
are taru yado wa	the house has fallen to ruins
tachibana no	only orange blossoms
hana koso noki no	flowering at the edge of
tsuma to nari kere	my eaves have invited you

11-3. From this verse, the woman who answers, the younger sister, is given her name: Lady Scattered Blossoms. Later Genji commits his orphaned son, Lord Evening Mist, to these sisters' care and upbringing, secure in the knowledge they will do it well.

11-4. Tsuma can mean either "edge" or "spouse."

12

SUMA

Third Month of Genji's twenty-sixth year to Third Month of his twenty-seventh year

After living such a charmed life, it suddenly seems all Genji's luck turns from him. Even the new Suzaku (Red Sparrow) Emperor, though Genji's half brother, who has promised his father to keep Genji by his side for advice and alliance once in power, allows himself to change. The Emperor's mother, Lady of the Beautiful Hall, whose position ascends with his, finally has the power to make life miserable for Genji. Although it is difficult for Genji to leave his many loves, his two young sons, and all his responsibilities for so many people, he decides it is best for him to go into exile. He travels to the then-remote coast at Suma (south of Kyoto, site of the modern seaport city of Kobe) with a selection of attendants, who move into a dreadfully rustic abode near the sea. Forlorn and bored, Genji wiles away his time painting the landscape, playing the harp, and writing poetry. At first he finds comfort in writing letters and poems to his many acquaintances who miss him in the capital, but Lady of the Beautiful Hall uses the strength of her position and demands that no one communicate with Genji. Only Murasaki and the First Secretary's Captain are able to ignore the edict.

12 - A

hito kouru	loving a lover
namida wo wasure	one forgets about the tears

ōumi e
hika re yuku beki
mi ka to omoi nu

I fear which
are enough for an ocean
left to tug on one's body

---

12 - 1

Due to changes in palace politics, Genji abruptly decides to leave for exile to the remote coast of Suma. Before leaving, he visits his deceased wife's residence, where his friend, the First Secretary's Captain, lives. While there, visiting with the women who had served his wife, Genji decides to stay the night with one of them. At dawn, the traditional time of parting is made even sadder by the knowledge Genji might never return here again. When the Great Princess sends him a note saying it is a pity he cannot stay to see his son Lord Evening Mist, Genji weeps, and whispers as if to himself:

toribeyama
moe shi kemuri mo
magou ya to
ama no shio yaku
ura mi ni zo yuku

if going to
shores where fisherfolk's
salt fires burn
there is smoke rising
as from the cemetery

---

12 - 2

Genji sends another note to the Great Princess, saying how sad he is to leave, and that the thought of his child makes him think of trying to withstand the hostility in the city just to be near him, yet he is resolved to leave. Standing in the light of the setting moon, he seems more elegant and handsome than ever before. With the sorrow of losing Genji added to the sorrow of her daughter's death, the Great Princess sends one more poem to Genji.

nakihito no
wakare ya itodo
hedatara n
kemuri to nari shi
kumoi naradewa

how long has it been
since we bid her farewell?
and now you
leave the very skies that
received her as smoke

12-1. Poor people, usually women, living along the coast derived some income from boiling seawater down for its salt or burning gathered seaweed for minerals contained in the ash to be used as fertilizer. Although the work was hard, wet, and dirty, poets found a wealth of images in the process: dripping wet sleeves, briny tears, fires on lonely beaches, smoke like that of the crematoriums. Mount Toribe *(toribeyama)* was the customary place of cremation and burial for Kyoto.

12 - 3

At his own residence, the empty courtyard and the dust on the tables announce the waste and neglect that will come to the house in his absence. Genji goes to Murasaki, who has been up all night waiting for him. First of all he must explain to her why he has been away though the two of them have so little time yet together. It has been rumored that many feel that now all of her favorable fates bringing her into Genji's household are also leaving her. As he combs his hair, and sees how he has already lost weight from the stress, he also sees in the mirror Murasaki sitting by a pillar behind him, crying.

mi wa kakute	in this way
sasurae nu tomo	though I wander afar
kimi ga atari	I'll be with you
sara nu kagami no	my image will stay
kage wa hanare ji	here in your mirror

12 - 4

Turning her tearful face to the pillar, Murasaki says, as if to herself:

wakare temo	though we part
kage dani tomaru	may your image remain
mono nara ba	a clear fact
kagami wo mi temo	as it is seen in a mirror
nagusame te mashi	that would comfort me

12 - 5

Instead of spending all of his last nights in the capital with Murasaki, now his official wife, Genji goes out to visit each of his lovers one more time. While leaving Lady Scattered Blossoms on her verandah, the bright moon shines on the deep purple of her gown. It is as if the moon is shedding tears that catch on her sleeves. Extending her arms, she whispers:

tsukikage no	moonlight
yadore ru sode wa	lodges on these sleeves

semaku tomo	even though narrow
tome te zo mi baya	they shall keep the gleam
aka nu hikari wo	I never tire of seeing

12 - 6

Although very sad himself, Genji tries to comfort Lady Scattered Blossoms.

yukimeguri	going away
tsuini sumu beki	yet in the end together again
tsukikage no	the moonlight
shibashi kumora n	goes for awhile into the clouds
sora na nagame so	so don't gaze at the sky absently

12 - 7

Genji even sends a note to Princess of the Night of the Misty Moon, whom he has not dared to visit since her father caught Genji in her bed. The scandal was made even greater because the princess was made a consort of the present emperor. "Remembering the crime to which I cannot plead innocent . . ." He can write nothing more, out of fear his note might be intercepted, but he wishes he could wipe away her tears.

oose naki	sunken in sorrow
namida no kawa ni	in the river of our tears
shizumi shi ya	we cannot meet
nagaruru mio no	drifting with the currents
hajime nari ken	we can only begin again

or

no chance to meet
shall I again sink into
a river of tears?
that deep current entered
when we began our affair

12-6. *Sumu* can mean "clear, shining brightly" or "to live" or "live as man and wife."

12 - 8

Deeply upset, Princess of the Night of the Misty Moon replies with shaky handwriting. There is something very fine about the hand disordered by grief.

namidagawa	a bubble floating
ukabu minawa mo	on the river of tears
kie nu beshi	will vanish
wakare te nochi no	before having a chance to
se wo mo mata zu te	meet at the lower crossing

12 - 9

On the night before his departure, Genji plans to visit his father's grave site in the northern hills. But first he goes to Lady of the Wisteria Apartment to discuss affairs concerning their son. When the tears begin to splash down from Genji's face, she finds him almost too handsome to resist. When he asks her if she has a message she wishes to have delivered to his father's grave, she is silent a long time as she attempts to control her tears with her sleeve-covered hand pressed to her lips.

mi shi wa naku	how sad it is
aru wa kanashiki	the one I served is gone
yo no hate wo	bound by these times
somuki shi kai mo	unable to become a nun
naku naku zo furu	my reward is more weeping

12 - 10

Their sorrow, in triple form because of their connections, is so great, there is no room for words. Yet Genji replies:

wakare shi ni	that parting from him
kanashiki koto wa	was such a sad occasion
tsuki ni shi wo	and yet it ended
mata mo kono yo no	this time leaving the child
usa wa masare ru	my torment is even greater

12-8. *Se* refers to either "shoals, crossing" or "chance." If one completely understands the phrase "meet at the lower crossing," one understands Genji's attraction to her.

12-9. This poem is notable for the use of *naku,* which occurs three times. *Naku* can mean "to weep" or "cease to exist." The full range of meanings is expressed by her grief.

Somuki refers to turning one's back on the world or becoming a priest or nun.

12 - 11

As Genji and his few attendants who accompany him into exile travel past Lower Kamo Shrine, one attendant dismounts, taking the bridle of Genji's horse. He recalls the day he acted as Genji's attendant at the Kamo lustrations, as he recites:

hiki tsure te	forced to go along
aoi kazase shi	with heartvine in our hair
sono kami wo	those bygone days
omoe ba tsurashi	bitter to remember at
kamo no mizugaki	Kamo Shrine's sacred fence

12 - 12

Dismounting, Genji bows toward the shrine in memory and farewell, saying:

ukiyo oba	from this bitter world
ima zo hanaruru	though forced to leave
todomara n	my name stays
na oba tadasu no	entrusted to the god here
kami ni makase te	who rights all wrongs

12 - 13

Coming to his father's grave, Genji feels he can almost see his figure before him. Weeping, Genji tells his father of the situations that are causing this trip into exile, but in the silence there seems to be no answer from beyond the grave. The moon sails behind a cloud, making the grove of trees dark and sinister. As he bows in farewell, a shiver passes through him and he seems to see his father as he had been in life.

naki kage ya	without existence
ikade miru ran	how does he look upon me?
yosoe tsutsu	does it compare to
nagamuru tsuki mo	my seeing the moon even
kumogakure nuru	when hidden by the clouds?

12-12. *Tadasu* means "to right or rectify" and also indicates the name of the place where Lower Kamo Shrine is located.

12 - 14

Back at his palace, Genji sends a last message to the Crown Prince by way of Lady of the Wisteria Apartment's lady-in-waiting, who has been put in charge of him. Tying his paper to a cherry branch from which all the flowers have fallen adds to the poignancy of his words.

itsuka mata	when shall I
haru no miyako no	a rustic mountain man
hana wo mi n	see again
toki ushinae ru	spring in the capital
yamagatsu ni shite	the prince of flowers?

12 - 15

The lady-in-waiting is the one who facilitated the illicit meetings between Lady of the Wisteria Apartment and Genji that resulted in the birth of the Crown Prince. Now she sees how much unhappiness this has brought for all concerned. She tells Genji she has given the Crown Prince his message and how the prince's sadness has only made Lady of the Wisteria Apartment even more despondent.

saki te toku	though it was sad
chiru wa ukere do	when the flowers scattered
yuku haru wa	as spring passed
hana no miyako wo	however when you return
tachikaeri miyo	the city will bloom again

12 - 16

Genji spends his very last day at home with Murasaki. When the moon rises, he urges her to say good-bye to him, telling her with forced lightness:

ike ru yo no	living in the world
wakare wo shira de	as if we knew nothing
chigiri tsutsu	of separations
inochi wo hito ni	my vows will last
kagiri keru kana	as long as you live

12-15. At this time, it was thought that the cherry trees flowered most beautifully in the capital.

12 - 17

Murasaki's farewell poem to Genji makes him wish to linger, but he does not want the city to see him leaving in broad daylight.

oshikara nu	no longer precious
inochi ni kae te	I would wish to exchange
me no mae no	this life
wakare wo shibashi	if it would delay our parting
todome te shigana	even for one minute

12 - 18

Murasaki's heartrending expression remains with Genji on the long journey. He is consumed by sorrow as he boards the boat that, with a tailwind and the long spring day, brings him yet that afternoon to the coast of Suma, where he is to live. There he passes Oe Station, which he has read about in *The Tales of Ise*, now in ruins, with only a grove of pines to mark where it had been.

karakuni ni	once upon a time
na wo nokoshi keru	a man left his name
hito yori mo	in old China
yukue shira re nu	will my destination
iei wo ya se n	be a place so far away?

12 - 19

Looking back from the boat toward the city, Genji sees that the mountains are shrouded in mist, making him feel as if he has traveled to a faraway realm. The ocean spray flying from the oars seems only to add to the sadness.

furusato wo	though misty peaks
mine no kasumi wa	hide my ancient village
hedatsure do	is the sky I see
nagamuru sora wa	the same one which
onaji kumoi ka	contains those clouds?

12-18. Oe Station, in the heart of present-day Osaka, had been established as overnight accommodations for the high priestesses on their way to and from the shrine at Ise.

Shikibu makes a bow of recognition to the poem-story that was popular about fifty years before her novel and was still avidly read by her contemporaries. She repeats some of the situations from *The Tales of Ise*, but greatly enlarges upon them while weaving them into a much more complex plot. The nameless hero of *The Tales of Ise* is thought to be Arihara no Narihira, a ninth-century cavalier poet who is responsible for about one-third of the poems in the story. One or two other men probably compiled the poems and wrote some of the prose headings to flesh out the stories. The mention fits well here, as the hero of *The Tales of Ise* had many of his amorous affairs while on a journey.

12 - 20

After Genji has settled into his rustic, but adequate, new home, the rainy season arrives, bringing him thoughts of his abandoned family. He thinks of his son, the Crown Prince, and his other son, Lord Evening Mist, but it takes him longest to write to Murasaki and Lady of the Wisteria Apartment, because his eyes keep misting over. Thinking of Lady of the Wisteria Apartment, who has become a nun, Genji writes to her:

matsushima no	in a nun's thatched hut
ama no tomaya mo	on the Island of Waiting Pines
ikanaran	think how it is
suma no urabito	for the one living on Suma Bay
shiotaruru koro	weeping briny tears all the time

12 - 21

Genji's letter to Princess of the Night of the Misty Moon is sent, as usual, to her lady-in-waiting, as if it were meant for her. Yet the words conceal another meaning directed to the princess.

korizuma no	at Suma Bay
ura no mirume no	on the beach is the sea grass
yukashiki wo	which one knows so well
shio yaku ama ya	what do the women boiling salt
ikaga omowan	from seawater think of it?

or

undisciplined
on the beach a chance to meet
for which we long
why are nuns burning seawater
and what will the public think?

12 - 22

Lady of the Wisteria Apartment responds to Genji's letter and poem with a poem of her own. It seems that with Genji

12-20. *Matsushima* is the name of a place in Miyagi Prefecture; it is a fixed poetic expression that plays on the two meanings of *matsu*, "pine," the tree, and "to pine, long or wait for." *Shima* means "island," and *ama* can refer to a nun, fisherman, or a woman pearl diver. *Matsushima no ama* thus implies "the nun who waits for me to come back."

12-21. *Suma* can be a place name or mean "to live."

so far away, she feels she has been too cool and rejecting during their farewells. Although always afraid of the effect of gossip on her life, having Genji farther away permits the empress to relax her tight control on her emotions. Thus, her response is more affectionate than usual.

shiotaruru	the burning issue
koto wo yaku nite	are the briny tears on sleeves
matsushima ni	on the Island of Pines
toshi furu ama mo	as the years go by the nun
nageki wo zo tsumu	accumulates more sadness

---

12 - 23

Princess of the Night of the Misty Moon tucks the following poem for Genji into the letter from her lady-in-waiting. The princess is able to match Genji's expressive ability, concealing her true feelings in her poem:

ura ni taku	fires on the beach
ama dani tsutsumu	yet the nun keeps to herself
koi dare ba	since being in love
kuyuru kemuri yo	the smoke of smoldering fires
yukukata zo naki	does not cheer one up at all
	or
	burning on the beach
	yet the nun keeps to herself
	because of love
	from fires that only smolder
	that cannot be cleared away

---

12 - 24

Murasaki has sent bedding and other supplies to Suma for Genji's household. In reply to Genji's letter, she sends some beautifully tailored robes that also contain this poem, which makes him long for her even more.

urabito no	fisherman
shio kumu sode ni	scooping seawater with sleeves
kurabe miyo	compare his to mine
namiji hedatsuru	though far from the ocean
yoru no koromo wo	just look at my night robe

12 - 25

Lady of the Sixth Ward sends a messenger from Ise to Suma with her letter containing many pages and several poems. She has sent a messenger to find Genji in his exile—to know more about the place to which he has confined himself. Her letter expresses the idea that he might soon be returning to the city, but that she, lost in sin, will not be permitted to see him.

ukime karu	cut sea weeds float
ise o no ama wo	like the nun at Ise
omoiyare	imagine saying
moshiho taru chō	sea grass burnt for salt
suma no ura nite	dribbles on the Suma beach

12 - 26

Unable to stop with one poem, Lady of the Sixth Ward adds another. Their situations, both living on remote coasts, are so very similar, yet they, as lovers, are so far apart.

iseshima ya	oh the isle of Ise
shiohi no kata ni	on the beach when the tide ebbs
asari temo	though one looks for it
iu kai naki wa	there's no answer in the shell
wagami nari keri	except one's own lot in life

12 - 27

The style of her calligraphy showed such unique breeding and cultivation that Genji begins to regret his not going with Lady of the Sixth Ward to live at Ise Shrine. There, too, he would have been far enough away from the capital for his exile but he would not have been as lonely as he is here on Suma Bay.

12-26. The poem refers to Ise as an island, but it is in fact a peninsula.

He was truly fond of her and perhaps it was wrong to let one incident drive them apart. The letter moves him so deeply he begins to feel a certain affection for the messenger she has sent and detains him for several days. Because the house is small, the messenger can observe Genji at close range and is moved to tears by his admiration of the man. After learning much of the life at Ise from the messenger, Genji's reply to Lady of the Sixth Ward includes these poems to her.

isebito no	with the one at Ise
nami no ue kogu	even a small boat could have rowed
obune nimo	on the tops of waves
ukime wa kara de	without having to cut the bitter
nora mashi mono wo	kelp through which I must row

---

12 - 28

Genji's second poem in his reply to Lady of the Sixth Ward:

ama ga tsumu	a nun collecting
nageki no naka ni	sorrow like driftwood while
shio tare te	the brine drips
itsu made suma no	how long is one lost in thought
ura ni nagame n	to go on living at Suma Bay?

---

12 - 29

Even Lady Scattered Blossoms sends her complaints, which seem sad yet comforting. After receiving this poem, Genji commissions workers to repair her roof.

are masaru	wasting away
noki no shinobu wo	ferns of remembrance
nagame tsutsu	at the eaves
shigeku mo tsuyu no	continually lost in thought
kakaru sode kana	many tears fall on my sleeves

2-27. *Uki-me* can be understood as "floating seaweed" or "bitterness."

12-28. *Nageki* can refer to "sorrow" or "driftwood."

12-29. *Shinobu* refers to either a kind of fern that grows on the eaves of thatched roofs or the verb "to recall or remember."

12 - 30

When the autumn storms come to the shores of Suma, the wind and waves are especially loud. Although Genji's house is some distance from the sea, the roaring wind seems to bring the surf right to his bedside. One night Genji wakes full of despair. He tries playing the harp, but it only makes him more despondent.

koiwabi te	waves dash on the beach
naku ne ni magau	with the voice of one weeping
uranami wa	who suffers from love
omou kata yori	is it because the wind blows
kaze ya fuku ran	from the direction of my love?

12 - 31

One evening in autumn, while Genji is on the verandah looking down the far coastline at the tiny fishing boats bobbing on the lonely sea, he brushes away tears caused by the splashing of the oars. The calls of the migrating wild geese as they pass overhead and the whiteness of Genji's hand holding the jet-black rosary beads bring comfort to his men so far from their families.

hatsukari wa	are wild geese
koishiki hito no	seeking the companions
tsura nare ya	for whom I long?
tabi no sora tobu	flying through the sky
koe no kanashiki	the journey of their cries

12 - 32

One of his attendants answers.

kaki tsurane	I know not
mukashi no koto zo	why they bring thoughts of old
omooyuru	migrating geese
kari wa sono yo no	even in those times were
tomo nara ne domo	never my companions

12-31. *Tsura* means either "in a line" or "company, companions."

12 - 33

Sir Reflected Brilliance recites:

kokoro kara	to willingly leave
tokoyo wo sute te	the country of my birth
naku kari wo	the wild goose's cry
kumo no yoso nimo	somewhere beyond the clouds
omoi keru kana	is the same as mine was then

12 - 34

The guard's officer, who remembered the day at the Kamo lustrations, offers:

tokoyo ide te	leaving one's country
tabi no sora naru	to journey through the skies
karigane mo	the wild goose also
tsura ni okure nu	has a line of companions
hodo zo nagusamu	and solace for a time

12 - 35

That evening the full autumn moon rises, bringing many memories for each of the men and making them even more dejected. Genji stares at the moon, calling it his oldest friend, and wonders if the people he loves are also staring at the same moon. He refuses to come inside, despite the lateness of the hour and his men's urgings.

miru hodo zo	while looking at it
shibashi nagusamu	I am for a time comforted
meguriawa n	that we'll meet again
tsuki no miyako wa	the moon over the capital
haruka nare domo	though it is so far away

12 - 36

Genji thinks of the Suzaku Emperor, of the last time he saw him, and recalls how, at their farewell, he reminded Genji so much of their own father. As he goes inside, he mentions that he still has a robe, a gift from his father, that he always keeps by his side.

ushi to nomi	a single robe
hitoeni mono wa	yet the two sleeves
omooe de	are wet with tears
hidari migi nimo	on one side bitterness
nururu sode kana	on the other affection

12 - 37

The Assistant Viceroy of Kyūshū passes Suma as he is returning to the capital accompanied by his wife and many daughters. From their boat they catch the strains of someone playing the harp. After messages have been exchanged between the visitors and Genji, one of the daughters, called the Gosechi Dancer, sends this in a note.

koto no ne ni	having been stopped
hikitome raruru	by the sounds of a harp
tsunadenawa	the boat's towing rope
tayutau kokoro	drifts like my hesitant heart
kimi shiru rame ya	my Lord, do you know why?

12 - 38

Genji replies with a smile that makes his attendants feel rather inadequate.

kokoro ari te	if your heart is
hikute no tsuna no	being tugged by a tow rope
tayutawa ba	because it's drifting
uchisugi mashi ya	how then can you pass Suma
suma no uranami	where the waves dash to the beach?

12 - 39

As winter comes and people in the city send fewer letters, Genji begins to miss Murasaki even more. He thinks of

12-36. *Hitoeni* means either "earnestly, entirely" or "a single robe."

having her brought to Suma but decides that the punishment is for him alone and she should not be subjected to such hardships. While observing someone unsuccessfully trying to light a fire with wet wood, Genji murmurs.

yamagatsu no	a mountain person
iori ni take ru	in this hut tried to light
shiba shiba mo	firewood many times
kototoi ko nan	just as often I have wished
kouru satobito	for the town folk I miss so

12 - 40

One night when the bright, rising moon is so low it shines in the farthest corners of his shallow-eaved room, Genji is reminded of one of Sugawara Michizane's poems. He had written "to the moon" while he, also, was in exile. Genji whispers as he quotes"The Moon Goes Always to the West:"

izukata no	so aimless
kumoji ni ware mo	is my journey lost in skies
mayoi nan	it shames me
tsuki no miru ran	to have the moon see
koto mo hazukashi	how very lost I am

12 - 41

Awake until dawn, Genji hears, while the others sleep, the cries of beach plovers. He repeats this poem several times to himself.

tomochidori	a flock of plovers
morogoe ni naku	cry in a chorus of voices
akatsuki wa	at the break of day
hitori nezame no	bringing comfort to the bed
toko mo tanomoshi	of one who wakes alone

12-39. *Shiba* is "firewood"; *shiba shiba*, "often, many times."

12-40. Sugawara Michizane (845–903) was a brilliant scholar in Chinese and gifted poet who was influential at court. With the ascent of Emperor Daigo (r. 897–930), Michizane's position waned to the point that he was exiled to the island of Kyūshū, where he lived in crushing poverty for two years while he continued to write poetry. It is generally agreed, judging from his last poems, that he died of starvation. After his death, a series of calamities in Japan were perceived by some to be an indication that the gods were retaliating for the way the emperor had treated Michizane. Thus, Sugawara Michizane became god-like himself and is today petitioned as Tenjin in temples near universities all over Japan for aid in getting good grades and advancement.

12 - 42

Shortly afterwards, when New Year's day comes to Suma, a cherry sapling Genji brought with him begins to bloom. The flowering tree brings to Genji many memories of the festivals at court. He thinks about the time his brother, the present emperor, had honored him by reciting one of his poems.

itsu to naku	still longing
ōmiyabito no	for my companions at court
koishiki ni	only the times
sakura kazashi shi	we put cherry blossoms
kyō mo ki ni keri	in our hair are here again

12 - 43

The First Secretary's Captain, Genji's oldest friend and former brother-in-law, misses him so much he risks slander and rejection by coming to Suma to visit Genji. At dawn, just when the two men are parting, a line of wild geese fly overhead. Genji says:

furusato wo	in which spring
izure no haru ka	will I return to see
yuki te mi n	my hometown?
urayamashiki wa	I envy the wild goose
kaeru karigane	keeping the tradition

12 - 44

Unwilling to leave Genji so soon, the First Secretary's Captain replies with one more poem.

akana kuni	hating to leave
kari no tokoyo wo	this temporary paradise
tachiwakare	yet I must go
hana no miyako ni	to the capital's flowers
michi ya madowa n	will I stray from my way?

12-43. It is still a rite of spring for the Japanese people to journey back to the place where they were born for a visit.

12-44. Kari is "wild goose" or "temporary." Kyoto lies north of Suma.

12 - 45

The First Secretary's Captain sadly wonders how long his friend will have to remain in exile. Genji's answer comes as a poem.

kumo chikaku	a crane flies across
tobikau tazu mo	clouds as high as the court
sora ni miyo	watch the skies
ware wa harubi no	to see me as undefiled
kumorinaki mi zo	as a clear spring day

12 - 46

Genji is confronted with the notion that someday he will have to go back to the court, but he recalls how difficult it will be to reestablish himself and wonders if he will be able to. The First Secretary's Captain recites this verse to comfort Genji.

tazukanaki	helpless and alone
kumoi ni hitori	in the imperial courts
ne wo zo naku	like a crying voice
tsubasa narabe shi	we once flew wing to wing
tomo wo koi tsutsu	the crane friend I still miss

12 - 47

On the first day of the serpent in the Third Month, one of Genji's men reminds him of the custom of "washing away one's worries" in a lustration ceremony. A soothsayer is engaged to transfer Genji's sins and tribulations onto a straw doll, which is then cast into the sea. As Genji watches the large doll floating helpless on the cold waves, he feels how much he is like the thing carrying sins and tribulations.

shira zari shi	unknowing
ōumi no hara ni	the vastness of the ocean
nagare ki te	so the sadness
hitokata ni yawa	comes drifting like
mono wa kanashiki	the sacrificial doll

12-45. Cranes were associated with writing, nobility, and longevity. *Kumoi* means "clouds" or "cloud-covered place," i.e., the Imperial Palace.

12-46. *Tazukanaki,* "helpless, unreliable," can also indicate the cry of a crane.

The brightness of the sunny seashore shows Genji to his men in a new light as he thinks of all that has happened to him and wonders what is ahead. His words seem much like a prayer.

yaoyorozu	eight million gods
kami mo aware to	will surely have pity also
omou ran	as they consider
okase ru tsumi no	that no crimes or sins exist
sore to nakere ba	which I may have committed

13

AKASHI

Third Month of Genji's twenty-seventh year to Eighth Month of his twenty-eighth year

As autumn comes to the rugged Suma coast where Genji is in exile, the weather worsens so that living in this remote place stops being romantic and actually becomes dangerous when the storms sweep in from the sea, one after the other, lasting for weeks. Genji and his men begin to fear for their lives as parts of the house burn from lightning strikes and then another section is blown away in a typhoon. Huddled together in the kitchen where they are trying to sleep, Genji dreams of his father, who tells him to leave this place by sea immediately.

The next morning, just as they are ready to make a hasty departure, the ex-governor of Harima, who has retired to be a monk on the coast at nearby Akashi, almost magically appears in a boat. Talking to him, Genji realizes that he has already heard of the man's daughter. Genji's party goes with the man to Akashi, again with magical speed, where they find conditions much more civilized. The former governor offers Genji a lovely home by the sea and, later, his daughter in his home on the hill. The girl is very afraid of someone so elevated and charming as Genji, and Genji feels a great deal of guilt about carrying on an affair when Murasaki misses him so much back at the capital.

While Genji is unsuccessfully wooing the rustic maiden—the Akashi Lady—the Emperor, back in the capital, has a dream in which his father appears to remind him of his vow to keep

Genji by his side. The Emperor wishes to revoke Genji's exile but his mother, Lady of the Beautiful Hall, insists that he not give in to Genji. As result of her intense hatred, the mother falls ill. As she weakens in health and power, the Emperor is able to send for Genji, and asks him to come home, thus fulfilling the prayers Genji had made at the temple at Sumiyoshi.

In the last months before parting, the Akashi Lady gives in to Genji's sexual advances, which makes their parting even more poignant. His joy of going home is now saddened by his having to leave the woman he has grown to love, the mother of his unborn child, and her father, to whom he has grown attached as a friend.

---

13 - A

warinaku mo	unable to avoid
wakare gatashi to	the pain of separation
shiratama no	beautiful white pearls
namida wo nagasu	seem to be tears shed
koto no ito kana	by the harp's strings

---

13 - 1

During the ceremony of lustration on the beach, a terrible storm suddenly descends upon Genji and his men. Without warning, the wind, waves, and rain swirl about them. The torrents and tempest go on so brutally for days that Genji begins to think of trying to move to a less remote place. He is scared to stay in this place, but he is ashamed to return to the city so soon for fear of what people will say of him. In the middle of this stormy time, a messenger arrives with a letter and poem for him from Murasaki.

urakaze ya	winds on the beaches
ikani fuku ran	how must they be blowing now
omoiyaru	I am concerned
sode uchinurashi	that sleeves are so dampened
namima naki koro	they cannot dry between waves

13 - 2

The winter storms, both here on the coast and in the capital, seem to increase in violence. Lightning strikes Genji's dwellings, burning part of his residence to the ground. Forced to seek shelter in the kitchen, Genji gives thanks as the storm finally passes away.

umi ni masu	without the grace
kami no tasuke ni	of the gods of the sea
kakara zu ba	to depend upon
shio no yaoai ni	we would have drifted
sasurae namashi	into giant whirlpools

13 - 3

Exhausted, Genji falls asleep leaning on a piece of old furniture and dreams his father has come to tell him to leave Suma. The very next morning, a boat arrives from Akashi, a point farther down the coast. Genji asks if he might return with the visitors. It happens that a wealthy man who has become a monk has several dwellings in the area, so Genji is offered a house on the beach. When they are barely settled in, Genji sends off Murasaki's messenger with this poem for her.

haruka nimo	worrying about you
omoiyaru kana	from a distant place
shira zari shi	not knowing
ura yori ochi ni	much beyond the beach is
urazutai shi te	one even farther away

13 - 4

By the Fourth Month, Genji feels quite at home in the old monk's carefully appointed abode. With the better weather, many messages arrive from the city. Here in Akashi, the sea is so calm and quiet, Genji almost feels he is looking out over his own garden. Yet these feelings make his longing to go home only greater. One night, while seeing the moonlight on the white sea foam, Genji whispers to himself:

13-3. Akashi was rustic and remote, but it had been established as a post station, one of the earliest, in 646, during Emperor Kōtoku's reign. It held horses and was maintained for traveling government officials. Thus it remained in closer contact with the capital than many areas much nearer to Kyoto.

awa to miru	seeing over there
awaji no shima no	Awaji like an island of foam
aware sae	sad and abandoned
nokoru kuma naku	in a forsaken corner at night
sume ru yo no tsuki	clearly shines the moon

13-5

In his loneliness, Genji brings out his harp, spreading a world of sad thoughts far and wide. Even the monk's household on the hill hears the notes of his harp joining the wind and waves. The monk comes running down to Genji's place to join him in playing and discussing music. Genji mentions that he feels women can get more emotion from a harp. From their talks, Genji is reminded that, though aged, the monk has a lovely young daughter who also plays the harp. At first Genji is afraid her father will not want her to meet him, a man in exile. So Genji carefully asks the old monk for only his companionship for the lonely evenings. The monk asks Genji:

hitorine wa	surely you know
kimi mo shiri nu ya	how lonely it can be
tsurezureto	to spend a night
omoi akashi no	on the shores of Akashi
urasabishisa wo	with only one's worries

13-6

The old monk and Genji then begin to compare their experiences on this remote and rugged seacoast.

tabigoromo	traveling garments
uraganashisa ni	are enough to make one sad
akashi kane	to spend the night on
kusa no makura wa	a grass pillow at Akashi
yume mo musuba zu	where even dreams do not come

13-4. The wordplay involves *a,* "that over there," and *wa,* indicating the subject, thus *a wa,* "as far as that is concerned," and the name of the island previously called Ahaji and now called Awaji, in which *awa* refers to "bubbles" or "foam." The tip of Awaji Island lies directly across the bay from Akashi. This strait, which was bridged in 1985 with the longest bridge in Asia, lies between the largest and the smallest islands of Japan.

13-5. Akashi refers to the place or to "pass or spend the night."

13-6. Kusa no makura indicates sleeping on a journey, from *kusa,* "grass," *no,* "of," and *makura* "pillow" or the times when one used grass for a pillow.

13-7

About noon the next day, encouraged by his talks with the old monk, Genji sends off an introductory note to the house on the hill among the trees where the daughter lives. He takes great care with his poem, written on fine saffron Korean paper.

ochikochi mo	lost in a sky
shira nu kumoi ni	of strange and far places
nagame wabi	a hint of a house
kasume shi yado no	and treetops in the mist
kozue wo zo tou	guide my way to you

13-8

The old monk's daughter, raised in such a remote area, is overwhelmed with the elegance of Genji's note and feels unable to answer. Very eager for a meeting to occur, an event for which he has fervently prayed, her father urges the girl to reply. She seems to be taking so long that finally he takes it upon himself to write the answering poem, even though he wishes she had been able to do it.

nagamu ran	she gazes
onaji kumoi wo	into the same skies
nagamuru wa	as you do
omoi mo onaji	may your thoughts also
omoi naru ran	come to be of one accord

13-9

The next day Genji tries to make a reply to the poem but he is disconcerted by the fact that it was the father who wrote to him instead of the girl. Thus, he writes, on soft, delicate paper, the words:

ibuseku mo	clouded
kokoro ni mono wo	by affairs of the heart
omou kana	I am lost

13-7. *Kasume* means "mist" or "hint, imply."

yayoya ikani to	hello! why doesn't someone
tou hito mo nami	ask how I am?

13 - 10

Again unwilling to attempt to respond to such a noble man's poem, the girl is reduced to tears and inaction. Yet she is forced by her father to write back to Genji. She chooses a perfumed lavender paper and takes great care with the gradations of the ink.

omou ran	how can you
kokoro no hodo ya	be lost in the gloom?
yayo ikani	hello! in what way
mada mi nu hito no	could one be so troubled
kiki ka nayama n	without even meeting me?

13 - 11

Finally, the father, with the help of astrology, picks the night Genji shall meet his daughter. As Genji rides his horse into the hills on the way to her house under the bright full moon, his longing for Murasaki increases so that he only wants to continue journeying on to the city where she is.

aki no yo no	on to the palace
tsukige no koma yo	oh roam colored horse
waga kouru	this autumn eve
kumoi ni kakere	take me to see her
toki no ma mo mi n	even just for a moment

13 - 12

At the house in the hills, the daughter, the Akashi lady, seems in no way eager to meet Genji and refuses to answer him when he speaks to her. Just as he feared, she is winning at this battle of wills. Then Genji hears a curtain cord accidentally brush against a harp string. He seizes upon the inspiration of the incident by asking her to play the harp for him and adds a poem to show his need for companionship.

mutsugoto wo	I wish for someone
katariawase n	who will kindly share with me
hito mogana	a heart-to-heart talk
ukiyo no yume mo	to be awakened halfway through
nakaba samu ya to	dreams of this bitter world

13 - 13

The Akashi lady's answer comes in a whisper, reminding Genji strongly of Lady of the Sixth Ward.

ake nu yo ni	the heart strays
yagate madoe ru	on an endless night
kokoro niwa	to another
izure wo yume to	how can one tell a dream
waki te katara n	from being awake?

13 - 14

Thus Genji begins his furtive affair with the Akashi lady. He dreads that the locals might discover his actions and he fears hurting Murasaki if she hears of his unfaithfulness. So, before this can happen, he writes to her, admitting the infatuation with a poem capable of having two meanings.

shio shio to	first of all it was
mazu zo naka ruru	natural to be slightly wet
karisome no	temporarily
mirume wa ama no	a fisherman meets someone
susabi nare domo	and decides to have some fun

or

first of all it was
natural to be slightly wet
when harvesting
sea grasses the fisherman
decides to have some fun

13-14. *Shio,* "salt"; *shio shio,* "slightly wet." *Mirume* can mean either "sea grass" or "to meet"; with *karisome,* the reference is to reaping sea grass or temporarily meeting someone.

13 - 15

Murasaki's letter is gentle and uncomplaining, yet the poem she encloses is enough to stop Genji from visiting the house of the Akashi Lady.

uranaku mo	naive of me
omoi keru kana	to believe you and yet
chigiri shi wo	you did vow
matsu yori nami wa	that this pine tree of ours
koe ji mono zo to	would not be inundated

13 - 16

At this time the country suffers from several great disasters. Believing them to be an indication of a fault of his, the Emperor becomes ill. Finally, in the Seventh Month, in an effort to right his wrongs, the Emperor grants Genji amnesty and orders him to return to the capital. In the Sixth Month Genji discovers that the Akashi Lady is pregnant with his child. Now Genji does not want to leave Akashi, but the Emperor issues another edict ordering him to return. Two days before his departure, he visits her again. Genji notices what a proud beauty she is. Together they watch as smoke from the salt-burner's fires draws faint lines in the sky as if all the symbols of loneliness have come together.

kono tabi wa	at a time like this
tachiwakaru tomo	when we must part
moshio yaku	smoke trails
kemuri wa onaji	from burning sea grass
kata ni nabika n	waft on the same route

13 - 17

The Akashi Lady speaks her poem while weeping pitifully, only because silence would seem to be rude.

kakitsume te	sea weeds piled up
ama no yaku mo no	for the woman to burn
omoi nimo	yet tender feelings

ima wa kainaki	are in vain now as
urami dani se ji	well as are grudges

13 - 18

Never in all their time together has the Akashi Lady played the harp for Genji. So on this, the eve of their parting, she does. He is so impressed with her skill that he gives her the harp he had brought with him from the capital as a keepsake. She replies:

naozari ni	small comfort
tanome oku meru	it seems I'm left to rely on
hito koto wo	one person's harp-word
tsuki se nu ne ni ya	the sound of its ringing
kake te shinoba n	will only be my weeping

13 - 19

Genji cannot let her reference pass:

au made no	until we meet again
katami ni chigiru	as a keepsake of our vows
naka no wo no	I leave this
shirabe wa kotoni	I hope the tone never changes
kawara zara nan	especially the middle string

13 - 20

On Genji's very last day, amidst all the moving activities, he manages to send the Akashi Lady a note.

uchisute te	leaving in sadness
tatsu mo kanashiki	waves dash against the shore
uranami no	leaving you
nagori ikani to	with such regrets
omoiyaru kana	worries me greatly

13-18. *Ne* means either "crying" or "a sound."

13-19. *Naka* means "middle" or "relationship."

13 - 21

The Akashi Lady, who has threatened at times to drown herself because of her conflicts over their affair, replies:

toshi hetsutsu	years have passed
tomaya mo are te	with the thatched-roof hut in ruins
uki nami no	it's a bitter wave
kaeru kata niya	that's returning to its place
mi wo tague mashi	I wish to go along with it

13 - 22

The old monk of Akashi makes a splendid ceremony of Genji's departure. He even has robes made by his women for each of Genji's men as farewell gifts. On one travel robe, the Akashi Lady pins a poem.

yoru nami ni	waves coming closer
tachikasane taru	when I cut and sewed
tabigoromo	this traveling robe
shiodokeshi toya	was made wet by tears
hito no itowa n	might this offend you?

13 - 23

As accompaniment to his thanks, Genji sends a poem to the Akashi Lady with one of his inner robes, one worn between underclothes and outer clothes and the garment normally worn while sleeping with a lover.

katami ni zo	just as a keepsake
kau bekari keru	why shouldn't we exchange
au koto no	our sleeping robes
hi kazu hedate n	restraining us from meeting
naka no koromo wo	are the countless days ahead

13 - 24

The old monk, who by his religious vows should have been more separated from the emotional affairs of the world, is very upset that he cannot accompany Genji back to the capital.

yo wo umi ni	weary of this
kokora shiojimu	world dipped in salt
mi to nari te	even I
nao kono kishi wo	am not able to leave
e koso hanare ne	behind this beach

13 - 25

Genji tries to explain away his own copious tears with:

miyako ide shi	leaving the capital
haru no nageki ni	in spring I wept in sorrow
otora me ya	isn't it just as sad
toshi furu ura wo	leaving this shore in autumn
wakare nuru aki	grown older with grief?

13 - 26

As soon as he is back in the capital, Genji visits the Emperor. Unable to tell him directly how he has been missed, the emperor tells him how he has missed having music and hearing the old songs. Genji's answer is equally oblique.

watatsumi ni	cast into the sea
shizumi urabure	I sank into my grief
hiru no ko no	like the leech child
ashi tata zari shi	without a leg to stand on
toshi wa he ni keri	yet the years went passing by

13 - 27

Touched and embarrassed, the Emperor forms his reply around the rest of the leech-child story, in which the couple return to the sacred shrine pillar to try again.

miyabashira	at the shrine pillar
meguri ai keru	where they met again by chance

13-24. *Umi* refers to the sea or to growing tired, weary of.

13-26. In the *Nihongi* is a version of the creation story of Japan in which the first parents of mankind meet at a sacred pillar. First the woman invites the man to circle it with her by telling him how handsome he is. Thereafter she bears children that are deformed, among them the "leech child" that has no legs. According to the legend, the couple are advised to try this ritual again, but letting the man speak first—to extend the invitation. This time their children are beautiful gods and goddesses. Knowing that Japan was first a matriarchal society, and later patriarchal, gives new understanding to the cruelty of this legend, a weight of embarrassment for the mother of every crippled child.

toki shi are ba	as we do now yet
wakare shi haru no	let us forget the spring of parting
urami nokosu na	and leave behind those feelings

13 - 28

When the retinue from Akashi is ready to return from accompanying Genji to the capital, Genji sends with them a tender poem for the Akashi Lady.

nageki tsutsu	are you still grieving
akashi no ura ni	from those nights spent
asagiri no	on Akashi's shores?
tatsu ya to hito wo	morning mists rise up as
omoiyaru kana	fears for the one I left there

13 - 29

Back in the capital, Genji receives an unsigned poem that he recognizes from the handwriting is from the Gosechi Dancer from Kyūshū, who has sent him a note while her boat was passing Suma.

suma no ura ni	once on Suma's shores
kokoro wo yose shi	you recall a heart came near
funabito no	someone in a boat
yagate kutase ru	wishes to show you the sleeves
sode wo mise baya	rotted from continuous tears

13 - 30

Her handwriting has improved but not enough to hide her identity. Genji's playfully replies to the dancing girl:

kaerite wa	on the contrary
kagoto ya se mashi	I'm the one with the grudge
yose tari shi	your approach
nagori ni sode no	has left me with such regrets
hi gatakari shi wo	that my sleeves are seldom dry

MIO TSUKUSHI
CHANNEL BUOYS

Tenth Month of Genji's twenty-eighth year to Eleventh Month of his twenty-ninth year

Now that the Emperor has seen the error of his ways in handling the Genji exile, he decides to abdicate in favor of the child (Genji's son) of Lady of the Wisteria Apartment. This restores Genji to prominence at court, with promotions. At the same time, Genji receives word that the Akashi Lady has borne him a daughter. Because a fortune-teller once predicted that all of his children would be emperors and empresses, Genji greatly regrets having let his first daughter be born in the provinces. With great care, he hires his hand-picked help to send to the Akashi Lady for the raising of the child.

Genji decides to make a pilgrimage to the shrine at Sumiyoshi to thank the local gods for answering his prayers by returning him to royal favor. While he is there, the Akashi Lady also arrives on her own pilgrimage, but when she sees the display of wealth and importance of the Genji party, she withdraws to another, smaller shrine. She and Genji exchange a series of poems about channel buoys and the finding of their own ways together.

Again Lady of the Sixth Ward enters Genji's life, but this time it is she who is ill. Visiting her brings again to the surface all of Genji's feelings for her. Her goal, though, is to get Genji to promise to look after her beautiful daughter, Lady Who

Loves Autumn. Lady of the Sixth Ward dies suddenly, which increases Genji's feelings of sadness. Genji uses his newly won power by helping his family into more positions. He gets Lady of the Wisteria Apartment to offer Lady Who Loves Autumn to the new Emperor (their own son) to prevent the retired Emperor from acquiring her, which would put her into their camp.

14 - A

mi wo tsukushi	like channel markers
awa n to inoru	entrusting one's life to prayers
mitegura mo	for wedded bliss
ware nomi kami ni	even offerings to the gods
tatematsuru ran	given by one who is alone

14 - 1

The Akashi Lady bears Genji a daughter on the sixteenth day of the Third Month. Wishing for a capable nurse to send to care for his child, Genji interviews a young girl at the court. The longer he talks to her, the less he wants to send her so far away from him. As he gives her his poem, he says, with a sly feeling in his words, "perhaps I should go with you."

kanete yori	since separating
hedate nu naka to	before having a chance to
narawa ne do	get to know you
wakare wa oshiki	it is a regretful thing
mono ni zo ari keru	that you are leaving

14 - 2

The nursemaid smiles as she gives an answer to Genji.

uchitsuke no	such sudden regrets
wakare wo oshi mu	upon parting are usually
kagoto nite	just an excuse
omowan kata ni	for one to continue longing
shitai yawa se nu	for the adored one, aren't they?

14-A. *Mi o tsukushi,* "entrust one's life to" or, read as *mio tsukushi,* the meaning is "channel buoys," from *mio,* "waterway," *tsu,* possessive case, and *kushi* "stake" or "marker."

14 - 3

Genji, having been admonished, is then all business as he reminds the new nursemaid how important his new daughter is to him.

itsushika mo	someday soon
sode uchikake n	my sleeves shall cover
otomego ga	the famed maiden
yo wo he te nade n	who measures the flight of time
iwa no oisaki	wearing away rock with wing touch

14 - 4

The Akashi Lady has been in despair since Genji's departure. However, with the arrival of the nursemaid, so attractive and cultured, along with so many splendid gifts, she begins to understand the position of her child in his life. When the nursemaid's escort prepares to return to the capital from Akashi, the Akashi Lady sends a letter to Genji with the following poem:

hitori shite	by being alone
nazuru wa sode no	my sleeves are too narrow
hodo naki ni	we await
oou bakari no	the cover of protection
kage wo shi zo matsu	of the very broadest one

14 - 5

Genji is astonished at how much his new little daughter is on his mind and how eager he is to see her. But then, fearing that Murasaki will learn of his new daughter with the Akashi Lady through rumors, Genji decides to confess everything to her, even telling her of their parting and the lines made in the sky by the smoke from the salt-burners' fires. Murasaki mutters to herself, "once we seemed a well-matched couple . . ." and this poem.

omou dochi	the couple in love
nabiku kata niwa	bend in the same direction
ara zu tomo	when not together

14-3. One of the classic definitions of a *kalpa* (a Buddhist eternity) is the length of time it would take for an angel's wing to wear away a gigantic rock when touching it only once in a millennium.

ware zo kemuri ni	I wish to be cremation smoke
sakidachi namashi	even before I have to die

14 - 6

Genji feels it is unpleasant for her to so lightly speak of her own death, so he answers her with:

tare ni yori	who was it
yo wo umi yama ni	in a world of mountainous seas
yukimeguri	went hither and yon
tae nu namida ni	floating on tears unceasing
uki shizumu mi zo	until at last my body sank?

14 - 7

As the baby's fiftieth-day celebration approaches, Genji sends off many gifts to arrive on just that day. His poem for the occasion is:

umimatsu ya	Sea Grass Princess
toki zo tomo naki	do remain unchangingly
kage ni ite	in the rock's shadow
nani no ayame mo	how to celebrate your day
ikani waku ran	on the iris's holiday?

14 - 8

The care and all the splendid gifts sent for the baby's celebration make the Akashi Lady slowly aware of what an important and special man Genji is. She sends this note back to Genji with the returning couriers.

kazunaranu	the cry of a crane
mishima gakure ni	hiding on this small isle
naku tazu wo	on her birthday
kyō mo ikani to	of fifty days no one
tou hito zo naki	comes to celebrate

14-7. The child's fiftieth-day celebration fell on the fifth of May, the day of the iris, or sweet flag, festivals in the capital. *Ayame* means "iris" or "step by step"; the Chinese ideograms can be read as *shōbu*, "sweet flag." *Ikani* can refer to either the interrogative adverbs why or who or the fiftieth day after birth celebration called the *ika* festival.

14-8. In societies with a high infant mortality rate, celebrations were held when the child had survived certain critical periods. Where we might give gifts for the birth of a child, this was postponed for seven days to make sure the child lived. In some ways, the fifty-day celebration could be viewed as the equivalent of a child's first birthday. Regardless of an individual's actual birthday, on New Year's Day every person becomes one year older. Thus, a baby born at the end of the year is one year old within a few days. However, the counting for the seven-day and fifty-day celebrations started from the day of the actual birth.

In *The Diary of Murasaki Shikibu,* the author describes in great detail the various ceremonies and celebrations of Empress Akiko's baby

14 - 9

During the long, rainy season of early summer, Genji has some respite from his many duties. He thinks of Lady Scattered Blossoms and decides to pay a visit to her. Just as they meet, a nearby water bird makes its tapping cry. She speaks very quietly.

kuina dani	if not for
odorokasa zu ba	knocking by a water bird
ikanishite	what other way
are taru yado ni	could the moon enter into
tsuki wo ire mashi	the lodging fallen to ruin?

14 - 10

Her soft voice trailing off into silence makes Genji pleased to be in her company again. Having so many charming women around him complicates his life, he thinks, as he sighs.

oshinabete	if you answered
tataku kuina ni	the tapping of every
odoroka ba	water bird
uwanosoranaru	even a wandering
tsuki mo koso ire	moon could enter

14 - 11

In the late autumn, Genji and his attendants make a pilgrimage to the shrine at Sumiyoshi to give thanks to the gods for answering their prayers. While in exile, they had visited the shrine with their petitions to be returned to the capital. One of his men, Sir Reflected Brilliance, hands this poem to Genji.

sumiyoshi no	at Sumiyoshi
matsu koso mono wa	these pines were the very things
kanashikere	we found so moving
kamiyo no koto wo	those days in which we lived
kakete omoe ba	in the neighborhood of the gods

son. From this account, one gets a clear picture of the usual pomp surrounding a royal birth.

14-10. In Shikibu's tale, as well as in others from this period, men are often portrayed as overly romantic, sentimental, and self-centered, especially as reflected in their poems. Women, on the other hand, are realistic and pragmatic and admired these qualities. Although it seems men admire childish women in the stories, the women do not reason as children.

14-11. Sumiyoshi, one of the oldest shrines in Kyūshū, was founded first at Kobe in A.D. 202 and later moved to its present site; as with many rural shrines, it is situated in a magnificent grove of cedar and camphor trees. From their age, it is obvious that the trees have been there much longer than the shrine and were surely the reason for situating it there. There is a fine view from the shrine to the Naka River. The shrine is dedicated to the four patron gods who protect seafarers, and thus these were the deities who protected Genji in exile on the seacoast.

14 - 12

Genji finds the poem very apt and gives this reply to his man.

arakari shi	roughed up
nami no mayoi ni	by violent wind and waves
sumiyoshi no	how can I forget
kami oba kakete	the gods of Sumiyoshi
wasure yawa suru	who saved me from this?

14 - 13

Later, one of Genji's attendants reports to him that a boat has come from Akashi but has been turned away from landing by the crowds of Genji's people on the beach. Genji feels it is not accidental that the Akashi Lady herself has come and gone away on this very day he is in the same area. The gods of Sumiyoshi are acting in his life again. While doing the lustration at Naniwa, Genji jots down a poem that he sends to the Akashi Lady by his most trusted attendant.

mi wo tsuku shi	I give myself
kouru shirushi ni	as a token of my love
koko made mo	to this place
meguri ai keru	we go roundabout to meet
eni wa fukashi na	due to the depth of our bonds

14 - 14

Because they had met on a joint pilgrimage, the Akashi Lady sends her reply tied with sacred cords.

kazunarade	out of the question
naniwa no koto mo	the incident at Naniwa
kainaki ni	was useless and yet
nado mi wo tsukushi	why did I give up my body
omoisome ken	devoting myself to you then?

14-14. Naniwa (rapid waves) was named by Emperor Jimmu after his legendary odyssey through the Inland Sea of Japan. Its great marshes, full of reeds, were later celebrated in many tanka. The most famous ones are by the monks Saigyō (*Shin Kokinshū*, 625) and Nōin (*Goshūishū*, 43).

14 - 15

Reading the Akashi Lady's note makes Genji long to see her again. Touching the paper of her note causes him to want to caress her skin. At evening, the tide comes flooding in and the cranes call from the shallows in the reedy marshes. Genji longs to go to her no matter what the people might say about him.

tsuyukesa no	as if wet with dew
mukashi ni ni taru	as it was in years gone by
tabigoromo	my traveling clothes
tamino no shima no	a straw rain cape of that isle
na niwa kakure zu	whose name cannot hide me

14 - 16

When Lady of the Sixth Ward is dying, she asks Genji to look after her daughter, Lady Who Loves Autumn, who was the high priestess at Ise. Shortly after the funeral, on a miserable winter day of high winds and driving sleet, Genji wants to send a poem to Lady Who Loves Autumn. He chooses a paper of cloudy azure, taking care to add details that he hopes will appeal to a young girl.

furimidare	always from the sky
himanaki sora ni	unceasing snow and sleet
nakihito no	the deceased one
amagakeru ran	seems to be flying upward
yado zo kanashiki	from this sorrowful house

14 - 17

Lady Who Loves Autumn does not know how to reply to Genji's poem and wishes to avoid doing so, but her women tell her she must reply to such a respected personage. She picks a richly perfumed gray paper and writes with all the proper modulations of ink in a calm and reserved hand.

14-15. Reeds were used not only for roof thatching but also for making raincoats.

Tamino means "field of the rain cloak" and calls to mind the place where the reeds for raincoats are grown. Genji's poem makes a connection by containing the hidden word *naniwa* in the first three sound units of the last line.

kiegateni	unable to vanish
furu zo kanashiki	snow makes one even sadder
kakikurashi	as it grows darker
wagami sore tomo	that is similar to being one
omooenu yo ni	who is not favored in this world

14-17. Lady Who Loves Autumn proved earlier to have been very aware that Genji had been her mother's lover. Being now fifteen years old, she does not know exactly what her relationship to him should be. From her mother she surely knew that he was supposed to care for her, but his note did not make clear whether he saw her as his daughter or if he saw her as a substitute for her mother as his lover. After a talk with Murasaki, it was agreed that she come to the palace on Second Avenue to live with them.

YOMOGI U

THE WORMWOOD PATCH

Autumn of Genji's twenty-eighth year to Fourth Month of his twenty-ninth year

Mogusa is a type of *yemogi*, or wormwood (*Artemisia absinthium*). A cottonlike fiber taken from the leaves was used for *moxa* treatments. These consisted of a small, woolly ball being laid directly on the skin and set afire. It was believed the treatment increased circulation of the blood and therefore was a cure for everything from pains in the legs to stomachaches. The treatment was also used as punishment for children who misbehaved. The burning always leaves a wound and then a small, white scar on the skin.

Just as Genji is firmly established in the capital again, another rustic scene is introduced. The orphaned Princess Safflower (the one with the bright red nose) has continued to live in poverty waiting for Genji's return from exile. The mansion she inherited from her father is in complete disrepair; her women have left her because of the isolation and poverty. Even her own family has tried to get her to move in with them, but she wishes to remain faithful to her memories of Genji. Genji, busy with his resumed life, does not know about this until one evening, on his way to another amorous encounter, he chances to pass her house and decides to pay her a visit. Even though she is not a beauty and her poetry is less than the ordinary, he feels guilty for abandoning her. He resolves anew to care for her and thus renovates her mansion, hires new companions, so that once again her home is a house of joy; she moves into Genji's palace two years later.

15 - A

michi mo naki	when not even a path
yomogi wo wake te	can be cut through the wormwood
kimi zo ko shi	nothing surpasses
tare nimo masaru	the supreme feeling I had
mi no kokochi suru	when you came as my husband

15 - 1

Princess Safflower retains her faith in Genji's promises to her. While he is in exile, her mansion falls into greater disrepair. The people Genji hired to repair her roof never arrived. When Genji first returns to the capital, he is too busy to visit her or to attend to her needs. An aunt of the the princess tries to get her old attendant, Jijū, to leave the dilapidated house, which family members jokingly call "The Wormwood Patch," and to go with her to the island of Kyūshū. Determined as she is poor, she steadfastly refuses to leave her old home. But because it is so sad and dreary living there, the last of the princess's attendants—Jijū—decides to go with the aunt. Thus, her leaving brings even more sadness. When the party is ready to depart, the princess has nothing suitable for a farewell gift for the long years of service, so she gives Jijū her cut-off hair that had been saved in a beautiful box. With her gift, Princess Safflower encloses a poem.

tayu majiki	not to be cut off
suji wo tanomi shi	lineage depends on memories
tamakazura	hair like jeweled vines
omoi no hoka ni	I never dreamed that they
kakehanare nuru	must now go so far away

15-1. The word *tamakazura,* which will later be used in the tale for the name of another orphaned daughter, can be understood as "jeweled" *(tama)* "vine" *(kazura),* and the compound thus becomes an aesthetic expression for a jeweled garland or wreath of flowers, as would be worn in the hair for the Kamo festivals. (Waley calls it a "jeweled hairpin" and Seidensticker calls it a "jeweled caplet," but garland seems a closer term.)

15 - 2

Jijū, the daughter of one of Princess Safflower's attendants, was raised in the old house. Thus, leaving it and the princess is very hard for her. She makes this promise to the old princess in her poem:

tamakazura	your jeweled garland
tae temo yama ji	cut off but not broken
yuku michi no	a farewell gift
tamuke no kami mo	that goes with me forever
kakete chikawan	I swear by the gods of the road

15 - 3

One night, on his way to visit Lady Scattered Blossoms, Genji passes the desolate Hitachi mansion, home of Princess Safflower. At the moment of Genji's passing, she is dreaming of her father and suddenly rouses herself to take care of some water leaking through the roof. Just as she is reciting this verse to herself, Genji's retainer is searching for a sign of life about the place.

nakihito wo	tears of longing
kouru tamoto no	for one who has departed
hodonaki ni	not so long ago
aretaru noki no	have ruined my sleeves
shizuku sae sou	even the eaves drip

15 - 4

After hearing the retainer's dismal report, Genji feels he should stop to visit Princess Safflower, but he hesitates to simply barge in on her. Yet he does not want to take the time for a lengthy exchange of notes before being admitted. He knows how long it takes her to write just one poem of reply, and, with the rain falling heavily, he fears everyone in his party will be soaked while they wait for her to compose her thoughts. At the same time, to simply walk through the overgrown weeds will get them equally as wet. Sir Reflected Brilliance offers to make a path through the underbrush and shake off the droplets of water. Genji mumbles to himself as he gets out of the carriage:

tazune temo	even if looked for
ware koso towa me	suppose I should go asking
michi mo naku	deep in the wormwood
fukaki yomogi no	without a path there exists
moto no kokoro wo	the roots of a heart to be found

---

15 - 5

Seeing her again, Genji speaks warm, affectionate words and renews his promises to Princess Safflower. As he is leaving (he chooses not to spend the night with her), he notices a pine tree planted by someone else, so many years ago it seems to have been in a dream.

fujinami no	waving wisteria
uchisugi gataku	one cannot pass them by
mie tsuru wa	as they seemed to me
matsu koso yado no	at your house like the pine trees
shirushi nari kere	a token of eternal waiting

---

15 - 6

Princess Safflower's reply:

toshi wo he te	the time spent waiting
matsu shirushi naki	like the pine tree did not bring
waga yado wa	you to my dwelling
hana no tayori ni	wasn't it the chance to see flowers
sugi nu bakari ka	that would not let you pass by?

SEKI YA
THE GATEHOUSE

Late autumn to Eleventh Month of Genji's twenty-ninth year

Back in the capital, Genji continues to reinstate his relationships with his former mistresses. While returning from an excursion to the provinces, Genji meets Lady of the Cicada Shell at the barrier gate to the frontier. She is returning, with her husband, to the capital. As previously, Genji uses her brother, Little One, to try to gain access to her. She again successfully eludes Genji. When her old and ill husband dies, Genji thinks that perhaps there is now a chance for him, but she quietly becomes a nun before he can meet with her in secret.

16 - A

ōsaka wa	on the slope of meetings
seki no shimizu mo	the millrace gatehouse dam
koibito no	holds back clear waters
atsuki namida mo	as well as the tears of lovers
nagaruru tokoro	which also flow at this place

16-A. The place name Ōsaka comes from *au*, "to meet" and *saka*, "slope," which is often used in lover's poetry for "the slope where we meet."

Seki is "checkpoint, gatehouse" or "dam."

16 - 1

Lady of the Cicada Shell marries a man who becomes the vice-governor of Iyo Province. It happens that on the same day in the Ninth Month as she and her husband's retinue come to Ōsaka Barrier, Genji is there on a pilgrimage to Ishiyama for a thanksgiving ceremony. Memories come flooding back to both of them. The lady is overcome by all the feelings she has held back over the years.

yuku to ku to	coming or going
sekitome gataki	it is not easy to hold back
namida wo ya	the tears, is it?
tae nu shimizu to	people will think my tears are
hito wa miru ran	a clear spring that never dries

16 - 2

When Genji went into exile, the brother of Lady of the Cicada Shell, Little One, severed his connections with Genji in order to advance himself politically. But now that Genji is back in power, Little One realizes that had he stayed with Genji his star would have risen faster. Genji nonetheless treats him with just the same consideration when he gives him a letter for his sister, recalling their meeting at Ôsaka.

wakuraba ni	by chance
yukiau michi wo	we happen to meet on the way
tanomi shi mo	though it's promising
nao kainashi ya	it's fruitless to ask for
shio naranu umi	a seashell from the lake

16 - 3

Impressed by Genji's gallant behavior toward him, the younger brother urges Lady of the Cicada Shell to answer. The years of her marriage have made the woman more reticent, but she is unable to ignore such a remarkable message.

ōsaka no	on the meeting slope
seki ya ikanaru	in what way does the gate
seki nare ba	hold anything back?
shigeki nageki no	trees grown thick as grief
naka wo waku ran	would divide in the middle

16-1. The meaning of the poem hinges on the double meaning of the word for barrier, alluding to the barrier that regulates the movement of people from place to place and to that which dams waters—as well as floods of memories.

16-2. Kai nashi means "fruitless" or "without seashells."

17

EAWASE
A PICTURE CONTEST

Third Month of Genji's twenty-ninth year

Genji's goal of getting Lady Who Loves Autumn to be the wife of the new, young emperor is crossed by his friend, the First Secretary's Captain, who has aspirations that his own daughter receive this honor. The Emperor loves paintings and story illustrations, so it is decided that the two ladies will hold a contest with Prince Firefly as judge. As the competition heats up, there is lively talk on painting and stories written on scrolls, and both sides seem very evenly matched, even though the two women exhibit very different tastes. At the last minute, Genji decides to bring out the scrolls he had painted while in exile at Suma, and everyone is deeply touched by his work and the sad memories of those times. Seeing his pictures of that rustic place gives Genji the idea that perhaps he should build a retreat for himself outside of the capital.

17 - A

ai gataki	it must have been
itsuki no miko to	as a royal virgin priestess
omoi teki	difficult to wed
sarani haruka ni	in addition to having
nari yuku mono wo	to move very far away

17-A. The high priestesses of both Kamo and Ise shrines had to be royal daughters. Sometimes they were as young as one year or as old as twenty-eight, but normally they were in their mid-teens. They could only be excused from the position (1) if the emperor died or stepped down, (2) if the priestess became ill or disabled, (3) either of her parents died, or (4) upon the loss of her virginity. The change in status to high priestess was reflected partly in the way the speech taboos were imposed. All words associated with Buddhism were naturally forbidden. In addition, death was called "recovery"; illness, "taking a retreat"; blood, "sweat"; a tomb, "an earth heap"; and meat was called "vegetables."

17 - 1

Fulfilling his promise to the dying Lady of the Sixth Ward, Genji takes the place of a father when her daughter, Lady Who Loves Autumn, is presented at the court as a consort for the new emperor. As Genji is looking over her gifts, he sees that the Suzaku Emperor (Genji's brother, who is now retired) has sent her combs with a poem in his own handwriting.

wakareji ni	under the pretext
soe shi ogushi wo	of putting a comb in your hair
kagoto nite	a token of farewell
harukeki naka to	when you were sent away
kami ya isame shi	is that why the gods banished me?

17 - 2

The Suzaku Emperor still wonders why the gods caused the misfortunes in his land that he felt had caused him to cease his reign. He was very much attracted to Lady Who Loves Autumn when he met her as high priestess, but he had denied his feelings when he placed the comb in her hair as a sign of her office and sent her off to Ise. And now Lady Who Loves Autumn has returned from her position only to be given as wife to the new emperor. They have missed their chance to be together. Thus Lady Who Loves Autumn writes to the retired Suzaku Emperor:

wakaru tote	"Proceed henceforth!"
haruka ni ii shi	was what was said long ago
hitokoto mo	just one word given
kaerite mono wa	to the contrary would've mattered
ima zo kanashiki	now there is only sorrow

17-2. Notice again and again how rational, honest, and down-to-earth are the replies of women in Shikibu's writing. In spite of the patriarchal society, the women of those times display incredible strength and wisdom.

17 - 3

While looking among his works of art, Genji finds the journals and sketchbooks he compiled during his exile and shows them to Murasaki. She is cruelly reminded of the pain of those days and yet wonders why he did not share them with her before.

hitori ite
nagame shi yori wa
ama no sumu
kata wo kaki te zo
miru bekarikeru

to be alone
remembering times when one
lived like a fisherman
pictures drawn on tidal flats
is what I should have been

---

17 - 4

As he looks at his old paintings, Genji also feels as if he is back at Akashi again. Yet his first thought is that he should show them to the empress, Lady of the Wisteria Apartment. Only by showing his paintings at court can he be assured that she will look at them.

ukime mi shi
sono ori yori wa
kyō wa mata
sugi ni shi kata ni
kaeru namida ka

feeling bitterness
even more than it was then
again this day
spent out on the tidal flats
coming back with more tears

---

17 - 5

The illustrations for various literary works are put forth by the two groups of court ladies, of the Left and the Right. The spokesman for the Left speaks in praise of *The Tales of Ise* and adds his poem.

ise no umi no
fukaki kokoro wo
tadora zu te
furi ni shi ato to
nami ya ketsu beki

The Tales of Ise
without tracing the profound
heart of the sea
will the waves wash away
all the tracks of the past?

---

17 - 6

The spokesman for the Right, with more fire and enthusiasm, defends *The Tale of Jōsammi* (no longer extant).

kumo no ue ni
omoi nobore ru

if one aims
at the cloud-shrouded palace

17-3. *Kata* means "form" or "tidal flats."

kokoro niwa	and ascends
chihiro no soko mo	the thousand-fathomed sea
haruka ni zo miru	seems to be very shallow

---

17 - 7

Lady of the Wisteria Apartment elegantly joins the fray when she defends *The Tales of Ise* by Prince Narihira. Yet her choice of words makes one wonder whether she is secretly referring to Genji.

miru me koso	seeing sea pine grass
urabure nu rame	one usually feels miserable
toshi he ni shi	recalling the years
ise wo no ama no	the fame of fisherfolk
na wo ya shizume n	of Ise is with us still

---

17 - 8

The excitement over the picture contest rises to such a pitch that even the retired Suzaku Emperor becomes involved. He has brought from storage a picture recording Lady Who Loves Autumn's departure for Ise as high priestess. He has the painting set in a special box and sends it to her to enter in the contest for her side. His poem is laid next to the painting of the Grand Hall, where he had stood on that fateful day.

mi koso kaku	so much like myself
shime no hoka nare	outside the palace confines
sonokami no	in the days of old
kokoro no uchi wo	remembering the heart inside
wasure shimo se zu	when sending you to the gods

---

17 - 9

Lady Who Loves Autumn sends her graceful answer by attaching it to a sacred comb and wrapping it in blue paper. She rewards the messenger with elegant gifts.

17-7. In *The Tales of Ise*, section 69, the story is told of the falconer of the emperor who goes to Ise Shrine to arrange a hunt. Due to the urgings of her mother, the high priestess takes extra care to entertain the falconer in a special manner. That night, unable to sleep, the priestess slips away to his rooms, where she stays the night but leaves before dawn. Her poem to him of the next morning has the famous lines: "did you come to me / or did I go out to you? / now I cannot tell / if it was a dream or fact / was I awake or sleeping?"

shime no uchi wa	all is much changed
mukashi ni ara nu	within imperial confines
kokochi shi te	the feeling I had
kamiyo no koto mo	in the days serving the gods
ima zo koishiki	is now one for which I long

MATSU KAZE
WIND IN THE PINES

Autumn of Genji's thirty-first year

Instead of beginning to build his planned retreat, Genji proceeds to remodel his palace at Nijō (Second Avenue) to accommodate his various mistresses. Everyone seems to be delighted by the changes except the Akashi Lady, who continues to feel slighted by Genji and is still very timid about the differences in their stations in society. Because of her refusal to come to the capital to live in Genji's palace, Genji takes an old property of his father's in the hills at the edge of the city and remodels it for the Akashi Lady. There she lives with her mother, the old nun who had left her husband at Akashi. Here, next to many old pines, which is very romantic, Genji keeps the Akashi Lady close enough for his occasional visits.

Originally he had planned for more visits, but Murasaki begins to assert herself as his wife by making demands on Genji's time and attention. As an excuse to his wife to come to the area, he decides to build his retreat here so he can go easily to see the Akashi Lady in secret. Finally, with this plan, Genji also gets to spend time with his new little daughter (now about two years old). He finds her so charming he wishes to bring her to the city as he knows he cannot leave her living out in these hinterlands if she is to be accepted into the society of the court. While Genji is secretly visiting the Akashi Lady, the First Secretary's Captain, and even the Emperor, suddenly discover the charms of this remote region. They come holding parties and excursions, which causes Genji no end of trouble as he is trying to keep the existence of the Akashi Lady a secret from the court and his wife. This proves impossible, so that in the end Murasaki finds out everything and becomes angry with Genji over his propensity to have affairs.

Another delicate situation between the two is the fact that Murasaki has never had a child. This endangers her hold on Genji and his attachment to her. Thus, when Genji asks her to take over the raising of the baby from the Akashi Lady, he can make use of her maternal instincts and get his daughter raised in a home with a proper lady. She gladly accepts the role as stepmother as a way to strengthen the ties between herself and Genji.

---

18 - A

ajikinaki	how melancholy
matsu no kaze kana	seems the wind in the pines
nake ba naki	weeping and weeping
ogoto wo tore ba	it's similar to the voice
onaji ne wo hiku	of one playing a small harp

---

18 - 1

In autumn, always a sad time of the year, Genji decides he wants to bring the Akashi Lady and his little daughter to the capital. The Akashi Lady's father, the old monk, who is seeing his dream come true (that his progeny become head of the land), is nonetheless brokenhearted at their parting. He is ashamed that as a monk he is still so touched emotionally. He holds his sleeve over his eyes.

yukusaki wo	praying for the future
haruka ni inoru	the destination far away
wakareji ni	when it's time to part
tae nu wa oi no	I could never tolerate
namida narikeri	the tears of the old folks

18 - 2

The monk's old wife, who is accompanying the Akashi Lady, also weeps as she leaves her husband and the shores where she has spent so much of her life.

morotomo ni	we were together
miyako wa ide ki	when we left the capital
kono tabi ya	this time on the trip
hitori nonaka no	going alone into the fields
michi ni madowa n	straying far from the path

18 - 3

They beg the old monk to go along with them, to act as their escort, but he refuses to leave his place by the sea. The Akashi Lady asks him:

iki te mata	how can you say
aimi n koto wo	when we leave to live again
itsu tote ka	we will meet once more?
kagiri mo shira nu	how can we trust in a life
yo oba tanoma n	that's not ours to trust?

18 - 4

The party sets sail and the old wife is filled with regrets as the shores of Akashi disappear in the mists of autumn.

kano kishi ni	that spiritual shore
kokoro yori ni shi	which the heart once so admired
amabune no	the nun herself
somuki shi kata ni	rowing a small boat to that
kogi kaeru kana	place to which she must return

18 - 5

Rapidly under way with the seasonal winds, the Akashi Lady finds herself accompanied by sad thoughts.

18-3. Iki, "to go away" or "to live, be alive, exist."

Although her father had been a monk for many years, he did not obey the precept to give up his interest in the affairs of his family. If he had, if he had not brought Genji here, if he had not encouraged Genji to become her lover, she would not be in the sad position she was in now. Again, it is a woman who is so rational in her poems.

18-4. Kano kishi alludes to the world of spiritual enlightenment, the opposite of the world in which we live. *Amabune* refers to the boat of a fisherman or the nun's own self.

ikukaeri	back and forth
yukikau aki wo	how many times has autumn
sugoshi tsutsu	been coming and going
ukigi ni nori te	as if riding on driftwood
ware kaeru ran	I suppose I'll return too

---

18 - 6

Once settled in a former prince's villa at Oi, the Akashi Lady waits for Genji to visit her. As days go by without his appearance, she idly takes up playing the seven-stringed harp that Genji had given her as a parting gift in Akashi. As she plays, her mother, who is resting nearby, laments:

mi wo kae te	the change to oneself
hitori kaere ru	back living alone again
yamazato ni	in a mountain village
kiki shi ni ni taru	all one hears as in the past
matsu kaze zo fuku	the wind blowing in the pines

---

18 - 7

The Akashi Lady adds her complaint to that of her mother's.

furusato ni	in one's hometown
mi shi yo no tomo wo	memories are seen as friends
koiwabi te	with love and worry
saezuru koto wo	chitchat or playing the harp
tare ka waku ran	who hears and understands this?

---

18 - 8

Finally Genji contrives, by telling Murasaki he has business at Katsura, to go to Oi to see the Akashi Lady. There he finds the gardens in need of repairs; he orders his men to set to work. He directs their efforts by clearing out the garden brook. He asks the Akashi Lady's mother for advice on how the garden had been in Prince Nakatsukasa's time. At just that moment, the brook, cleared of leaves and litter, gushes forth—free and sparkling.

sumi nare shi	feeling at home
hito wa kaeri te	the one who has returned
tadore domo	gropes about even though
shimizu zo yado no	the clear waters of this home
arujigao naru	appear to be like the master

18 - 9

Genji, impressed with the old woman's gentility and courtly behavior, observes:

isarai wa	a garden's small brook
hayaku no koto mo	even in the days of old
wasure ji wo	one could not forget
moto no aruji ya	the origin of the household
omo gawari se ru	though the image has changed

18 - 10

In the evening, the Akashi Lady brings out the harp Genji had given her when he asked that the middle string not be changed. As he plays it, he is touched to see the harp tuned as it had been when he had vowed his troth with this gift.

chigiri shi ni	as it was promised
kawara nu koto no	the tuning of the harp string
shirabe nite	remains unchanged
tae nu kokoro no	in the same way may you know
hodo wa shiri ki ya	nothing has changed in my heart

18 - 11

The Akashi Lady's reply shows Genji that she is very competent with such exchanges, in spite of his view that she was of inferior social status.

kawara ji to	never to change
chigiri shi koto wo	the words of the promise have
tanomi nite	been my talisman

18-11. The Akashi Lady expresses herself making a play on the word *koto,* which can mean either "harp" or "words."

matsu no hibiki ni | added to the pine tree's sound
ne wo soe shi kana | is the memory of my sighs

18 - 12

Before returning home, Genji and his party go to Katsura, where they are joined by a group of revelers from the court. They bring a poem from the Emperor showing his envy of the party in the autumn countryside.

tsuki no sumu — clearly the moon dwells
kawa no ochi naru — in a distant place by a river
sato nare ba — in a village named
katsura no kage wa — Katsura with the image
nodokekaru ran — which I am sure is lovely

18 - 13

Genji's reply is a hint for the Emperor to join the party in Katsura.

hisakata no — heavenly radiance
hikari ni chikaki — of the light hereabouts
na nomi shite — is merely its fame
asayū kiri mo — even night and morning mists
hare nu yamazato — do not leave the mountain village

18 - 14

Thinking of the poems other poets have written about the moon, and even the one he wrote at Akashi, Genji speaks:

meguri ki te — we've returned
te ni toru bakari — now near enough to touch
sayakeki ya — the bright light
awaji no shima no — from far away Awaji
a wa to mi shi tsuki — look! over there! the moon

18-12. Katsura still exists as an imperial villa on the Katsura River. It is possible to visit this lovely park with advance arrangements with the Imperial Household. The site was chosen for the construction of the villa because of its natural beauty; the villa was built in 1658 for Prince Hachijo Toshihito, brother of Emperor Goyozei. The stipulation was that no expense should be spared, the building should take as long as it needed, and he prince and his retainers could not visit the place while the work was in progress.

In legends, the *katsura* tree (*Cercidiphyllum japonicum*) was reputed to grow on the moon. Some authorities identify it as the Judas tree or (properly enough) the love tree. The leaves were also used in the decorations for the Kamo festivals. The flowers were used as a spice in pickling.

18-13. Hisakata is a *makura kotoba*, or "pillow word," which is used as an epithet or poetical phrase. In this case, *hisakata* is used for describing celestial elements such as the moon, sun, clouds, rain, and so on.

18-14. See 13-4.

18 - 15

The reply to Genji's poem is given by one of his attendants.

ukigumo ni
shibashi magai shi
tsukikage no
sumihatsuru yo zo
nodokekaru beki

floating clouds
obscured for awhile
the moonlight
in the night the skies cleared
there shall be peace in these times

or

thus our noble Genji
owing to disagreeable affairs
had concealed himself
now settled in the capital
bright times shall be more calm

18 - 16

An attendant who had served Genji's father adds his poem.

kumo no ue no
sumika wo sute te
yoa no tsuki
izure no tani ni
kage kakushi ken

where in the clouds
has he gone to live
the midnight moon
in which hidden valley
was his image concealed?

18-15. Yo refers to "night" or "this world" or "these times."

18-16. The "midnight moon" refers to Genji's departed father, the Paulownia Court emperor.

USUGUMO
A RACK OF CLOUDS

Winter of Genji's thirty-first year to autumn of his thirty-second year

The Akashi Lady has never completely trusted Genji's actions or his motives, so when he comes with the news that he is taking her baby to the city to be raised by his wife, she is devastated by his decision. She and her mother are cut off from their family by living in this out-of-the-way place so far from their home at Akashi, and now they must give up the joy of having the child with them. The parting of mother and child causes a heartbreaking scene that overshadows Murasaki's delight in adopting the sweet little girl.

Genji makes plans to retire, but the death of the Minister of the Left (his first father-in-law) forces him to become an imperial adviser. The country is experiencing unusually devastating earthquakes and storms, which seem to be an indication of a foreboding evil. Then Lady of the Wisteria Apartment, who had often been ill, suddenly dies. The whole court goes into mourning, but Genji, who had loved her the most, must now hide the depth of his grief, which makes her passing even harder for him to bear.

A priest, who had been the confidant of the Empress, comes to the funeral services and takes the opportunity of telling the young Reizei Emperor that Genji is his real father. The Emperor is aghast that he is on the throne while his true father is not. He believes that the country's natural disasters are the result of his unwitting breach and decides to abdicate. But Genji quietly talks him out of the action—restoring the balance within the family. Genji again immerses himself in his domestic affairs.

19 - A

sakura chiru	cherry blossoms fall
haru no yūbe no	in an evening of spring
usugumo no	the thin cloud cover
namida to nari te	changes into being the tears
otsuru kokochi ni	which also fall in sadness

19 - 1

It is decided that Genji's daughter should leave her mother, the Akashi Lady, to come to the palace to be raised by Murasaki. This means that the nursemaid Genji sent to Akashi, who had become a companion to the Akashi Lady, will return to the capital with the child. On the day of her departure it is snowy and very cold. The Akashi Lady says to the nursemaid:

yuki fukaki	deep snows
miyama no michi wa	in the mountain pass
hare zu tomo	are not cleared
nao fumi kayoe	even so do send letters
ato tae zu shite	tracks without an ending

19 - 2

The nursemaid makes a promise to the child's mother.

yukima naki	were you to go
yoshino no yama wo	high on Yoshino Mountain
tazune temo	where snows never melt
kokoro no kayou	where all tracks are extinct
ato tae me ya wa	my heart would still come to you

19-1. *Fumi* means "letter" or "to step, tread upon."

19-2. Mount Yoshino was known for its drifts of snowy cherry blossoms in spring as well its deep snows in winter.

19-3

When it comes time for the nursemaid and the child to get into the carriage with Genji, the child tugs on her mother's robes, wanting her to climb in, also. The Akashi Lady's voice breaks before she finishes reciting her poem:

sue tōki	far in the future
futaba no matsu ni	this seedling pine princess
hiki wakare	from whom I part
itsuka kodakaki	when shall I be able to see
kage wo miru beki	her grown as a tall tree?

19-4

Genji is very touched by her tears and her feelings. The image comes to his mind of the two famous pines of Takekuma, whose intertwining roots and branches and long survivial had become legendary.

oi some shi	since starting to grow
ne mo fukakere ba	the root was deep and thick
takekuma no	twin pines of Takekuma
matsu ni komatsu no	for a thousand years may we
chiyo wo narabe n	be the pines beside her

19-5

After taking her only child from her, Genji worries about the Akashi Lady. Although he knows a visit to her at Oi will make Murasaki jealous, he wants to go anyhow. Just as he is preparing to leave, Murasaki overhears him humming the tune of an old folk song in which the lyrics portray a man taking a boat over to see his lover, and so she sends out her lady-in-waiting with a message for Genji.

fune tomuru	where will the boat dock
ochikatabito no	if there is no one over there?
naku ba koso	in that case I suppose
asu kaeri ko n	you will return tomorrow
sena to machi mi me	the husband for whom I wait

19-4. *Takekuma* is both the name of a place in Miyagi Prefecture and a poetic reference to pine trees, because a huge tree at that place was considered to be twin trees that had grown from one root.

19-5. The *saibara* (ribald folk song) known as "Cherry Blossom Girl" is first sung by a man's voice: "Stop that boat, cherry blossom girl. / I will row to the island. / I've a twenty-acre field, / And I'll be back tomorrow." Then the woman sings: "You say you'll be back tomorrow. / You've a woman over there. / You won't be back tomorrow. / No, you won't be back tomorrow."

19 - 6

Genji tries to reason with Murasaki.

yuki te mi te	let's see how it goes
asu mo sane ko n	how it will be tomorrow
nakanakani	how it will really be
ochikatabito wa	if the person over there
kokorooku tomo	is attached to me by heart

19 - 7

In late spring, Lady of the Wisteria Apartment, who was gravely ill, suddenly dies. Her funeral and the mourning engage the whole court. Not wanting to show the unseemly depth of his grief publicly, Genji goes to his newly made temple at Katsura, where he weeps the whole day. At evening, standing on the verandah, he looks out over the hills. The trees on the far ridge are in clear, bright light. Below, wisps of clouds shroud the darkened valley in a dull gray.

irihi sasu	the evening sun
mine ni tanabiku	shines over the mountain peaks
usugumo wa	thin clouds
mono omou sode ni	as if lost deep in thoughts
iro ya magae ru	the color of mourning clothes

19 - 8

While talking through a screen of slatted bamboo with Lady Who Loves Autumn, Genji becomes strangely excited and attracted to her. Her soft, hesitant answers make him wish to take her in his arms. As she feels his passion growing, she becomes more quiet and unresponsive. The room darkens during their silence. Genji is afraid she will use the gloom to slip away from him, so, in an effort to engage her in conversation, he asks her whether she prefers the season of spring or of autumn. She responds that she prefers autumn because it seems to link her to her mother, Lady of the Sixth Ward. She is quite dismayed when she hears Genji's poem implying that he loved her mother as deeply as she did.

kimi mo sawa	in that case you too
aware wo kawase	share the very same feelings
hito shire zu	no one else knows
waga mi ni shimuru	how deeply I am stung by
aki no yū kaze	evening winds of autumn

---

19 - 9

Genji prefers to have the Akashi Lady live closer to the palace, but she feels inferior to the society there and refuses to move. Thus, in order to see her, Genji has to journey to Oi, which is not always easy for someone in his position, and so his visits are rarer than both of them would wish. One night, the two are watching cormorant fishermen working in the light of the lanterns on their boats. Genji finds the scene strange but interesting, whereas the Akashi Lady sees it in a different light.

isari se shi	when they were fishing
kage wasura re nu	one couldn't forget the images
kagaribi wa	made by the torches
mi no uki fune ya	was bitterness in the boat
shitai ki ni ken	when following me here?

---

19 - 10

Genji's answer to the Akashi Lady turns her gentle complaint against her.

asakara nu	they are not shallow
shita no omoi wo	the deepest feelings of the heart
shira ne baya	why can't you see it?
nao kagaribi no	the way the torches flicker
kage wa sawage ru	is nothing to worry about

19-9. *Uki* means "to float" or "bitter."

ASAGAO
MORNING GLORY

Ninth Month of Genji's thirty-second year to a snowy day that winter

Although Genji is in deep mourning for Lady of the Wisteria Apartment, and he is fascinated with Murasaki's raising the new baby, yet he cannot resist having another affair. For years he has pursued his own cousin, Princess Morning Glory, without success. When he hears that her father has died and that she must now retire from her position as high priestess at Kamo Shrine, Genji decides to visit her. He makes an excuse to Murasaki that he is seeing his maternal aunt and takes off with high hopes of a quick conquest. However, Princess Morning Glory, though thoroughly capable of exchanging excellent poems with him on religious themes, resists his advances. Even when Genji sends her a faded, withered blossom with a poem that suggests that this is what she will become without him, she is not moved. The princess continues to be resolute, which only fans the flames of Genji's passion. Rumors begin circulating of their having an affair, and this makes the situation very uncomfortable for Genji because the truth is, he is the rejected lover. Murasaki hears the gossip and is heartbroken, not knowing the complete truth.

In this predicament, Genji meets up with the old Woman of the Bedchamber, who again pursues him avidly, but her bold manner repulses him so that he leaves her rooms early. He goes back home to Murasaki, and between them they discuss his various affairs in a companionable way that quiets her fears that Genji might abandon her. Yet, when he goes to sleep, after thinking of Lady of the Wisteria Apartment, Genji dreams she leans over him scolding him for his part in bringing so much shame into her life with his amorous actions.

20 - A

mizukara wa
aru ka naki ka no
asagao to
iinasu hito no
wasura re nu kana

what would it be like
to be one who called herself
a morning glory?
one who would dare to say that
could never be forgotten

20 - 1

The high priestess of Kamo, Princess Morning Glory, has been relieved of her position and is now living at Momozono Palace. Using the excuse of visiting other members of the family, Genji manages to get into her living quarters. She claims to be not yet settled in enough to begin a relationship with him. Genji makes this complaint to her.

hito shire zu
kami no yurushi wo
machi shi ma ni
kokora tsurenaki
yo wo sugosu kana

secretly
waiting for permission for you
to leave the gods
I've spent so much time
in this heartless world

20 - 2

Firmly determined not to get involved romantically with Genji, Princess Morning Glory replies:

nabete yo no
aware bakari wo
tou karani
chikai shi koto wo
kami ya isame n

the gods warn me
that I've broken my vows
even if visiting
this world of emotions
with the slightest contact

20 - 3

Feeling deeply rejected, Genji returns home to spend the night. The next morning while looking over his garden, he sees a morning glory vine bearing two faded, frostbitten blooms. He breaks them off to send with his poem to Princess Morning Glory.

mi shi ori no	recalling that time
tsuyu wasura re nu	I cannot forget the dew on
asagao no	the morning glory
hana no sakari wa	the flower at its very best
sugi ya shi nu ran	has it now passed away?

20 - 4

It is only at the urging of her ladies-in-waiting that Princess Morning Glory responds to Genji's poem.

aki hate te	the end of autumn
kiri no magaki ni	fog by the bamboo fences
musuboore	becomes entangled
aru ka naki ka ni	like a question not yet asked
utsuru asagao	the morning glory fades

20 - 5

Even though Princess Morning Glory's reply is not very interesting or encouraging, Genji is unable to put it down. He doesn't know if it is the handwriting or the soft gray-green paper, or the elegance of both, that compels him. Thus he continues to visit Momozono Palace, presumably to see the very old Fifth Princess. The unused gate through which he enters seems to have aged also.

itsu no ma ni	in which of the ages
yomogi ga moto to	have the stalks of the wormwood
musuboore	become entangled
yuki furu sato to	now snow falls on the village
are shi kakine zo	as the hedges yield to ruin

20 - 6

During his conversation with the old Fifth Princess, she nods off and falls asleep. Gleefully Genji begins to creep away, eager now to seek out Princess Morning Glory. Suddenly, from the darkness, he is stopped by another voice, one from his past. Woman of the Bedchamber, the old granny who had been his father's consort, speaks from out of the gloom.

toshi fure do	though the years go by
kono chigiri koso	my longtime bonds to this child
wasura re ne	cannot be forgotten
oya no oya to ka	how you asked to call me
ii shi hito koto	your own father's mother

20 - 7

Genji, in his irritation, puts her off, suggesting they can talk another time.

mi wo kae te	in the next world
ato mo machimiyo	we'll have to wait and see
kono yo nite	in this world
oya wo wasururu	to forget one's parents
tameshi ari ya to	is not possible is it?

20 - 8

As Genji continues on his way to Princess Morning Glory's chambers, he sees the snow in the garden dazzling under the moon's bright light, but the wind blows and it is very cold. The princess, Genji finds, turns out to be as cold as the night. In his frustration, he says to her:

tsurenasa wo	years of coldness
mukashi ni kori nu	have not taught lessons
kokoro koso	to this heart
hito no tsurasa ni	to the one who is bitter
soe te tsurakere	only bitterness is added

20 - 9

The women around Princess Morning Glory chorus their belief that Genji is suffering mistreatment. Still resolute not to admit him, however, she fires back her answer.

aratame te	not to mention
nanikawa mie n	why I shouldn't meet you
hito no ue ni	I've heard of
kakari to kiki shi	the other women's sadness
kokorogawari wo	who have been betrayed

20 - 10

Back in his own palace, Genji spends the wintry night talking to Murasaki. As the moon rises higher, the scene brightens and the world becomes snow quiet.

kōri toji	ice freezes over
iwa ma no mizu wa	the water between the rocks
yuki nayami	slowing the flow
sora sumu tsuki no	yet the brightness of the moon
kage zo nagaruru	drifts in a stream of light

20 - 11

As Murasaki moves forward to look at the garden, Genji sees her profile and is reminded again of Lady of the Wisteria Apartment, her aunt, and is filled with feelings of urgent passion. Just then a water bird calls out.

kakitsume te	thus are piling up
mukashi koishiki	the memories of long ago
yuki mo yo ni	on a snowy night
aware wo souru	feelings increase as a bird
oshi no ukine ka	sleeps floating on the water

20 - 12

That night Genji dreams that the Empress, Lady of the Wisteria Apartment, comes accusing him of letting out the secret that he is the father of her child, the present emperor. When the image of the furious empress attacks him, Genji panics and wakes with his heart pounding and sweat pouring off of him. In his fear, he wakes Murasaki to comfort him. She wonders what has frightened him so much. Genji, too, is worried about the images in his dream, but he does not admit this to Murasaki or tell her what he has seen in the dream.

toke te ne nu	awake since midnight
nezame sabishiki	unable to sleep and lonely
fuyu no yo ni	on a winter's night
musuboore tsuru	I was attacked only by
yume no mijikasa	the brevity of a dream

---

20 - 13

Genji fears that Lady of the Wisteria Apartment is in hell, where she is being tormented by her sinful affair with him. He wants to commission extra services for her but is afraid to attract attention to their relationship and perhaps embarrass the Emperor. He gives himself over to invoking the holy name for Buddha again and again. All he wishes for was that they might share the same lotus in the next world.

nakihito wo	longing for one
shitau kokoro ni	who has passed away
makase temo	if unable
kage mi nu mizu no	to see her watery image
se niya madowan	lost in the River of Death?

20-13. According to the Japanese belief system, the deceased must cross a river, called *sanzu no kawa*—reminiscent of the Styx in Greek mythology—to reach the Land of the Dead.

21

OTOME
THE MAIDEN

Fourth Month of Genji's thirty-third year to Tenth Month of his thirty-fifth year

Lord Evening Mist, Genji's son with Lady Heartvine, is now twelve years old and ready to enter adult life and the court. Much to his chagrin, his father refuses to confer a high rank on him, and instead has him enter into more studies of the Chinese classics, that is—remain a lowly student. Since the death of his mother shortly after his birth, Lord Evening Mist has been raised by his grandmother, the Great Princess, in the same house where the First Secretary's Captain's daughters have grown up. The Great Princess's favorite, Lady Wild Goose in the Clouds, is also the dearest childhood friend of Lord Evening Mist. When another of the First Secretary's Captain's daughters, who has been competing with Lady Who Loves Autumn to be the wife of the emperor, loses, the First Secretary's Captain angrily decides that he wants to save Lady Wild Goose in the Clouds for an auspicious marriage connection. He does not want Lord Evening Mist to behave toward his unwed daughter in the manner that he and Genji did when they were young. Thus he suddenly denies Lord Evening Mist access to her rooms and requests that Lord Evening Mist go live with Genji. However, Lord Evening Mist is very different from his father, in that he is a serious, steadfast lad. And he loves Lady Wild Goose in the Clouds. The young, motherless boy misses his association with these two most important females in his life and shows his distress with poems and tears.

In the meantime, Genji is occupied with the selection of a Gosechi dancer for a festival at court. Again Genji and the First Secretary's Captain are in competition, and again Genji wins when it is his own retainer's daughter who is chosen. While she is being prepared for her role, she moves into Genji's quarters, and Lord Evening Mist, following an illicit peek at her, falls in love again. Yet, his deepest desire is to take his place at court, and he grumbles to everyone of his lack of success.

Genji now acquires the old Sixth Ward mansion and is at last able to gather around him all of the ladies for whom he provides. There is still a competitive spirit between Lady Who Loves Autumn and Murasaki, which manifests itself in the way in which they compete with their gardens. Murasaki prefers spring, so she has her garden planted with the flowers that are their best early in the year. Lady Who Loves Autumn tries just as hard to create the feeling of fall on a deserted moor as representative of her personality. The ladies exchange gentle gibes, poems, and gifts as they try to outshine one another.

21-A. Yosano's poem skillfully condenses this chapter by beginning with a reference to Lady Wild Goose in the Clouds and ending with a lovesick boy—Lord Evening Mist. She makes her poem seem an instant in reality as she crystalizes the chapter into five lines.

21-1. Genji's poem turns on the idea that the water has returned to the river shoals as well the persons performing lustration, or purification rites, prior to participating in religious services. These rites range from only washing the hands or rinsing out the mouth to bathing the whole body and changing clothes. The removal of mourning clothes, with their gray, dirty colors, relates to washing away the grime of the world and its sad hold on a person.

---

21 - A

kari naku ya	the cry of wild geese
tsura wo hanare te	leaving together in a row
tada hitotsu	only one seems to
hatsukoi wo suru	have fallen in love for
shōnen no goto	the first time like a young boy

---

21 - 1

Winter gives way to spring, and at the time of the Kamo Festival, the mourning for Lady of the Wisteria Apartment ends. On the morning of the lustration rites, Genji remembers Princess Morning Glory by sending her a spray of wisteria with this poem, written on lavender paper that was carefully folded.

kake ki ya na	did you expect
kawase no nami mo	the return of the waves

tachikaeri	at the river shoals
kimi ga misogi no	for purification rites
fuji no yatsure wo	would remove mourning clothes?

---

21 - 2

Princess Morning Glory's simple reply to Genji :

fujigoromo	how quick to change
ki shi wa kinou to	the sad garments of grief
omou ma ni	yesterday—today
kyō wa misogi no	the shallow waters
se ni kawaru yo wo	of purification rites

---

21 - 3

Genji's son, Lord Evening Mist, is old enough to begin to have romantic thoughts about his cousin, Lady Wild Goose in the Clouds. Her father, the First Secretary's Captain, is not happy with this situation and tries to get his mother, the Great Princess, to thwart Lord Evening Mist's ambitions. As a result, Lord Evening Mist finds the doors to Lady Wild Goose in the Cloud's quarters locked against him. All he can do is stand outside and recite his poem in a loud voice.

sayonaka ni	now at midnight
tomo yobi wataru	calls from a migrating friend
karigane ni	cries of a wild goose
utate fukisou	are added to the violence
ogi no uwakaze	of wind blowing over the reeds

---

21 - 4

The father of Lady Wild Goose in the Clouds, the First Secretary's Captain, is determined that Lord Evening Mist, who is too young and of too low a rank for a relationship with his daughter, shall not succeed. Thus he demands that she leave her grandmother's place to stay with his family where he can watch over her more closely. The grandmother, who feels kindly

21-2. *Fuji* refers to "purple" or "wisteria" and is also the abbreviated form for *fujigoromo,* "mourning garments." The phrase also echoes the name of Lady of the Wisteria Apartment (Fujitsubo).

Princess Morning Glory is not portrayed as a brilliant writer, so Murasaki Shikibu intentionally makes her poem closely echo Genji's. It is as if she is following him stroke by stroke, image by image. Her only addition is to show her almost depressive opinion that everything, in the end, gets washed away—even grief.

21-3. Although Lord Evening Mist shows some education in his poetry—he is skillful enough to call himself a friend and mention "wild goose" so Lady Wild Goose in the Clouds knows to whom the poem is directed—one can feel the fervor of youth (at the time Lord Evening Mist is twelve years old). It is hard to read the poem without howling.

toward her two grandchildren, arranges one last meeting for the pair. When one of the attendants of Lady Wild Goose in the Clouds finds them together, she creates a scene and insults Lord Evening Mist by saying his sleeves are green. Lord Evening Mist's hotheaded response is:

kurenai no	dyed the deepest crimson
namida ni fukaki	from the depth of many tears
sode no iro wo	the color of sleeves
asamidori toya	how can one call them light green?
ii shioru beki	gossip like that should be punished

21 - 5

Lady Wild Goose in the Clouds tries to console Lord Evening Mist with her poem.

iroiro ni	dyed various hues
mi no uki hodo no	the bitterness of one's rank
shiraruru wa	is easily known
ikani some keru	in what way have our clothes
naka no koromo zo	been dyed by our relationship?

21 - 6

The attendants take Lady Wild Goose in the Clouds away and Lord Evening Mist cries all night. While it is still dark enough to hide his tear-reddened face, Lord Evening Mist goes back to Genji's palace on Second Avenue. On this night, under cloudy skies, there is a heavy frost.

shimo kōri	frost becomes harder
utate musube ru	in the darkness before dawn
akegure no	it has turned to ice
sora kakikurashi	darkening these very heavens
furu namida kana	with the mass of falling tears

21-4. Again, the poem from Lord Evening Mist betrays its youthful author. The use of a cliché like tears of blood could only come from one new to writing and be the result of reading old romance stories. His call for punishment for the woman who made the demeaning remark is out of a child's repertoire of how wrongs are handled—by punishment. The reason the woman's comment hurt him so deeply is because he had been forced by his father to continue his studies instead of assuming a position at court. The varying degrees of rank at court were indicated by the colors the person was permitted to wear. Evidently she has lowered him even lower than he was.

21-5. Lady Wild Goose in the Cloud's verse makes clear she understands his anger and, like a good peacemaker, tries to remind Lord Evening Mist that their relationship is much more important to her. Knowing that dampened fabric has a brighter hue, one wonders to what she is referring. We can only speculate.

21-6. By morning Lord Evening Mist is dampened and his emotions are hardened by tears. He draws a parallel with the weather and the hardness of frost. In his unhappiness, he sees the frost coming from gloomy skies filled with tears. The poem shows he has moved from referring to himself to seeing the whole world as having his emotional state.

21-7. Lord Evening Mist's poems continue to show they are written by a very young man. His calling the dancer "a messenger of the Sun Goddess" (perhaps a bit pompous?) and declaring that his heart is on her sleeve (this image is also in the poem) are securely in the repertory of a young man.

Shime means "sign, marker" or "occupancy."

---

21 - 7

Genji is responsible for furnishing the costumes and accoutrements for one of the Gosechi dancers for the harvest festival in the Eleventh Month. The dancer is the daughter of his favorite retainer, Sir Reflected Brilliance. After the festival, she is to be presented at court. When she moves into the residence at Second Avenue with her retinue, it causes much excitement. In the disorder, Lord Evening Mist is able to sneak a peek at the her. Instantly he becomes enamored of this little beauty. He becomes so bold, he actually tugs at her sleeve protruding from under a screen and later sends her a poem.

ama ni masu	oh messenger
toyookahime no	of the Goddess of the Sun
miyabito mo	who is in heaven
waga kokorozasu	do not forget the sign that
shime wo wasuru na	a heart is pinned on your sleeve

---

21 - 8

All the activities surrounding the Gosechi dances remind Genji of the Gosechi Dancer who, in passing him during his exile on Suma, sent him a note after hearing from across the water the notes of his harp. In remembrance, he sends to her gifts and a poem.

otomego mo	another young girl
kamisabi nu rashi	in sleeves of the angel-wing robe
amatsu sode	who looked so solemn
furuki yo no tomo	to a friend from times long gone
yowai he nure ba	growing older and more holy

---

21 - 9

The Gosechi Dancer is touched that Genji should have remembered her in conjunction with the present celebrations, so she replies with a poem written on a blue paper that matches the dancer's dress.

kake te iwa ba	now as then it seems
kyō no koto to zo	the dances are the reason
omooyuru	for one's thinking of
hikage no shimo no	the garland vines of sunlight
sode ni toke shi mo	melting the frost on our sleeves

21 - 10

Lord Evening Mist maintains his interest in the Gosechi Dancer, whom he has seen so briefly. He hears she has been appointed to the Empress's staff. This removes her even farther from his approach, but still he persists in his attempted affair by sending a poem to her with her brother. It is written on a delicate blue, folded in papers of several colors.

hikage nimo	did you not see when
shirukari keme ya	wearing the garland of vines
otomego ga	as a young maiden
ama no hasode ni	in the angel's feather robe
kake shi kokoro wa	a heart was pinned to your sleeve?

21 - 11

In the Second Month, the Emperor, Genji's secret son, makes a visit to the Suzaku Palace, home of the retired emperor, who is Genji's half brother and the one who had sent him into exile for several years. Each of these powerful men carries strong emotional ties to Genji, who is also in attendance at the palace. As part of the festivities, held under blooming cherry trees, the dance of the "Spring Warbler" is performed. Genji is reminded of seeing the springtime dance under other circumstances—when his father was alive. He offers a cup of wine to the Suzaku Emperor with the verse:

uguisu no	the nightingale's
saezuru haru wa	singing in the spring remains
mukashi nite	as it was long ago
mutsure shi hana no	our esteem in the cherry's light
kage zo kaware ru	is completely different

21-9. *Hikage:* "sunlight, "vines of sunlight." Spangled cords designed to catch and reflect the sunlight to increase the feeling of warmth and brightness hung from both sides of the dancer's headdress.

21-11. The *uguisu* is another bird of Japan for which we have no precise English equivalent. Sometimes *uguisu* is translated as "bush warbler," but because its call is so esteemed, it is often rendered "nightingale," whose hauntingly beautiful call and association with royalty capture better the image of *uguisu* than "bush warbler." The *uguisu* is always associated with spring.

21 - 12

The Suzaku Emperor replies:

kokonoe wo
kasumi hedatsuru
sumika nimo
haru to tsuge kuru
uguisu no koe

separated by mists
from the Imperial Palace
even at my place
the song of the nightingale
comes to tell me it is spring

21 - 13

Prince Firefly, filling the Emperor's cup, adds his poem:

inishie wo
fuki tsutae taru
fuetake ni
saezuru tori no
ne sae kawara nu

many years ago
the art was given to us
of the bamboo flute
the singing of a bird
also stays unchanged

21 - 14

The Reizei Emperor replies with awesome diplomacy.

uguisu no
mukashi wo koi te
saezuru wa
kozutau hana no
iro ya ase taru

the nightingale's
song of lament
as it flies
from tree to tree is it
because of fading colors?

21 - 15

In the Ninth Month, Lady Who Loves Autumn's moorlike garden is at its very best, resplendent with autumn colors. On an evening of calm winds, she arranges some flowers and leaves on the lid of an ornamental box and sends them, with a verse, to Murasaki, whose garden has been tidied up and covered over with straw mats for winter.

21-12. The emperor's name, Suzaku, or "Red Sparrow," is a clue to this poem.

21-13. It was considered most admirable when the song "Spring Nightingale" was played on a bamboo flute just at sunset.

21-14. Kozutau hana, "fly from flowering tree to tree," refers to the Reizei Emperor's reign. *Iro ya ase taru,* "are the colors fading?" refers to the question of a decline of the present rule. By humbling himself, the Reizei Emperor tries to console the retired Suzaku Emperor.

kokoro kara	following your heart
haru matsu sono wa	your garden waits for spring
waga yado no	at my place
momiji wo kaze no	the winds of autumn colors
tsute ni dani miyo	ask you to please come and look

21 - 16

In the spirit of the competition between these two women and their gardens, Murasaki quickly replies and, with her poem, sends Lady Who Loves Autumn an arrangement depicting the scene of a small pine tree set on moss before clifflike rocks. Lady Who Loves Autumn's serving women are impressed with Murasaki's ingenious response.

kaze ni chiru	before the wind can
momiji wa karoshi	easily scatter autumn leaves
haru no iro wo	the colors of spring
iwane no matsu ni	ask to be compared to
kake te koso mi me	a pine standing among rocks

21-16. Shikibu again, like an experienced serial writer, introduces at the end of the chapter another subject in another mood to pique the reader's interest into unrolling the next scroll.

TAMAKAZURA

THE JEWELED GARLAND

End of Genji's thirty-fourth year

Through all these years Handmaiden, the gentlewoman of Lady Evening Faces, has been supported by Genji in gratitude for her help when her lady had unexpectedly died in his presence. At the time, the other women attendants of Lady Evening Faces, who had not been taken along during the abduction and who had stayed with Lady Evening Faces's small child, never knew what had happened to Handmaiden and her Lady Evening Faces.

When Lady Evening Faces did not return and the father of the child offered them no support, the women were scattered, seeking other positions. The nursemaid, who had been left with the care of the child, later marries. Her husband is given a position in a remote area, and, not knowing what to do with the small child, the simple nurse takes her along and raises her together with her own daughters. When the child, Jeweled Garland, reaches marriageable age, the nurse is frightened when a tough local youth begins courting her. Certain of his success, his attitude becomes even more menacing as he obtains, he thinks, aid from the gods.

Desperate, the nurse, her own daughter, and Lady Jeweled Garland board a boat in the dark to sail away to safety in Kyoto. The young yokel is so determined, he sails after them and keeps the women in a state of panic. When the three women arrive in

Kyoto, they realize they have nowhere to go and no one to help them. Consequently, they head for the famous shrine at Hatsuse to pray for help and guidance.

There, by accident, Handmaiden encounters them and recognizes the nursemaid. Handmaiden leads them to Genji, and he takes Lady Jeweled Garland into his home as if she were a long-lost daughter and places her, as he had Lord Evening Mist, under the care and tutelage of Lady Scattered Blossoms.

For Lady Jeweled Garland, an orphan raised in the provinces, life at Genji's palace is very different. Raised without knowing her mother or father, the young girl feels she has no one she can turn to for advice. She realizes how fortunate she is to have landed in Genji's care and how dependent she is on his good will. Yet she is very confused by his attitude toward her. He often makes salacious remarks to her, in conversation and in his poetry. And he certainly seems to be attracted to her good looks and young body. Because most people suppose she is Genji's child, he has complete access to her and her rooms. The girl wavers between accepting his advances out of gratitude and attempting to protect her virginity.

22 - A

hi no kuni ni	since having been born
oiide tare ba	in the land of volcanic fires
iu koto no	everything one does
mina hazukashiku	or says is so shameful
ho no soma ru kana	cheeks are naturally tinted

22 - 1

Many years ago, Genji had kidnapped Lady Evening Faces. The night after her abduction and sexual assault, she died in his presence. Afraid of the gossip this unusual situation could generate for someone in his political position, and aware he has been made ritually unclean, Genji had his retainer take her body to a remote temple, where it was buried secretly. Her baby daughter was left in the care of a nursemaid, who did not know where the mother had been taken or what had happened to her. Out of her sense of duty, the nursemaid continued to care for

22-A. *Hi*, "fire," *no*, "of," *kuni*, "country" or "hometown"; together, as *hi no kuni*, forms another name for Higo Province, whose volcanic mountain, Aso, is still active today.

Yosano's tanka works with the idea that people living far from the capital have ruddy complexions, not because of exposure to sun and air, but from blushing for their blunders and countrified ways. She adds to the hyperbole by including the fact that it is the heat of the volcanoes that causes the rosy cheeks of one from a country of smoking mountains. Unusual explanations of nature, as here, are one of the treasured techniques of Japanese poetry, as they work as linkage: something is because something else is. When the device provokes the reader think, "Can that be so? Oh, surely not," the poet has engaged the reader into the poem beyond mere reading.

the child of her lady. When the young child is about four years old, the nursemaid decides to take her along with her own daughters as they journey to the province of Kyūshū, where her husband has been appointed deputy viceroy. As they voyage on the sea to Kyūshū, the nursemaid ponders:

funabito mo	even the sailors
tare wo kouru ya	are longing for someone?
ōshima no	at Ōshima
uraganashiku mo	those on the beach also
koe no kikoyuru	are hearing their sad voices

22 - 2

When the abandoned child asks if they are going to her mother, the daughters of the nursemaid look at one another and weep. Finally getting her tears under control, one of the daughters recites:

ko shi kata mo	totally at sea
yukue mo shira nu	not knowing from whence we come
oki ni ide te	or where we are going
aware izuko ni	alas, wherever can she be
kimi wo kou ran	the lady for whom we long?

22 - 3

It so happens, then, Lady Jeweled Garland, the daughter of Lady Evening Faces and the secret child of the First Secretary's Captain, is raised in Kyūshū. When she is about twenty years old, a rough young local fellow begins to court her. The nursemaid tries to discourage him, saying the girl is not right in her head, but he persists in trying to gain admittance to her quarters. He insists on being able to at least leave a verse for Lady Jeweled Garland.

kimi ni moshi	if my heart changes
kokoro tagawa ba	he can do with me as he wants
matsura naru	God of the Mirror

22-1. *Ōshima,* literally "big island," was in Tsukushi Province, present Fukuoka Prefecture in Kyūshū.

22-3. Not only is the nursemaid frightened by the strong figure of the unwanted lover, but that he would have the audacity to include the very gods into his plans with a sacred vow makes her feel that, with the gods behind him, he will be more than she can withstand. The young man's vow, vows being considered binding, shows that he is not a trifler, but a serious suitor. Still, the nursemaid feels he is the wrong match for Lady Jeweled Garland.

kagami no kami wo	at Matsura where I have
kake te chikawa n	taken a vow to be true

22 - 4

The nursemaid is truly frightened by the close presence of this tall, powerful young man, so she hastily composes an answer for the girl.

toshi wo he te	having spent many years
inoru kokoro no	praying our hearts out
tagai naba	if he should fail us
kagami no kami wo	the Mirror God of Matsura
tsurashi toya mi n	will seem to be heartless

22 - 5

The nursemaid's family is also in jeopardy because the unwanted suitor is of the warrior class and not, therefore, someone they could afford to insult. He could potentially cause a great deal of trouble for her husband and their families. Backed into a corner, she decides to send Lady Jeweled Garland back to the capital rather than let this uncouth lover have her. During the night, the younger of the nursemaid's daughters leaves her husband and family to board the ship with her mother and Lady Jeweled Garland. As their vessel leaves Ukishima, they leave their dear ones in the care of the gods of Matsura:

ukishima wo	from a floating isle
kogi hanare temo	we row away in gloom
yukukata ya	not knowing
izuku tomari to	where our destination
shira zu mo aru kana	harbor can be found

22 - 6

Lady Jeweled Garland looks as sad and forlorn as her poem:

22-4. Matsura is the present Karatsu City, Saga Prefecture.

The nursemaid tries to scare him off by implying that the lady and her attendants have also petitioned the same god. The poem is not as polished as the nursemaid's usual work—showing the extreme stress she is feeling. So she uses the exaggeration "pray our hearts out," instead of finding a more subtle expression, hoping to make a strong impression on the suitor.

22-5. This poem and the next two all make use of the name of one of the islands. *Ukishima*: *shima* refers to "island" and *uki* to "gloomy" or "floating." Both aspects of the name are explored in the following poems. Ukishima lies across the water from Ôshima.

yukusaki mo	so like the future
mie nu namiji ni	we cannot see the sea lanes
funade shi te	our sailing outward
kaze ni makasuru	abandons us to the wind
mi koso uki tare	where we go drifting about

---

22 - 7

When a boat seems to be following them, they are unsure if it is a pirate or the unsuitable ruffian. They agree they would rather be accosted by a pirate than the jilted lover. As they pass Hibiki (Echo Bay) in Harima, Lady Jeweled Garland says:

uki koto ni	with the gloomy thoughts
mune nomi sawagu	that assail my troubled heart
hibiki niwa	merely an echo
hibiki no nada mo	are the dangers of Echo Bay
na nomi nari keri	which seem only a rumor

---

22 - 8

Finally on shore, Lady Jeweled Garland and her party make a pilgrimage to the shrine at Hatsuse on the Furukawa (Old River). While there, Handmaiden, the attendant who had been with Lady Jeweled Garland's mother the night she died, recognizes the young girl's nursemaid. Finally, after an exchange of stories, Lady Jeweled Garland learns of the circumstances of her mother's disappearance, and Handmaiden is very happy to find the long-lost child of her lady. As they look down on the streams of pilgrims by the river, Handmaiden says:

futamoto no	two cedar trees twine
sugi no tachido wo	in this place by the old river
tazune zu ba	if I had never
furukawa no be ni	come to see them I suppose
kimi wo mi mashi ya	I would have never found you

22-6. *Uki:* "to drift or float"; "gloomy, bitter, hard."

22 - 9

Lady Jeweled Garland replies, her weeping making her even more beautiful.

hatsusegawa	of the old river
hayaku no koto wa	and the troubles long ago
shira ne domo	I know so little
kyō no ōse ni	yet today with our meeting
mi sae nagare nu	I'm overflowing with tears

22 - 10

As soon as Handmaiden tells Genji of Lady Jeweled Garland's existence, he wants to have her brought to his new palace in the Sixth Ward, without informing her rightful father, the First Secretary's Captain. Genji has assembled many robes for gifts to go with his note and poem. Yet, he is a little worried, wondering what kind of person he is inviting into his home.

shira zu tomo	without seeing
tazune te shira n	you will surely know
mishimae ni	at Three Island Bay
ouru mikuri no	where the marsh rushes grow
suji wa tae ji na	are the ties which are never cut

22 - 11

Lady Jeweled Garland does not understand why she cannot go to her father, why she is to go live with a stranger. But Handmaiden sets about convincing her that to go to Genji is the best thing for her to do. The girl is timid and very aware of her countrified upbringing, but Handmaiden urges her to send a response. Lady Jeweled Garland finally replies to Genji on a richly perfumed Chinese paper in a faint, delicate handwriting.

kazunaranu	since insignificant
mikuri ya nanino	what does the reed with
suji nare ba	strings and lines
uki ni shimo kaku	have to do with the sad way one
ne wo todome ken	has taken root in a muddy marsh?

22-9. Here is a nice use of a pivot. *Furu*, "old" and *kawa* (*gawa* when part of a compound), "river" refer both to the river and to Lady Jeweled Garland's weeping, thus expressing the idea that women's tears are also a very old river. The shrine was called Hatsuse, and later the river took on the same name. The question is why the nursemaid uses one term for the river's name and Lady Jeweled Garland uses another. Perhaps Shikibu wished to show Lady Jeweled Garland was cultured enough to want to use a different name, one whose sounds fit with the other words in her poem?

22-10. Mishimae is located along the Yodo River in present Takatsuki City, in Ōsaka Prefecture.

22 - 12

After meeting Lady Jeweled Garland and finding her to be very desirable, Genji has to find room in his crowded house for her. Dismantling an unused library, he is able to install her in a remote and slightly gloomy corner of the west wing. Of course now he has to tell Murasaki about her and confess the long, sad story about her mother. As they are talking, Genji reaches for an inkstone in order to jot down a verse.

koiwataru	through endless
mi wa sore nagara	longing for another
tamakazura	a line was drawn
ikanaru suji wo	which attaches me to one
tazune ki tsu ran	called a garland of jewels

22 - 13

For the New Year's celebration, Genji gives each of the women in his household a robe with patterns and coloring especially chosen to fit each lady's personality. Princess Safflower, still living at the Second Avenue palace, sends with her thank-you verse an old gown slightly discolored from wear at the sleeves. The poem is written on official stationery, heavily scented and also yellow with age.

ki te mire ba	just wearing this
urami rare keri	turns me to having tears
karagoromo	the high court robe
kaeshi yari ten	I return to you is perfect
sode wo nurashi te	except for dampened sleeves

22 - 14

Murasaki and her women begin to make fun of the Princess Safflower's gifts and poems. Genji explains to them how much she has studied from the books left to her by her father and how he, too, is conservative and slightly old-fashioned. Even after a long explanation of her style of poetry, Genji nonetheless thinks she lacks originality and does not want to

22-12. Genji, recalling his passion for Lady Evening Faces, is now greatly attracted to her daughter, Lady Jeweled Garland. He sees lives and loves revolving around him like a jeweled garland of women.

respond to her poem. But because he is, at heart, a kind man, he finally dashes off a poem to the Princess Safflower.

kaesa n to	return you have said
iu ni tsuke temo	but it's turn you mean
katashiki no	night clothes
yoru no koromo wo	spread where you lie alone
omoi koso yare	causes me to worry about you

22-14. A popular belief at the time was that to sleep on a robe turned wrong side out brought dreams of one's lover.

HATSUNE
THE FIRST SONG OF THE NIGHTINGALE

New Year's season of Genji's thirty-sixth year

This chapter describes the New Year's celebrations at Genji's new palace in the Sixth Ward. Genji is extremely satisfied with his life. Although he thought for many years that he would have no children, or at least none he could openly claim, he is now surrounded by attentive women and just the right amount of sons and daughters. He even has the pleasure of outdoing his old rival, the First Secretary's Captain, by giving the latter's unacknowledged daughter, Lady Jeweled Garland, the care, support, and education that she has lacked all her life. As the visitors come by the palace, leaving poems and congratulations, Genji and Murasaki seem especially close and contented. Genji makes the customary calls the season demands to each of his ladies. Finding Princess Safflower, lacking warm undergarments, again has a cold and drippy nose, he makes certain she is properly cared for. Genji is feeling very good about himself until Lord Evening Mist and his best friend, Lord Rose Plum, one of many sons of the First Secretary's Captain, come by caroling. Genji thinks the son of the First Secretary's Captain sings better than his own son, so he gets out the musical instruments, encouraging his family to practice more. Genji's competitive spirit lives on with renewed vigor.

23 - A

wakayaka ni	it makes one young
uguisu zo naku	the song of the nightingale
hatsuharu no	the beginning of spring
kinu kubara re shi	when we shared our silk clothes
hitori no yō ni	we became the image of one

23 - 1

On New Year's Day, Genji's palace is open to distinguished visitors. On a beautiful cloudless day, with the green grass beginning to show among the patches of snow, everyone seems filled with happiness. After greeting callers all morning, Murasaki and Genji sit together before her charming garden as Genji congratulates her on their happiness.

usu kōri	at last the thin ice
toke nuru ike no	has melted from the pond
kagami niwa	the mirror reflects
yo ni taguinaki	an image unequaled in
kage zo narabe ru	these times of two side by side

23 - 2

And Murasaki replies to Genji:

kumorinaki	how clear it is
ike no kagami ni	in the mirror of the pond
yorozuyo wo	these images of
sumu beki kage zo	ten thousand generations
shiruku mie keru	which remain vivid forever

23 - 3

In his daughter's room, Genji finds that her mother, the Akashi Lady, has sent a very fine "bearded" basket that contains a small pine tree with a nightingale in it, along with her poem.

23-A. For many years in Japan, people slept, not under blankets, but under or in the long-sleeved, wide robes similar to those worn in the daytime. In winter these night robes were heavily padded, but when the weather turned warm, the padded robes were put away for lighter, silk ones. Lovers snuggled together under one robe instead of the usual two and thus looked like one person in a robe as well as being united as one entity.

23-1. As one looks over the difficult times Genji and Murasaki have survived—his exile, her righteous jealousy of other women, her lack of her own children, and her total acceptance of Genji's illegitimate daughter—one realizes how apt is his phrase "at last the thin ice / has melted from the pond." The rest of the poem is about as close to meaning "I love you" as one finds in these old *waka.* Also, it is rare for *waka,* or tanka, to contain the happiness of love. Usually, they deal with the sadness of the pain of love. Thus, this poem has even more appeal.

23-2. Murasaki's modesty shows in her reply. Instead of openly returning Genji's love, or taking his words as a compliment to her, she focuses on the hope that the family line will clearly be "ten thousand generations." It is this grace, this delicacy, that makes the characters in the story so beloved that the tale has served for generations as a model of refined behavior.

23-3. The basket the Akashi Lady sent to her daughter was called a "bearded basket" because the ends of the woven reeds were not tucked in but were allowed to jut forth, giving the basket a hairy appearance. Just as it is an accomplishment to weave a basket with every end firmly tied in place, when one is really skilled, one can make a thing look even better by ignoring the rules. But this type of basket, looking so rough and almost primitive, also spoke of the Akashi Lady's humility about her own uncultured background and the fact that she has lived most of her life outside of the capital.

23-4. In her answer, the Akashi Lady's daughter not only acknowledges her mother—her "nest"—but also refers to "the roots of the waiting pine," surely meaning her grandparents. This shows sensitivity for the lineage of her mother and the feelings for her family. For a

toshi tsuki wo	a year of months
matsu ni hika re te	simply gazing at the pine
furu hito ni	the old one just waits
kyō uguisu no	for today to hear the song
hatsune kika se yo	of the spring's first nightingale

23-4

Genji encourages his daughter to write a poem to thank her mother for the gift as he hands her the brush and inkstone. Cheerfully, she jots down the first thing that comes to her mind.

hikiwakare	years of separation
toshi wa fure domo	older since the nightingale flew
uguisu no	away from its nest
sudachi shi matsu no	but how can one forget
ne wo wasure me ya	the roots of the waiting pine?

23-5

In his rounds of holiday visiting with all the women he cares for, Genji stops by the rooms of the Akashi Lady, who is not there. As he looks over her things lying strewn about, he sees among her practice notes a poem in response to her daughter.

mezurashi ya	how wonderful it is
hana no negura ni	nesting among the flowers
kozutai te	hopping tree to tree
tani no furusu wo	the nightingale has called
toe ru uguisu	over the valley to its old nest

23-6

Later, when the busy days are over, he goes to visit Princess Safflower. Genji discovers she is feeling the cold, so he orders new quilted undergarments and has them sent to her. It is very quiet now on Second Avenue since he and the rest of the family have moved. He is touched when he visits the garden, where there seems to be no one to appreciate the rose-colored plum that was just beginning to bloom. He murmurs quietly, hoping the princess does not catch the full implications of his poem.

furusato no	coming to see
haru no kozue ni	spring in the treetops
tazune ki te	of the old village
yonotsune naranu	in this world it's uncommon
hana wo miru kana	to see such a flower

child to be so deeply aware of this that it comes into a verse jotted down quickly shows how well the child has been instructed about her life.

23-5. The Akashi Lady's phrase "nesting among the flowers" is ambiguous, so one does not know if she is referring to herself or her daughter, as both are now "nested" among the flowers in Genji's care. Her first joyous phrase serves to give Genji some satisfaction that both she and her daughter are now happy with the living arrangements Genji has devised, even though mother and daughter are not together in the same place.

23-6. Princess Safflower, it will be recalled, has a tendency to catch colds and have a red nose that goes with them. Genji's poem contains a pun on the word *hana*, which can be either "flower" or "nose." As always, this princess, who lives on the edge of poverty, seems to be the butt of Genji jokes.

KOCHŌ
THE BUTTERFLIES

Third and Fourth Months of Genji's thirty-sixth year

When spring comes, Murasaki's garden unfolds into its own magnificence. Delighted with the results, Genji orders boats built so people can row out on the charming little lake to admire the total view of the cherry trees and the thickets of yellow globeflowers. The occasion to celebrate becomes a party for Murasaki's friends. As the guests are drifting about on the new boats, they compose poetry in praise of the garden and their hostess. Lady Who Loves Autumn, who has now become the Empress, for some reason does not attend the event. To make a show of goodwill, Murasaki dresses children up as birds and butterflies and sends them to the Empress with bouquets of her spring blossoms. Very regal, and somewhat miffed, Lady Who Loves Autumn fears she has lost the contest of who has the best garden.

If there had been a contest as to who was the most interesting person in Genji's entourage, Lady Jeweled Garland would have won. Not only does she have Genji's complete attention, the air of mystery about her, her good looks, and her natural reticence cause a great many men to attempt to get acquainted with her. Genji tries to advise her, but his job is complicated by his desire to keep her heritage a secret. One of her suitors is Lord Oak Tree, the oldest son of the First Secretary's Captain, who is her own brother. Lord Evening Mist is also interested in her, but thinking she is his sister, he regretfully takes her off his list. As Genji works to find the perfect mate for Lady Jeweled Garland, he himself falls more deeply in love with her. Pretending to be educating her, as he did with Murasaki, he draws closer and closer to her. Thinking he can deflower her as easily as he had Murasaki, he begins to make his moves. However, this lady is wiser and more wary, perhaps having learned a lesson from her mother's actions. Genji does not know whether to admire her skill at handling amorous men or nurse his rejection.

---

24 - A

sakari naru	the very best time
miyo no kisaki ni	for offering to the empress
kin no chō	the gold of butterflies
shirogane no tori	the silver of the birds
hana tatematsuru	with the gift of flowers

---

24 - 1

To celebrate the perfection of Murasaki's spring garden, court women are invited to come for a party. On the artificial lake, small, decorated boats are poled about, giving various views of the garden and the palace. Many women take the occasion to write poems.

kaze fuke ba	as the breezes blow
nami no hana sae	even waves seem to be flowers
iro mie te	as colors appear
ko ya na ni tate ru	shall we name this place
yamabuki no saki	the Cape of Globeflowers?

---

24 - 2

Another lady drifting in a boat on the small lake recites her poem.

haru no ike ya	do springs of this pond
ide no kawase ni	flow into the Ide River?
kayou ran	yellow globeflowers

24-A. In this chapter, when Murasaki sends children bringing bouquets of spring flowers to Lady Who Loves Autumn, it is assumed that the vases are gold and silver, but Akiko Yosano turns this idea and creates an image of gold butterflies and silver birds. A very sensitive twist to the story, and, in itself, a lovely idea. Truly a tanka worthy of being part of this story.

24-1. The poetess has carefully observed how the colors on the decorated boats blend and stand out as they are reflected on the waves, so that the water itself seems to have colorful flowers floating on it.

The flower she refers to in her poem, *yamabuki*, is translated as globeflower. The plant is grown in the United States and often called by its Japanese name. A thornless yellow rose, it is similar in growth habit to spirea and forms a large, thicketlike shrub. The flowers are less than an inch across and petalled like small, open yellow roses. The yellow flowers cluster along the stems and make a striking appearance. Many of the flower's attributes could also be applied to Murasaki, which may be why, of all the spring flowers, *yamabuki* is the focus of

kishi no yamabuki	growing at the water's edge
soko mo niohe ri	shine brightly in the depths

24-3

Another lady recites her poem to honor Murasaki's garden.

kame no ue no	no need to visit
yama mo tazune ji	the top of Turtle Mountain
fune no naka ni	here in our boats
oi se nu na woba	where no one grows old
koko ni nokosa n	we'll name the place—Ageless

24-4

Another lady adds her verse:

haru no hi no	the sunlight of spring
urarani sashi te	shining in so beautifully
yuku fune wa	as our boat proceeds
sao no shizuku mo	water dripping from the poles
hana to chiri keru	seems to be scattered petals

24-5

The news that Genji has a new lady on the premises, Lady Jeweled Garland, brings out the men, who seek her acquaintance. Among them is the widowed Prince Firefly. At a party, he pretends to be in discomfort and refuses any more wine with this verse.

murasaki no	the reason is thus
yue ni kokoro wo	since the color lavender
shime tare ba	holds my heart so
fuchi ni mi nage n	I plunge into the depths
koto ya oshike ki	no matter what they say

this series of poems. The place most famous in Japan for displays of *yamabuki* was Yamashiro.

24-2. In the name Ide River, there is *i*, "spring" and *de*, "hand." It seems the lake at the palace was perhaps fed by an underground spring.

24-3. This poem contains a nice link to the previous one by building on *yama* (mountain) in *yamabuki*. Folk wisdom held that if one climbed to the top of Turtle Mountain one would be blessed with a long life, such as turtles have. However, the poem extends the idea to say that one can live longer by being on these boats, where time does not seem to exist.

24-5. In Japan, as well as in other countries, lavender is the color of older love—pink with its added shades of wisdom. We might say pink is closer to our red heart symbol for love, but lavender stands for a sensitive shade of love.

24 - 6

Prince Firefly divides his sprig of wisteria to put a small cluster in Genji's cap. Genji smiles as he suggests:

fuchi ni mi wo	wait before you throw
nage tsu beshi ya to	yourself into these depths
kono haru wa	of a spring like this
hana no atari wo	think of the flowers all around
tachisara de mi n	which you would be leaving

24 - 7

After the festivities in celebration of Murasaki's garden, there is to be a reading of the sutras in Lady Who Loves Autumn's autumn garden. Murasaki sends little girls dressed as birds or butterflies and carrying vases of cherry blossoms and globeflowers to Lady Who Loves Autumn. Lord Evening Mist himself carries this poem from Murasaki.

hanazono no	a flower garden
kochō wo sae ya	of butterflies are asking
shitakusa ni	the cricket who waits
aki matsu mushi wa	in the undergrowth of autumn
utoku miru ran	if they are seen with scorn

24 - 8

After making lavish gifts to all the participants, Lady Who Loves Autumn entrusts to Lord Evening Mist her reply to Murasaki.

kochō ni mo	if not your idea
sasowa re namashi	to make a fence of flowers
kokoro ari te	to separate us
yae yamabuki wo	I think the butterflies
hedate zari se ba	would have invited me

24-6. Genji's response to Prince Firefly is ambiguous enough so that one does not really know if this is Genji's suggestion to the prince to refrain from courting his adopted daughter or if Genji wants him to think that he should court only one woman at a time. The fact that Genji is laughing at the time he speaks only adds to the mystery.

24-7. Depending on how one takes this verse, one can either understand a lessening or escalation of the competition between the two prime ladies in Genji's palace. The contrast between the soft colors of spring and the sere hues of autumn perhaps offers clues to the personalities of these two women and the seriousness of their competition.

24-8. Lady Who Loves Autumn's lavish gifts can be seen as overcompensation for not being invited to the party. It also seems, from her verse, that Murasaki has used the thicketlike qualities of the globeflowers to put up a wall between the lake and Lady Who Loves Autumn's quarters so she could not see what was happening.

24 - 9

While Genji visits Lady Jeweled Garland's room, he discusses with her how to handle the many messages men are sending her. He notices a bit of blue Chinese paper tied in a knot that has not yet been opened. Genji opens the note himself and sees that the handwriting is strong and masculine. When he asks Lady Jeweled Garland whose note it is, she shyly turns her head away and does not answer him.

Genji calls in her lady-in-waiting to give her a lecture on how to manage the notes Lady Jeweled Garland receives and how she should answer their authors in order to keep the proper men interested but at a distance. Young triflers should be discouraged, and it is the lady-in-waiting's job to maintain the proper decorum. She promptly claims it is another of the gentlewomen who has accepted this note—from Lord Oak Tree.

omou tomo	you can never know
kimi wa shira ji na	the depth of my feelings
wakikakaeri	the way the colors
iwa moru mizu ni	in water are hidden when
iro shi mie ne ba	it seethes over the rocks

24 - 10

Genji continues, much longer than desired, it seems, his lecture to the lady-in-waiting and the young Lady Jeweled Garland on the flaws of the various men he considers marriage prospects. Lady Jeweled Garland is very uncomfortable with having to sit listening to him drone on and on, so she becomes very quiet and withdrawn. In Genji's visits to Lady Jeweled Garland he sometimes acts as her father and at other times seems to be trying to be her lover. The poor girl, who is so indebted to Genji for her protection, hardly knows how to answer him. In the uncomfortable silence among the women, he steps out onto the verandah to admire some bamboo shoots swaying in the breeze nearby.

mase no ura ni	the bamboo root
ne fukaku ue shi	firmly planted inside the fence

24-9. The poem by Lord Oak Tree shows an acute observation—how water loses its blue color when it boils over rocks—and then associates this fact with his inner emotional reality. This is classic *waka* imagery used at its best but in a very new way. The verse is good enough to make Genji jealous of the young man's talents.

24-10. Very new bamboo shoots have the pale look of a root that has broken through the ground, seemingly growing upward instead of downward. One might wonder whether it is a sprout or a root and in which direction it is growing.

take no ko no	becomes a sprout
onoga yoyo niya	for future generations to grow
oi wakaru beki	will you have to depart from me?

24 - 11

Lady Jeweled Garland gives her answer and slips away before Genji can detain her.

imasarani	now when it's too late
ikanaran yo ka	it is not the question to be asked
waka take no	by the young bamboo
oi hajime ken	why should I be interested in roots
ne oba tazune n	which are too far away to uncover?

24 - 12

The more Genji sees of Lady Jeweled Garland, the more she reminds him of her dead mother, Lady Evening Faces, and the more he loves her. He begins to talk to Lady Jeweled Garland about her mother more and more as the two women fuse in his mind into one person. One day, while talking to Lady Who Loves Autumn, Genji sees an orange in a basket before them and he reveals the following to her.

tachibana no	just such a fragrance
kaori shi sode ni	of oranges I once knew
yosou re ba	was worn on sleeves
kaware ru mi tomo	I cannot think of you being
omooe nu kana	any different from her

24 - 13

When Genji takes her hand and asks her not to dismiss him for his rudeness, Lady Jeweled Garland tries to maintain her composure as she makes the following verse

sode no ka wo	because of wearing
yosou ru karani	the sleeves with the fragrance
tachibana no	of that orange

24-11. Again Shikibu slips into the mind and heart of this confused child and writes a very appropriate verse. Basically, she acquiesces to Genji's position by saying she knows he is not her father but that she cannot figure out who her real father is.

24-12. The *tachibana,* usually translated as orange, is actually a smaller fruit with loose skin like that of a tangerine.

mi sae hakanaku	I feel that my body also
nari mokoso sure	may not live very long

24 - 14

Then late one night, when Genji is visiting Lady Jeweled Garland, he suddenly, with only the slightest breeze rustling the bamboo, throws off his robes. He is so practiced he can do this without making a sound, so that Lady Jeweled Garland is surprised when he pulls her down against his body. Frightened and overwhelmed, the girl begins sobbing so uncontrollably that Genji is forced to turn all of his efforts to comforting her—without success. She is so shocked she is unable to reply or even move. Genji takes her silence to be coldness and therefore rejection. As he gathers up his clothes and creeps away, he cautions her not to tell anyone of what has happened. The next morning she finds his note, written on prim, white paper hidden among her bedding.

uchitoke te	unable to join
ne mo mi nu monowo	or even see the root
wakakusa no	young grass-girl
kotoarigao ni	your gloomy face looks
musuboworu ran	as if we had tied the knot

25

HOTARU
FIREFLIES

Fifth Month of Genji's thirty-sixth year

Feeling he must get Lady Jeweled Garland married off soon and out of his reach before he ruins her chances of a good match, Genji insists she receive the attentions of Prince Firefly. Just when the prince thinks he has her, the cautious girl escapes to another room. Still determined, Genji coaxes her back into the room, where she believes his presence will protect her from any sexual attempts by the prince. Instead of protecting her, Genji uses the opportunity to show her off by releasing a net of fireflies in the dusk so the prince can get a better glimpse of her beauty. Genji's action is a deep breach of conduct, and thus the lady again has reason to be wary and very angry with him.

Unsatisfied with the results of his pursuit of the young girl, Genji visits Lady Scattered Blossoms. Although they exchange excellent poems, have a satisfying talk about the good old days, and spend the night together, they sleep in separate quarters. Genji begins to feel very old.

The next day, to raise his spirits, he goes again to Lady Jeweled Garland, where he finds her reading romance stories. Adding to her confusion of how to relate to him, Genji at first berates her for reading such stories and then, later, admits that fiction is a legitimate art form.

Meanwhile, the interest in the mysterious lady in Genji's house spreads farther and farther. Even the First Secretary's

It is useful to note that Japanese courtship occurred in the dark. If there was light, it was from either a very small, shaded lantern or the moon. Heian court women were extremely careful to not let any man see them, so even if there was light, a woman would keep her body turned so that her face was kept in the darkest corner. Genji's plan, which involved catching many fireflies and putting them in a cloth bag, also meant that he had to be closer to Lady Jeweled Garland than her suitor, his brother Prince Firefly. Devising his plans like a general, he was able to surprise both of them and make his brother feel he was trying to help his courtship with her. There is of course the utterly romantic idea of being illuminated by a cloud of fireflies. It is from this incident that Prince Firefly takes his name.

Captain begins to wonder about her. One night he has a dream in which he believes he is faulted for not taking care of an unsupported daughter. He actually tells his sons to be on the watch for a young girl claiming him as her father.

25-A. Akiko Yosano demonstrates one of the classic aspects of tanka in this poem. In spite of all the words in a language's vocabulary, there are many things in our lives that have no designated terms—especially in the area of feelings and emotions. Here, Yosano shows that the color of a firefly's glow is the color of the pain suffered from unrequited love. Rather than stating this overtly, she lets the reader absorb the impression from the implied comparison.

25-2. The reference to cries of insects, from the Japanese word *koe,* in Prince Firefly's poem links back to the last poem in chapter 24, which has the word *ne,* meaning "root" or, as in this poem, "to cry" or "weep."

25-3. On the fifth day of the Fifth Month, the Japanese celebrated what is normally called "Boy's Day." Instruments of warfare were displayed in homes in order to encourage boys to become manly. The swordlike leaves of the iris, or sweet flag (*Iris laevigata*), were used by small boys for their imitative battle plays. Aside from the beauty of its purple flower, the iris

---

25 - A

mi ni shimi te	for one's body
mono wo omoe to	love is the thing that stings so
natsu no yo no	on a summer's night
hotaru honokani	the faint glow of fireflies
ao hiki te tobu	leaves a pale blue-green trail

---

25 - 1

One summer evening, when Genji's brother Prince Firefly comes calling on Lady Jeweled Garland, Genji takes a particular interest in orchestrating the events of the visit. All at once, when he is sure the prince is looking in the lady's direction, Genji releases a cloud of fireflies from a cloth bag. Suddenly, in this very romantic way, illuminated by the unearthly glow, the prince can see how beautiful the girl truly is. Deeply moved by the display, Prince Firefly recites the following poem:

naku koe mo	one cannot hear the cry
kikoe nu mushi no	of a bug such as a firefly
omoi dani	even with longing
hito no ketsu niwa	how could you extinguish
keyuru mono kawa	the fire in someone's heart?

---

25 - 2

Lady Jeweled Garland's embarrassment is so great that she makes a hasty reply and rushes from his presence.

koe wa se de	unable to cry out
mi wo nomi kogasu	even when the body burns
hotaru koso	like the firefly
iu yori masaru	silence far surpasses
omoi naru rame	speaking of one's love

25-3

On the day of the Festival of the Iris—the fifth day of the Fifth Month—Prince Firefly sends Lady Jeweled Garland a poem on white tissue attached to an iris root. At first the poem seems very impressive, but upon repeating it, some of her gentlewomen feel it is rather ordinary.

kyō sae ya	why is it today
hiku hito mo naki	no one pulls up that which is
migakure ni	hidden in waters
ouru ayame no	the roots of the iris plants
ne nomi naka re n	as well as my deep crying

25-4

Genji urges Lady Jeweled Garland to answer the note from Prince Firefly, and her women agree with him that she has no choice but to respond. So she writes in her faintest handwriting:

araware te	it appears to be
itodo asaku mo	all the more shallow as it
niyuru kana	seems to be unable
ayame mo waka zu	to understand about iris
naka re keru ne no	or the roots of the crying

25-5

Genji goes to spend the holiday night with Lady Scattered Blossoms. Although they are companionable and discuss many things, they part to sleep in separate places—he on her robes and she on robes laid outside the curtain. Lady Scattered Blossoms says:

sono koma mo	even that pony
susame nu mono to	which naturally never does things
na ni tate ru	to spread gossip
migiwa no ayame	iris at the water's edge
kyō ya hiki tsuru	would you pull out today?

was also valued for its roots, which were dried and used as starch. *Ayame* is both "iris" and "patterns."

The fifth line, *ne nomi naka re n,* is quoted from a poem in the *Manyōshū*, vol. 5, no. 897, by Yamanoue no Okura.

25-4. A freshly dug iris root, all wrinkled and crooked, brown and scabby-looking, is not a pretty sight. Lady Jeweled Garland compares herself to this root, the root of her problems (her mother's death), and alludes to the fact that she is the illegitimate daughter of someone she does not know. The fourth line is taken directly from the *Kokinshū* imperial anthology, volume 1, on the theme of love. There, *ayame mo shira zu* could be translated as "without the distinction of things," as it is through the patterns of things that we can distinguish one from another.

25-5. Mention of a pony is, in Japanese literature, a euphemism for the male organ. The allusion to plants growing along the water's edge relates to the grassy places of the female where a pony would most like to graze. It is a slight connection to the damp places where irises grow, but in this poem the author makes it work.

25-6. *Niodori,* "water bird," also expresses "two in a row." Genji's poem adds a new element to the talk of grasses, ponies, and iris growing on the bank of a stream. It successfully creates the image of Genji and Lady Scattered Blossoms as two birds resting peacefully on the water, instead of the lustier image the lady projected.

25-7. It is interesting that instead of using the word for tales, *monogatari,* the word *ato* is used, which means footsteps, whereabouts, or keepsake. This implies that the old tales were not made up stories but are the accounts of actual lives.

25-8. The statement preceding the poem that Genji is stroking Lady Jeweled Garland's hair gives new meaning to the use of *kakaru,* which, as in English, means to either lean on or rely on a thing or person. Lady Jeweled Garland could neither physically lean on nor rely on Genji not to rob her of her virginity. At this point she suspects Genji might be her father. He acts as her father, and yet she feels he knows the secret of her heritage and is thus permitted to pursue her as a lover.

25-6

Genji is touched by Lady Scattered Blossom's comment, but his own poem lacks excitement.

niodori ni	like a pair of birds
kage wo naraburu	our images line up side by side
waka koma wa	with the young pony
itsuka ayame ni	how can one be separated
hikiwakaru beki	from the iris like that?

25-7

Lady Jeweled Garland loved to read and often discussed literature with Genji. One night, while they are talking about old romance novels, Genji presses closer and closer to her. He jokingly suggests that they write up the story of their lives, the truth of which would jolt the world. She hides her face as she tells him the whole world surely already knows their situation without going to the trouble of writing it down. Smiling and playful with thoughts about their curious affair, he presses his body even nearer to her.

omoiamari	so beside myself
mukashi no ato wo	I have searched the keepsakes
tazunure do	of ancient former times
oya ni somuke ru	no one is equal to you
ko zo taguinaki	for disobeying a sire

25-8

Even as Genji strokes her long, black hair, he reminds Lady Jeweled Garland that she is breaking one of the commandments. Refusing to look up at him, she manages finally to reply.

furuki ato wo	I too have searched
tazunure do geni	the old traces through and through
nakari keri	yet nothing is there
kono yo ni kakaru	a parent on which I can
oya no kokoro wa	rely in these present times

26

TOKONATSU
WILD CARNATIONS

Summer of Genji's thirty-sixth year

One hot day while lying by the pond where Lord Evening Mist and his young friends are swimming, Genji overhears the news that the First Secretary's Captain has actually found one of his long-lost daughters. It is rumored that she was raised at Ōmi and is very provincial—in fact, she has turned out to be quite brash and outspoken. Genji and the First Secretary's Captain are thus again in competition about who can best raise the abandoned child of an affair.

Genji thinks of letting the First Secretary's Captain know he has the latter's child in his home, wondering if it would make it easier for Genji to get into her bedroom if she knew he is not her father. But he realizes that any success he might have in deflowering her will reduce her chances for making a good marriage. Still, if the First Secretary's Captain takes her over, she will have to leave his house, and he will have no access at all to her. As Genji gives Lady Jeweled Garland a lesson on the harp, he finds her so charming and so attractive, he decides he simply cannot give her up to another man.

The First Secretary's Captain does not know what to do with his daughter from Ōmi now that he has brought her to his home in the capital. She is so loud and boisterous that he fears he will never find a proper husband for her. It is too late for him to educate her correctly, so he finally sends her off to court to

It is interesting that in Western traditions, carnations are seen as the flower that carries grief—almost as if they were designed to carry what cannot be endured on the jagged edges of their petals. Dew as a symbol of tears is so common, a poet needs only to mention dew for the mind to include its reference to tears. The observation is made that water on a flower deepens its hue. Also brought to mind is the correlation between wild carnations and illegitimate children, of which of course Lady Jeweled Garland is one. Also, the small, wild carnations grow in puffy "cushions" of leaves and flowers reminiscent of a bed.

live with one of his other daughters, hoping the atmosphere there will refine her behavior by example.

One can see how the wild carnations in the chapter title refer to the love children born of the promiscuous affairs of the men from the high court and what troubles they can cause later when plucked from their rustic environments.

26-A. Yosano seems to be expressing the sadness such children carry their whole lives as a result of their parents' irresponsible behavior.

26-1. By mentioning that the carnations grow at the root of the hedges, the idea is conveyed that Lady Jeweled Garland's origins are hidden, as she herself is protected by Genji as if she had a hedge around her. Wild carnations grow very low to the ground, so this is the natural place for them to appear.

26-2. Lady Jeweled Garland's poem underlines the fact of her unknown lineage when it asserts that even an uncultured mountain rustic would not look for carnations on the top of a hedge. If someone came looking for her, he would have to look at her roots, and if she was to make a proper marriage, her lineage would have to be revealed. In Heian times, the support of a family was most important to young people, but especially to women, who had no other way to support themselves. To be living in the unstable milieu of the court and not have a system of males to care for her left a woman in a very desperate situation. Even though young, a woman, or her attendants, would

---

26 - A

tsuyu oki te	the falling of dews
kurenai itodo	deepens the reds more and more
fukakere do	just as thick and dense
omoi nayame ru	as the worries which trouble
nadeshiko no hana	the wild carnation flowers

---

26 - 1

One evening Genji is instructing Lady Jeweled Garland on the harp, and he lets drop the information that her own father is a better harp player than he. This makes her even more eager to meet her father. But Genji strangely keeps himself between her and the First Secretary's Captain as well as her gentleman callers. The longer they talk, the quieter and more out of sorts grows Lady Jeweled Garland. Genji mentions that perhaps he should show her garden, with its cushions of wild carnations growing at the edge of her verandah, to his best friend, the First Secretary's Captain.

nadeshiko no	if he just knew
toko natsukashiki	the unchanging attributes
iro wo mi ba	of the carnation
moto no kakine wo	at the root of the hedges
hito ya tazune n	wouldn't he come asking?

---

26 - 2

Genji acts as if he has been protecting her by keeping her a secret from her father. She seems so young and gentle as she brushes aside her tears and speaks:

yamagatsu no	what mountain rustic
kakio ni oi shi	would search the tops of hedges
nadeshiko no	for wild carnations
moto no nezashi wo	whose roots were hidden
tare ka tazune n	as is her own lineage?

26 - 3

In the meantime, the First Secretary's Captain discovers another of his daughters being raised in the province of Ōmi. Eager to obey the prophecy of his dream, he quickly brings her to his home in Kyoto before even meeting her. She turns out to be very chatty, outspoken, and totally lacking in the social graces. When her father urges her to write to her half sister, the daughter of the First Secretary's Captain now at court, she inappropriately sends a kitchen maid with her note.

kusa wakami	as grasses are young
hitachi no umi no	on the sea of plains at Hitachi
ikagasaki	Cape How is asking
ikade aimi n	how the wave will ever meet
tago no ura nami	on the Farmer's Daughter's Beach

26 - 4

Her sister's ladies-in-waiting at court find the overuse of place names in the poem to be simply hilarious, so to continue the joke, they reply:

hitachi naru	hey you waves leaving
suruga no umi no	for Hitachi's sea of grassy plains
suma no ura ni	at Suruga
nami tachiide yo	on the beach of Suma the
hakozaki no matsu	pine trees of Hakozaki wait

be cognizant of these facts.

26-3. Shikibu again introduces a comical interlude. The daughter from Ōmi has been taught the tanka technique of using place names to enrich a poem. In her eagerness to impress her half sister at court, however, she goes overboard and includes three place names and an inappropriate metaphor. "Young grasses," designating a young girl, is not an expression a girl would use in reference to herself, and her choice makes her appear both uneducated and pert. The use of Tago no Ura (a place in Suruga Province), which translates as "beach of the farmer's child," reveals the Miss of Ōmi to be the rustic she is. Shikibu must have had a marvelous time writing such a poem.

26-4. They have outdone her with four place names! These two poems hardly hold together enough to make sense of them and should be seen as poking fun at a tanka technique carried to its ridiculous, but comical, end.

KAGARIBI
FLARES

Seventh Month of Genji's thirty-sixth year

As the unkind talk about the Miss of Ōmi circulates, Lady Jeweled Garland, who knows now that the First Secretary's Captain is her father, realizes how fortunate she is to be in her more favored position. Even though it is difficult dodging Genji's advances, he is offering a superior place from which she can live her life. When the first hints of autumn and loneliness come, Genji begins to spend even more time with Lady Jeweled Garland. Genji again attempts to give her an intimate lesson on the harp. After a while, they lie down side by side to rest, and Genji is very attracted to her. Just then he notices that the flares in her garden have burned down, so he calls a guardsman to relight them. The girl is so lovely in the flickering light from the garden, he does not ever want to leave her. As they sit together they hear flute music coming from the verandah where Lord Evening Mist and his friends are holding an impromptu concert. Genji invites them to come to the verandah before Lady Jeweled Garland's rooms. Lord Oak Tree, who has been one of her suitors, is finally persuaded by Genji to play on the harp. It is as if Genji knows the conflict that she will feel when she hears a young man serenade her in the garden on an autumn evening, who, unknown to himself, is her half brother.

27 - A

ōkinaru	how lovely it is
mayumi no moto ni	the glow of the flare fire
utsukushiku	by the giant roots
kagaribi moe te	of the bow-wood spindle tree
suzukaze zo fuku	yet what a cool wind blows

27 - 1

Autumn brings Genji even more often to Lady Jeweled Garland's rooms. One evening as he is about to leave, he notices that the flares have burned low in her garden under the arching spindle tree. He calls for attendants to have them refueled—in part so he can see her loveliness better. He reminds her that she should always have flares in her garden on moonless nights so she will not be frightened. However, she is more frightened by his words:

kagaribi ni	in burning flares
tachisou koi no	there is a kinship to love
kemuri koso	the way the smoke
yo niwa tae se nu	refuses to leave this world
honoo nari kere	see the flame is still here

27 - 2

Lady Jeweled Garland's reply, "I am sure we are the subject of much curious comment," is spoken with her poem:

yukue naki	if your heart's smoke is
sora ni kechi te yo	akin to the bonfire's fume
kagaribi no	put it into the sky
tayori ni tagū	where all destinations
kemuri to nara ba	even futures are extinguished

27-A. *Mayumi* refers to the spindle tree *(Euonymus sieboldianus)*, from which archery bows were made.

27-2. If one accepts the erotic aspects of the previous poem, one can deduce that the reply is telling Genji to take himself, his feelings, and his attentions elsewhere—into the sky. This may be a rather earthy interpretation of the words, but Shikibu was capable of being, at times, quite matter-of-fact about the human body. Still, the poem does give other connotations—deeper meaning—by returning to the crematory smoke image. All humans and their varied destinies float off to be absorbed and lost in the vastness of the skies.

28

NOWAKI
THE TYPHOON

Eighth Month of Genji's thirty-sixth year

As autumn arrives, Lady Who Loves Autumn prepares to show off her garden as Murasaki did in spring. But before her party can be arranged, a typhoon blows in and her garden is badly battered, making it unfit to be shown. Like the good son he is, Lord Evening Mist makes his way through the high winds to see how his father's family is faring in the storm. At Genji's palace, Lord Evening Mist observes a group of women attempting to control a wind-blown screen and sees, for the very first time, Murasaki. He is overcome by her beauty and understands why Genji has kept her hidden from him. A few days later, during another lull in the storm, when Lord Evening Mist arrives before daybreak, he accidentally overhears Genji and Murasaki talking together as they lie in their bed. This forbidden glimpse into their private life greatly adds to his thoughts and fantasies of his stepmother. While accompanying his father on his rounds to check on each of the women in the household, Lord Evening Mist observes how Genji acts toward Lady Jeweled Garland. He quickly recognizes that his father's behavior toward her is not parental and begins to think with great pity and compassion on Murasaki. While still making these rounds, Lord Evening Mist remembers the lady he loves and feels his responsibility to get a note off to her. While in the empty room of the Akashi Girl, he asks her women if he can borrow her inkstone and paper for a note to Lady Wild Goose in the Clouds. When the Akashi Girl comes back into the room, having slept elsewhere because of her fears during the storm, Lord Evening Mist hides behind some furniture so that he finally gets a peek at her. In these ways he becomes aware of the several beautiful women with whom his father has surrounded himself.

28 - A

kezayaka ni	how lifelike it is
medetaki hito zo	the typhoon has blown open
imashi taru	the scroll of pictures
nowaki ga akuru	so the Most Magnificent One
emaki no okuni	lives again in his homeland

28 - 1

After the terrors of the typhoon, Genji goes around visiting his various ladies to see how they have fared the storm. As he approaches the Akashi Lady's garden, he sees young girls are already at work straightening the trellis for the morning glories, and the Akashi Lady is sitting on the verandah playing her harp. She slips a cloak over her robes when Genji sits down beside her. After he hurriedly leaves her, she whispers to herself:

ōkata no	maybe the sound
ogi no ha suguru	of the wind rustling the leaves
kaze no ne mo	of reeds in the water
ukimi hitotsu ni	feels the sting of this person's
shimu kokochi shi te	most painful fate in the world

28 - 2

As Genji continues his rounds, checking on his household after the typhoon, his son Lord Evening Mist accompanies him. The typhoon had blown aside a curtain, permitting Lord Evening Mist a forbidden glimpse of Murasaki, which excites him and causes him to wish for more peeks at Genji's women. While Genji is in Lady Jeweled Garland's rooms, Lord Evening Mist raises a curtain to find he has a clear view of the intimacies

28-A. Akiko Yosano's idea that the wind blowing the hanging scroll gives it breath and thus animate the figures depicted there is strikingly original. The painted figures moving in response to the wind reinforces the idea. Homeland can mean either that the figures are again home or that they are in their ghostly homeland, in which the wind permits the author to see them.

28-1. While it is common in English poetry to give the things of nature human attributes—personification—here the poem takes this technique to a new level. The pain that the lady feels is so intense that the stiff action of the reeds blowing in the wind seems to express that they are in pain—expressing her pain. When one sees how reeds actually move, because of the way they are constructed, one can easily imagine the pain of their stiff, jerky movements.

between his father and Lady Jeweled Garland. The girl has just recited a poem to Genji, spoken too quietly for Lord Evening Mist to hear, but then Genji repeats it more loudly, as if to himself, but he wants his son to be sure to hear it.

fuki midaru	blown into disorder
kaze no keshiki ni	from the wind and my mind
ominaeshi	the maiden flower
shiore shinu beki	droops with its intention
kokochi koso sure	to die and just pass away

---

28 - 3

Lord Evening Mist is revolted by the meaning of her poem and hopes he has misunderstood the intent of his father's answering poem. It sounds as if his father has been intimate with her!

shiratsuyu ni	if it would consent
nabika mashika ba	in this case to shining dews
ominaeshi	the maiden flower
araki kaze niwa	would not fear the withering
shiore zaramashi	by the violence of wind

---

28 - 4

By now it is nearly noon and Lord Evening Mist is eager to write a note to Lady Wild Goose in the Clouds, his childhood sweetheart. Needing an inkstone and paper, he goes into his sister's room, that of the daughter of the Akashi Lady. She is sleeping late in another part of the villa, so he simply sits down to borrow her things. He writes his note on purple tissue and attaches it to a branch broken in the storm.

kaze sawagi	even on a night
murakumo mayou	when the winds rage and clouds
yūbe nimo	become disordered
wasururu ma naku	there was no time to forget
wasura re nu kimi	you whom I cannot forget

28-3. *Ominaeshi*, maiden flower, is one of the celebrated "seven herbs of autumn." The others are *hagi* (bush clover), *susuki* (Chinese silver grass), *kuzu* (arrowroot), *nadeshiko* (wild carnation), *fujibakama* (Chinese agrimony), and *hirugao* (bindweed).

29

MIYUKI
THE ROYAL OUTING

Twelfth Month of Genji's thirty-sixth year to Second Month of his thirty-seventh year

The last six chapters covered Genji's thirty-sixth year and have been called by some "the year of Lady Jeweled Garland." Genji is still tormented by his amorous feelings for her and knows intellectually that if he does not get her married off soon he will do the regrettable act that will cause both of them to be the object of scandal and gossip. One day when the Emperor and his court set out for an excursion to the snowy mountains, the ladies of Genji's palace ride out in palanquins to watch the procession. The occasion gives Lady Jeweled Garland a chance to observe all the men in her life—even the young Emperor, splendid in his bright red robes amid the flakes of snow. Suspecting the inclination of her heart, Genji offers Lady Jeweled Garland the opportunity of going to court to perhaps become a mistress of the Emperor. To do this, however, Genji will be forced to reveal the lady's identity to the First Secretary's Captain.

Gathering up his resolve, Genji goes to the First Secretary's Captain's villa to tell him but finds the mother of the First Secretary's Captain, the Great Princess (Genji's first mother-in-law), is gravely ill. Under these circumstances he cannot hope to engage his friend in such a serious discussion, and so the opportunity for the two men to talk passes. Genji continues fighting with himself, torn between his desires for the girl and his fear of gossip. Genji goes ahead with the initiation ceremony, after which Lady Jeweled Garland will be sent to court as the lady of the bedchamber. When the other illicit daughter of the First Secretary's Captain, the Miss of Ōmi, hears of this, she reacts in jealous rage because she thinks she should be given the same honor and attention.

---

29 - A

yuki chiru ya	the falling of snow
hiyori kashikoku	in fine weather is splendid
medetasa mo	as magnificent
uenaki kimi no	as jewels on the palanquin
tamano onkoshi	of the finest emperor

---

29 - 1

In the middle of winter the nobles are invited to accompany the Emperor on an outing to Ōharano for hunting. Not wishing to go, Genji claims to have a defilement that prevents him from joining them. The Emperor sends Genji a brace of pheasants with a poem.

yuki fukaki	in the deepest snows
oshio no yama ni	of Fine Salt Mountain
tatsu kiji no	a pheasant has flown
furuki ato wo mo	yet today you should have been
kyō wa tazuneyo	searching for ancient footprints

---

29 - 2

Genji receives the messenger with great ceremony and then sends back his answer.

oshioyama	the noble snows
miyuki tsumore ru	on Fine Salt Mountain gathered
matsubara ni	in the pine forests
kyō bakari naru	today why should my tracks
ato ya nakara n	mar the grand royal outing?

29-A. One of the most amazing sights in Japan happens on a clear, cold day, with sun and blue skies. Suddenly one will be aware of large, fluffy snowflakes drifting down out of those cloudless skies. Snow always feels like a blessing, but when it comes out of the blue, it seems extra special. Meteorologists explain that moisture, carried aloft by warmer winds, chills and falls as snow. Because this happens at high altitudes, the flakes compound, creating large, fluffy flakes. They are called *yuki no hana,* "flowers of snow."

29-1. Oshioyama, or Mount Oshio, can be translated as "small" or "fine" *(o)* "salt" *(shio).* The mountain is located to the west of Kyoto. There is a certain correctness in going on a snowy day to a mountain with such a name.

29-2. Miyuki is a wordplay meaning (1) snow belonging to the nobility, (2) deep snow, or (3) a royal outing. Thus, the last line could also be read as "mar the royal snows" or "mar the deep snow." Genji is also referring to his defilement—some taboo situation that has made him unfit to be in the presence of members of the court—in a way that reminds the Emperor

29 - 3

Genji writes a note to Lady Jeweled Garland, who was a spectator at the occasion, asking if she noticed the Emperor and if she was inclined in his direction—meaning would she like to go to court to become one of his consorts. She is surprised Genji has been able to read her heart and, in her reply, cloaks her feelings in a reference to the overcast day.

uchikirashi
asagumori se shi
miyuki niwa
sayaka ni sora no
hikari yawa mi shi

a morning of fog
has clouded up the outing
of the royal party
how can one see such
a radiance in a clear sky?

29 - 4

Genji presses Lady Jeweled Garland to make up her mind as to whether she wishes to be presented at court.

akanesasu
hikari wa sora ni
kumora nu wo
nadote miyuki ni
me wo kirashi ken

the scarlet shining
in the daytime sky
has not clouded up
have you been blinded by
the royal outing in deep snow?

29 - 5

On the sixteenth of the Second Month, Genji plans to have Lady Jeweled Garland ritually presented to the family gods as an adult. He tries to incorporate the First Secretary's Captain into the ceremonies, but his mother, the Great Princess, is ill, so the First Secretary's Captain uses her condition as an excuse to refuse to attend. Genji then has to go to their home to inform both of them of Lady Jeweled Garland's existence and ask permission to present her at court. On the day of the ceremonies, the Great Princess sends a very old-fashioned comb box to Lady Jeweled Garland with a letter and a poem.

futakata ni
ii mote yuke ba

two persons—two lids
the story boils down to that

that it is not his choice that he did not attend the outing.

29-4. The word *akanesasu* is from *akane*, the name of a plant whose root is used for making a scarlet dye, and *sasu* , "to shine, pour in." Thus *akanesasu* is a poetic reference to the sun, daytime, or the emperor. The Emperor robed in scarlet and viewed in the snow on a cloudy day would appear as the sun. Until 1945, the official opinion held that the Emperor was the direct descendent of the sun goddess.

29-5. Special boxes were made to hold women's combs, and, like every other thing, they were stored away when not in use. When looking at them in a museum, one could mistake them for jewelry boxes. The word *kakego* refers either to an inner box fitted into another, lipped box or a dependent child or child relative. This word's nuances are what make the Great Princess's gift and poem so apt. With her gift, she is literally fitting the child into her family. In the story, it is related that Genji makes fun of the verse because it contains three references to boxes: *futa*, "lid," *tama-kushige*, "jeweled comb box," and *kakego* "inner box."

29-6. In the Heian period, the various classes of nobility were differentiated by restrictions allowing certain colors and items of clothing to be worn only by members of that rank. The official court garments were called poetically "Chinese robes" in reference to the origin of the style. Because Princess Safflower is one of the lesser members of the court, she is excluded from wearing certain garments, an exclusion that deeply hurts her. This psychological wound occurs repeatedly in her poems with her fixation on clothes.

29-7. While working on this tanka, the echo of Gertrude Stein's "rose is a rose is a rose" came to mind. She was only 900 years behind Murasaki Shikibu.

29-8. Perhaps in an effort to seem as educated and refined as Genji, the First Secretary's Captain loads his poem with poetic epithets and double entendres. *Tamamo* can mean jeweled sea grass or indicate the train of a woman's long robe. With this thought in mind, one can imagine both a woman pearl diver emerging from the sea dragging long strands of shining kelp behind her and a woman wearing a robe with a train.

tamakushige	a jewel box for combs
wagami hanare nu	like a part of myself
kakego nari keri	is related to this child

29 - 6

When Princess Safflower hears of the preparations for Lady Jeweled Garland's ceremony, she insists upon sending gifts, even though the two women have never met. Attached to a jacket was another of the princess's poems about clothes.

wagami koso	I myself
urami rare kere	in the past bore a grudge
karagoromo	against court robes
kimi ga tamoto ni	thus I worry that your sleeves
nare zu to omoe ba	will never get to know mine

29 - 7

Genji, always eager to practice his unkind wit on Princess Safflower, takes over Lady Jeweled Garland's job of sending a reply and writes the following:

karagoromo	a Chinese robe
mata karagoromo	once more a Chinese robe
karagoromo	a Chinese robe
kaesugaesu mo	over and over again
karagoromo naru	it is a Chinese robe

29 - 8

Not until the ceremony of initiation for Lady Jeweled Garland did the First Secretary's Captain finally get a glimpse of his beautiful daughter. Genji handles every detail of the ceremony so admirably, even making certain there is enough light for the First Secretary's Captain to see her clearly, that the First Secretary's Captain can complain only that Genji did not introduce him to Lady Jeweled Garland sooner.

urameshi ya	it's bitter bitter
okitsu tamamo wo	the heart of the woman diver
kazuku made	underwater
isogakure keru	behind rocks until she wears
ama no kokoro yo	jeweled grasses of the sea

---

29 - 9

Being in the company of two such splendid gentlemen, Lady Jeweled Garland can only remain silent. So Genji gives the First Secretary's Captain the answering poem.

yorube nami	because there was no
kakaru nagisa ni	safe haven for the waves
uchiyose te	thus the sea grasses
ama mo tazune nu	for which the fisherfolk seek
mokuzu tozo mi shi	were said to be beach litter

In the third line, *kazuku* can mean "put on, wear"; "dive down, retrieve"; "make one go underwater." We also have *isogakure,* meaning "disappear behind rocks on a beach," as well as *ama,* mentioned previously, meaning "nun" or "woman diver" or "fisherfolk." It is almost more than one small poem can bear.

30

FUJIBAKAMA
PURPLE SKIRTS

Eighth and Ninth Months of Genji's thirty-seventh year

The chapter title comes from the flower called *fujibakama*—*fuji,* "wisteria" or "purple," and *hakama,* a pleated garment for men worn like a skirt under short robes. For this reason, perhaps, Edward Seidensticker translates the term as "trousers," but in truth the garment is more like a divided skirt. The flower is asterlike, purple, and blooms late in autumn.

Since her initiation, and because of the fact that everyone now knows the hidden story of her parentage, Lady Jeweled Garland's relationships with the males in her life begin to shift and change. The First Secretary's Captain's son, Lord Oak Tree, her strongest suitor, must withdraw because he is her half brother. This leaves the way open for Lord Evening Mist, who is now no longer considered her brother. He brings her a large bouquet of *fujibakama* and his best poems, but she is not impressed by him. Upset by her rejection, Lord Evening Mist goes to Genji for a father-son talk and learns much more about his father than he may have intended. In the end, Lady Jeweled Garland, who is surrounded by a wreath of male suitors, looks at the notes from each one, realizing that the sooner she makes her choice, the better off she will be. She is eager to end the constant threat of a man, any man, breaking into her rooms to deflower her before she makes a choice. Still no one man really appeals to her.

30 - A

murasaki no
fujibakama woba
miyo to iu
futari naki taki
kokochi oboe te

plant of purple dye
for the formal pleated skirt
explain it to us
how the sad feelings of two
persons can be felt by all

30 - 1

One of the results of the clarification of Lady Jeweled Garland 's paternity is that she will go into official mourning, as granddaughter, for the death of the Great Princess, and the other is that Lord Evening Mist now knows she is not his sister. The view he had of her the morning after the typhoon is such a pleasant memory for him. He picks a large bouquet of flowers, *fujibakama* ("purple skirts") and writes a poem. He pushes the bouquet and poem to her under the curtains, and, as she reaches for them, he grabs her sleeve.

onaji no no
tsuyu ni yatsururu
fujibakama
aware wa kakeyo
kagoto bakari mo

ruined by dew
like cast-off rags
purple skirts
do show some sympathy
even just a mere token

30 - 2

Unsure whether Lord Evening Mist is just being friendly or making himself a suitor, Lady Jeweled Garland responds and then quickly withdraws deeper into her rooms.

tazunuru ni
harukeki nobe no
tsuyu nara ba
usu murasaki ya
kagoto nara mashi

in case you ask
if it grew in distant fields
because of dew
I wonder if the pale
color is an apology

30-A. The Latin name for the *murasaki* plant is *Lithospermum erythrorhizon*, a *Boraginaceae*, or gromwell. The roots of the plant were long used for dyeing fabric a claret, a reddish purple, that was highly esteemed. Thus *murasaki* is also the color royal purple. There is even a berry called *murasakishikibu.* It is a poetic tradition to address plants, asking them for their secrets. What makes this tanka so excellent is Yosano finding the connection between the plant, Genji's second wife, and the author Murasaki Shikibu's art to make people, even centuries later, feel the pain the characters in the story seem to have felt.

30-1. If one turns the flower of an aster upside down, one can imagine the purple pleats of a dyed skirt. The character of Lord Evening Mist, who earlier was upset when his lack of advancement committed him to wearing a robe of a color not as highly respected as he wanted, seems to share a concern about clothes with Princess Safflower. Thus, when Lord Evening Mist sees the purple skirt of an aster, he sees cast-off clothing worn by someone in his rank. Both he and Lady Jeweled Garland are in

30-3

One of Lady Jeweled Garland's suitors has been Lord Oak Tree, the First Secretary's Captain's son. He now attempts to get even closer to her under the excuse of being her brother, but she is very wary and wise. When he comes to visit, she sends out her lady-in-waiting instead of letting him come close enough to speak to her. Lord Oak Tree's poem is a response to this treatment, spoken to the lady-in-waiting.

imose yama	on Sibling Mountain
fukaki michi woba	along the path through the deep
tazune zu te	I did not visit
odae no hashi ni	on Interruption Bridge with my
fumi madoi keru	footsteps straying from the path

30-4

Lady Jeweled Garland feels it is futile to complain about unhappiness that is of his own making and responds, through her lady-in-waiting, as follows.

madoi keru	how do you know that
michi woba shira zu	the way was even lost while
imose yama	on Sibling Mountain
tadotadoshiku zo	for me it is not yet clear
tare mo fumi mi shi	who took a step one can see

30-5

When the Ninth Month comes, it brings one of those magical bright mornings filled with a brilliant sun after a night of frost. One of Lady Jeweled Garland's suitors, Black Beard, sends a poem of his desperation.

kazu nara ba	if among those who
itoi mo se mashi	act as if they hate the number
nagatsuki ni	of the ninth month moon
inochi wo kakuru	why risk one's very life
hodo zo hakanaki	for such a lonely status?

the purplish-gray robes of mourning for their grandmother.

30-3. One of the poetic places of literary Japan is Mount Imose. *Imo* is an affectionate term for a woman and *se* can mean husband or lover. Implied is the love between a woman and man, husband and wife, younger sister and elder brother—the caring relationship that could exist between these couples. There are several mountains in Japan bearing this name.

The use of *Odae no Hashi,* Bridge of Interruption, is clear. However, the name seems to come from *o,* "ridge," "flax thread," or "string," and *dae,* derived from the verb *tayu,* "to cut, break off."

30-5. The Ninth Month is called *nagatsuki (naga,* "long" and *tsuki,* "moon"). It may mean that the moon seems to be seen longer because of the earlier evening times after summer. Black Beard seems to be saying that it does him no good to have longer moonlit evenings when he must spend them alone. As another of the characters in *The Tale of Genji* with a good education but lacking in innate talent, he seems to have his problems with poetry, also.

30 - 6

Another suitor, Prince Firefly, sends his poem attached to a sprig of bamboo still covered with glistening frost crystals.

asahi sasu	morning sun shines in
hikari wo mi temo	light beams seen as if coming
tamazasa no	from bamboo jewels
ha wake no shimo wa	on the leaf blazed by frost
keta zu mo ara nan	I hope it never vanishes

30 - 7

A brother of Murasaki who holds a position in the guard's commission is also interested in Lady Jeweled Garland and sends her a long list of his complaints, along with a poem.

wasure nan to	trying to forget
omou mo mono no	yet worrying about this affair
kanashiki wo	because of sadness
ikasama ni shi te	what should be done
ikasama ni se n	to make myself forget?

30 - 8

Although her women are greatly impressed by the efforts of her many suitors in writing their poems, and their choices of papers and inks, Lady Jeweled Garland decides to write a reply only to Prince Firefly.

kokoro mote	with a feeling heart
hikage ni mukau	it heads for the sunshine
aoi dani	even the heartvine
asa oku tsuyu wo	on which morning dew falls
onore yawa ketsu	tries to clear itself

30-6. In the story text, it seems the attendants make fun of Prince Firefly, his messenger, and the frozen bamboo twig—all seem a bit too old, hard, and bent with age. This poem, with its upbeat images of sunlight and warmth, however, is the most successful as poetry in spite of the opinions of the attendants.

30-7. We find a poem with no connection to the natural world, one concerned only with feelings and human acts. Still, the tone of the poem is apropos to a guardsman—a pragmatist, a realist.

30-8. Rereading Prince Firefly's poem, one sees how Lady Jeweled Garland finds a connection to his sentiments but is able to twist the elements just enough to make the poem's realities mirror her deepest feelings. One feels how refreshing she finds his sunshine motif, befitting a younger person, and instinctively turns in his direction, like the heartvine. Incredible honesty, mixed with the distance of knowledge, makes her poem a very special response.

MAKIBASHIRA
THE BLACK PINE PILLAR

Tenth Month of Genji's thirty-seventh year to Tenth Month of his thirty-eighth year

Much to Genji's chagrin, Lady Jeweled Garland takes for her husband the least likely candidate, Black Beard. True, he is a very powerful man whose career is on the rise, but he is already married to the daughter of Prince Director of Military Affairs and has several children. Complicating the situation is the fact that the wife, in fits of madness, lashes out violently against her husband. As if in a modern-day soap opera, the reader is shown the battles between errant husband and furious wife. One night, in winter, the wife actually assaults her husband by dumping incense embers on his head.

After this outburst of rage, the wife returns to her father's villa, taking her children. The young daughter is old enough to dimly perceive the situation and yet loves her father and cannot understand why her home must be broken up. At her favorite place in the house, by a pine pillar, she sticks up a poem for her dad. Without awareness of the child's feelings, Black Beard prepares to install his new wife, still dwelling in Genji's palace, in his quarters.

The Reizei Emperor, who has seen Lady Jeweled Garland, is eager for her to be presented at court, so Genji reluctantly lets her go. She spends one fabulous day and night at the Imperial Palace before Black Beard makes arrangements to have guards bring her to his home. The Emperor is greatly attracted to her, but Black Beard leaves no questions about her availability. She settles down with him and later in the story bears him several charming children.

31 - A

koishisa mo	even longing can
kanashiki koto mo	become a pitiful thing
shira nu nari	to avoid this
maki no hashira ni	I wish to be changed
nara mahoshikere	into a pillar of black pine

31 - 1

Lady Jeweled Garland chooses, of all her promising suitors, Black Beard, a married man with children. No one really understands her reasoning, but having the issue settled proves to one and all that Genji has not dallied with her before letting her be taken by this man. As Lady Jeweled Garland slowly realizes how superior Genji is to the man she has picked, she becomes so unhappy with her decision that her health is affected. When Genji makes a visit to her, in Black Beard's absence, he peeks through her curtains and sees that she is even more beautiful than he remembered and regrets giving her up so easily.

oritachi te	having disembarked
kumi wa mi ne domo	I scoop up without looking
watarigawa	water at the crossing
hito no se to hata	because I didn't think you'd cross
chigira zari shi wo	this stream with another lover

31 - 2

Lady Jeweled Garland's reply to Genji is made as she hides her face, saying, "this is unbelievably strange."

mitsusegawa	before crossing
watara nu saki ni	the river in the Land of the Dead
ikade nawo	my only wish is

31-1. There is an allusion to the Mitsuse River, in the mythical Land of the Dead, which echoes the mythical Greek River Styx. In Japan, however, there was the legend that a woman was helped across this river by her first lover. As relieved as everyone is that Black Beard has taken this position, Genji is eager to show Lady Jeweled Garland that he regrets not being able to help her after death in this way. The idea that he scoops up with his hand water from the river of death is a detail that poignantly evokes the many feelings he had while restraining himself from violating her. It is in such poems as this one that one understands the depth of feeling that these small poems can convey.

Kumi, from *kumu,* "ladle, scoop," can also mean "to consider." *Se* refers to "husband, lover" or "shoal, fording."

31-2. Next to Genji's poem, Lady Jeweled Garland's response comes off as almost glib and self-centered. This may have been Shikibu's intent—to show that Lady Jeweled Garland was not, in fact, worthy of being Genji's lover because she lacked the depth of feeling and

namida nomi wo no	that my stream of tears
awa to kie nan	may vanish like the foam

31 - 3

While Black Beard is involved in establishing his new relationship with Lady Jeweled Garland, he is having more troubles with his first wife. He wants to bring Lady Jeweled Garland, as his second wife, to his own home, because he finds the grand atmosphere in Genji's fine palace daunting, but his wife seems too unstable to risk bringing another woman into the household. One snowy evening, after dutifully perfuming Black Beard's robes with incense in preparation for his nightly visit to Lady Jeweled Garland, the wife opens the censer and dumps the smoldering embers and ashes on his head. Unable now to make his planned visit because he smells of singed hair, Black Beard sends a poem with his regrets to Lady Jeweled Garland.

kokoro sae	my heart as well
sora ni midare shi	as the sky is confused
yukimoyo ni	by falling snow
hitori sae tsuru	I have slept alone and cold
katashiki no sode	in the embrace of my own sleeves

31 - 4

The embers from the censer burn small holes in Black Beard's robes, making his clothes smell strongly of smoke and singed fabric. One of his women attendants whispers:

hitori i te	living alone
kogaruru mune no	because of the painful
kurushiki ni	burning in the heart
omoi amare ru	she didn't know what to do
honoo tozo mi shi	when these feelings flared up

ability to verbalize mature insights. The idea of wanting "to vanish like the foam" was already by this time a poetical cliché.

31-3. The combination of falling snow and falling ashes is perfect for this poem. The pivot also works admirably to then lead into Black Beard's complaint of having to sleep alone on such a cold night.

31 - 5

When she adds that he has been so unlike himself that even the servants cannot watch in silence, Black Beard responds to the lady-in-waiting:

uki koto wo	such dreadful events
omoi sawage ba	as if worry makes a noise
samazama ni	the sight of the scene
kuyuru kemuri zo	smolders with the noxious fumes
itodo tachisou	that also rise within me

31 - 6

It is decided that Black Beard's wife shall return to the home of her father, Prince Director of Military Affairs. She takes with her the three children: a girl of thirteen and two younger sons. The girl loves her father very much and fears she will never see him or her home again. She hopes to see him at least one more time before she is forced to leave, but he is with his Lady Jeweled Garland at the time. Desperate to make contact with her father, the girl writes a poem on a wood-colored paper and pins it with a needle to the pine pillar where she most often sat.

imawa tote	in these last moments
yado kare nu tomo	before I must leave this house
nare ki tsuru	oh pine pillar
maki no hashira wa	that I've come to know so well
ware wo wasuru na	do not ever forget me

31 - 7

The mother does not share her daughter's regret and is eager to place the blame where she feels it belongs.

nare ki to wa	though knowing it well
omoi izu tomo	you need to remember too
nani ni yori	the exact reason
tachi tomaru beki	for having to leave behind
maki no hashira zo	this pillar of pine

31-6. Murasaki Shikibu again shows in a poignant way how the contemporary morals of the society adversely affect children. That the girl sees the relationship between the pillar that holds up the house and her father adds resonance to the poem, and the fact that she does not leave her poem in his place in the home but on the spot where she most often sat underscores her despondency.

31-7. One certainly feels the righteous indignation of the wronged wife here. The depth of feeling is so accurate one wonders what the author experienced in order to so convincingly portray the emotions of such a moment. Still, the poem is perfectly constructed, with "the exact reason" being the centerpiece and crux of the situation, as well as the pivot of the poem.

31-8. In the story text, it is mentioned that the departing servants walk among the flowers and trees—bidding them farewell as they will probably never see them again. Chūjō's verse seems overloaded with images and ideas, to the extent that even her metaphors are perhaps mixed. It is not clear if she is referring to Black Beard's actions (being shallow) or using the image of clear water to instruct Moku on her duties and behavior in a compromised situation. The verse can be interpreted in many different ways.

31-9. Moku skillfully untangles the mysteries in Chūjō's verse by stating her opinion of what needs to be done to Black Beard as she compares him to the water between the rocks. She closes the poem with the admirable stance of pretending she is not important and is not long for this world.

31-10. Prince Firefly's poem seems rather contrived, as it must be to embrace his feelings that "his bird has flown" and to tie them in with the singing. It is interesting that Lady Jeweled Garland does not seem to reply to him. Shikibu shows how even princes can get stuck on one image. Often Prince

31 - 8

The breakup of Black Beard's family also means a separation for the servants. Moku, who is in Black Beard's service, will stay behind, but her best friend, Chūjō, has to leave with the wife and children. Chūjō bids farewell in a poem to Moku:

asa kere do	though shallow
iwama no mizu wa	water between the rocks
sumi hate te	yet clear to the end
yado moru kimi ya	you shall guard the house
kage hanaru beki	for the one who must leave

31 - 9

Moku did not know what to say.

tomokakumo	at any rate it seems
iwama no mizu no	the water between the rocks
musuboore	needs to be tied down
kage tomu beku mo	I don't think my shadow will
omooenu yo wo	linger longer in this world

31 - 10

Just before the New Year's celebrations, Black Beard, Genji, and the First Secretary's Captain have Lady Jeweled Garland presented at court and installed in her new rooms on the east side of the Shōkyōden Pavilion. Prince Firefly has come to court for the ceremony of songs but his attention is riveted on Lady Jeweled Garland. He thus takes the opportunity to send her a note.

miyamagi ni	in mountain trees
hane uchi kawashi	with their wings touching
iru tori no	birds alight
mata naku netaki	all the while chirping loudly
haru nimo aru kana	ah it is spring!
	or

in mountain trees
with their wings touching
birds alight
and I am very jealous
ah it is spring!

31 - 11

When the Reizei Emperor comes calling on Lady Jeweled Garland and she sees him in the moonlight, she is shocked at how much he resembles Genji. (He is, of course, Genji's son, not his brother, as others in the tale believe.) She is quite overcome in his presence by her feelings for Genji. When he asks her if she is grateful for his favors, she does not know what he means and hides her face behind her fan; the Emperor softly recites his poem to her:

nadote kaku	why am I so drawn
hai ai gataki	creeping with difficulty
murasaki wo	to lavender grass?
kokoro ni fukaku	has something deep in my heart has
omoi some ken	begun to move toward love?

31 - 12

Lady Jeweled Garland is unacquainted with the complicated ranking system at the palace and the various colors designating them. Has she already been advanced to the Third Rank? What does his talk of purple in his poem mean? She is very unsure of herself.

ikanaran	not even knowing
iro tomo shira nu	the meaning which the color
muraski wo	of lavender has
kokoroshi te koso	but watching it carefully
hito wa some kere	this one's heart is deeply touched

Firefly's poems have birds fluttering from tree to tree, just as Princess Safflower always has elegant robes in her poems.

31-11. For a young girl raised without a mother who has had to fend off men like Genji as well as her suitors, it must have been very disconcerting to find that, though now married, she is sent to court and basically offered as a consort to the Emperor. In addition, he looks and acts like Genji, whom she has repulsed for so long. It is no wonder that she finds it difficult to let the Emperor approach her.

31-12. Here we have another poem concerned with colors and ranking at court. It must have been very confusing, as the system often changed with regimes, and yet it was so very important. If the Emperor took a liking to a person, he could change their rank in order to make them more proximate to himself.

31 - 13

Black Beard is determined that his new wife will not fall into the arms of the Emperor, so he brusquely demands that Lady Jeweled Garland not stay a second night at the palace. Black Beard also wants to take this opportunity to bring her, not to Genji's villa, but to his home. The Emperor, however, is quite taken with Lady Jeweled Garland. Thus, when she is forced to leave, he follows her out to the carriage, where Black Beard is lurking. The Emperor finds her far more beautiful than it had been rumored and wishes he could say more to her. As he speaks his poem to her, he comments on how closely she is being guarded.

kokonoe ni	since nine-fold mists
kasumi hedate ba	hide the Imperial Palace
ume no hana	may not plum blossoms
tada kabakari mo	which are also hidden
nioi ko ji toya	leave behind a scent?

31 - 14

The Emperor asks if he may write to her, and, reluctant to make the him unhappy, Lady Jeweled Garland replies:

kabakari wa	only a fragrance
kaze nimo tsute yo	carried by a breeze calls you
hana no eda ni	to a flower branch
tachinarabu beki	standing side by side
nioi naku tomo	my perfume evaporates

31 - 15

Genji still feels that he has mishandled the affairs of Lady Jeweled Garland. He also believes Black Beard to be guileful and fears him. In spite of this, Genji wants to keep up his association with Lady Jeweled Garland, but dreads the repercussions if a big man like Black Beard should become jealous. Thus, one night, bored with the rain, Genji secretly sends a note to her lady-in-waiting, who was long in his service but has now gone with Lady Jeweled Garland to her new home.

31-13. The Emperor seems, in his allusion to the heightened enticement of plum blossoms that can only be detected by their fragrance, to be asking Lady Jeweled Garland for a promise of not forgetting him even though she has not seen him intimately.

kakitare te	falling so very hard
nodokeki koro no	in the quiet of these times
harusame ni	spring rain comes
furusatobito wo	asking if you remember
ikani shinobu ya	this friend in the old village

31 - 16

The lady-in-waiting shows Genji's poem to Lady Jeweled Garland in a moment when no one else is nearby. Not knowing if the lady-in-waiting knows or even suspects how unseemly Genji's behavior once was, Lady Jeweled Garland is too embarrassed to respond. Still, she is concerned enough to not want Genji to worry about her, so she writes:

nagame suru	continuous rain
noki no shizuku ni	makes a dripping from the eaves
sode nure te	and my sleeves as well
utakatabito wo	why shouldn't I miss a friend
shinoba zara me ya	even one as fleeting as foam?

31 - 17

Genji continues to think with renewed longing of Lady Jeweled Garland. In the Third Month, when the globeflowers bloom by her previous apartment, he stands looking at them and thinking of her. With no one near to hear, he speaks to himself, recalling a poem from the old anthologies about "wearing the robes of gardenia with a silent hue."

omowazu mo	it's still a surprise
ide no nakamichi	how on the road at Ide
hedatsu tomo	there was this parting
iwade zo kouru	the globeflowers somehow speak
yamabuki no hana	and are at the same time silent

31-17. The poem refered to is in the *Kokin Rokujō*. The Japanese name for gardenia literally means "mouthless flower." Japanese use the seeds of the gardenia as a food dye even today.

31 - 18

Genji has received a clutch of duck eggs, and he prepares a basket of some of them to send to Lady Jeweled Garland, with this verse— sounding as if he is her father.

onaji su ni
kaeri shi kai no
mie nu kana
ikanaru hito ka
te ni nigiru ran

this is like the nest
which hatched a bird's egg
now gone
what kind of a person has
taken it up in his hands?

31 - 19

Black Beard smiles wryly when he sees the gift and the note. He suspects Genji's motives at once and warns Lady Jeweled Garland about the inadvisability of visiting him. She is unhappy with Black Beard's behavior, so she merely says she does not know how to answer. Black Beard offers to write the reply, and she meekly assents.

su kakure te
kazu nimo ara nu
kari no ko wo
izukata ni kawa
torikakusu beki

hidden in a nest
and not counted among the eggs
was the wild-bird chick
how can it be said to have
been taken away and hidden?

31 - 20

In the meantime, the Miss of Ōmi, the other long-lost daughter of the First Secretary's Captain, continues to astound people with her unrestrained behavior. One evening in autumn, when several young gentlemen are gathered in her sister's rooms at court, she spies Lord Evening Mist among them and insists on offering her poem to him in such clear, loud tones, it is heard by all.

okitsu fune
yorube namiji ni
tadayowa ba

boat upon high seas
if you are drifting without
a harbor or course

saosashi yora n	give me a call and I'll row
tomari oshie yo	out to teach you about ports

31 - 21

Lord Evening Mist is startled to hear such uncouth words in these elegant rooms, but, as a proper gentleman and Genji's son, he is able to fend her off:

yorube nami	even a boatman
kaze no sawagasu	driven off course by winds
funabito mo	would not want to land
omowa nu kata ni	on the rocky shore that lies
iso zutai se zu	in that unthinkable place

32

UME GA E
A BRANCH OF PLUM

New Year's Day to Third Month of Genji's thirty-ninth year

With the settling of Lady Jeweled Garland's affairs, Genji is free to concentrate on the elaborate preparations to offer his own daughter to the Emperor. Even such a small thing as the fragrance the Akashi Princess will use is a concern for the whole household. Genji declares a contest in which every lady will concoct a fragrance from old or new recipes. To Genji's surprise, Princess Morning Glory joins the contest and enters her concoction in a jar with a painted plum branch. Prince Firefly is the judge, and afterwards there is a party with music. This concert introduces the younger son of the First Secretary's Captain, Lord Rose Plum, who takes his name from a song he sings about "a branch of plum."

After the party, Genji continues his preparations for presenting the Akashi Princess at court. He orders scribes to begin copying scrolls for her personal library—another delay that makes the Emperor only more eager to meet her. Finally the ceremony is held, to great success, which re-ignites the old rivalry with the First Secretary's Captain, whose daughters did not do as well.

The First Secretary's Captain also feels his plan to keep Lord Evening Mist from his daughter Lady Wild Goose in the Clouds has backfired, since Lord Evening Mist has rapidly risen in rank and has had several promising offers from fathers eager to marry off their daughters. He is also unaware that Lord Evening Mist is very different from what his father, Genji.

32 - A

ametsuchi ni	in heaven and earth
haru atarashiku	the freshness of spring again
ki tari keri	has come to be
hikaru genji no	beautiful for the noble daughter
mimusume no tame	of the radiant Prince Genji

32 - 1

Among the activities in preparation for sending the Akashi Princess to court, Genji initiates a contest among his household members to concoct a perfume for the princess. Each woman sets to work grinding secret ingredients from old recipes. Princess Morning Glory has kneaded her scents into two rather large balls. One she places in a jar with pine decorations and the other in one with a painting of a plum branch. She attaches her poem to a plum branch from which most of the petals have fallen.

hana no ka wa	the flowers' scent
chiri ni shi sode ni	faded from the sleeves
tomara ne do	unable to stay
utsura n sode ni	when the sleeves change
asaku shima me ya	since it sank in too little?

32 - 2

Genji's answer to Princess Morning Glory, composed on rose-colored paper, is tied to a sprig of red plum blossoms.

hana no eda ni	the branch of flowers
itodo kokoro wo	still more dear to my heart
shimuru kana	perfumes so deeply
hito no togamuru	people will suspect
ka oba tsutsume do	I'm hiding a secret

32-2. The poem's implication is that people will think he is seeing a lover secretly, because his robes were so deeply scented by her when their romance was active. This is not true, because Princess Morning Glory never gave in to Genji's desires, but it seems the two are now reminiscing as if the affair meant more to them than it did.

32 - 3

On the night before the Akashi Princess is to be initiated into the court, Genji holds an informal musical evening at his palace. His family and many young men attend, bringing harps and flutes. Prince Firefly recites a poem as the wine is being brought in.

uguisu no	will I be carried
koe niya itodo	farther away by the voice
akugare n	of the nightingale?
kokoro shime tsuru	I'm already enchanted by
hana no atari ni	the neighboring flowers

32 - 4

Genji replies to Prince Firefly:

iro mo ka mo	honor us
utsuru bakari ni	by sharing our blossoms
kono haru wa	this spring
hana saku yado wo	don't leave until you've taken
kare zu mo ara nan	on their hue and fragrance

32 - 5

Lord Oak Tree is the eldest of the First Secretary's Captain's sons and a close childhood friend of Lord Evening Mist. As Lord Oak Tree pours wine for Lord Evening Mist, who has played his flute so splendidly that evening, he recites:

uguisu no	though the nightingale's
negura no eda mo	nest is made of only twigs
nabiku made	it starts to flutter
nao fuki tōse	even at midnight due to
yowa no fuetake	the sound of the flute

32 - 6

Lord Evening Mist replies:

kokoro ari te	now what do you want?
kaze no yogu meru	the wind should be kept from
hana no ki ni	the flowery tree
toriae nu made	or just until that moment
fuki ya yoru beki	when I should begin to blow?

32 - 7

Lord Rose Plum, the younger brother of Lord Oak Tree, laughs as he adds his verse to the festivities.

kasumi dani	if the haze had not
tsuki to hana to wo	come out to go in between
hedate zu ba	the moon and flowers
negura no tori mo	otherwise even the bird nests
hokorobi namashi	might have burst into blossom

32 - 8

At dawn, when Prince Firefly is ready to leave, Genji has two sealed jars of perfume and a set of informal court robes sent to his carriage.

hana no ka wo	the scent of flowers
enaranu sode ni	on these most elegant sleeves
utsushi temo	no matter how it comes
koto ayamari to	will not my lady accuse
imo ya togame n	me of having misbehaved?

32 - 9

Genji comments, "How sad!" and recites this response.

mezurashi to	how splendid it is
furusatobito mo	even for an old acquaintance

32-8. *Imo* is a familiar way for a man to refer to women he is related to, a sister, wife, or lover. Prince Firefly is not married, and his verse thus has a twist of comic irony.

machi zo mi n	to experience
hana no nishiki wo	the master of the house coming
ki te kaeru kimi	home in flowers and brocades

32 - 10

Since childhood, Lady Wild Goose in the Clouds and Lord Evening Mist have been close friends. Unable to live with their parents, they were raised in the palace of their grandmother. When they reached their teen years, though, they were separated on the command of her father. Lord Evening Mist nonetheless continues to send Lady Wild Goose in the Clouds affectionate notes. Suddenly there is a palace rumor that Lord Evening Mist is going to marry the daughter of Prince Nakatsu. Lady Wild Goose in the Clouds is on her verandah weeping at the thought, when a note from Lord Evening Mist arrives. Reading it, she can detect no change in his manner.

tsurenasa wa	such a heartlessness
ukiyo no tsune ni	as is often in this world
nariyuku wo	happens and yet
wasure nu hito ya	is not a person who cannot
hito ni kotonaru	ever forget you not different?

32 - 11

Lady Wild Goose in the Clouds shows her unhappiness with Lord Evening Mist for not admitting of his new affair. Try as he may, Lord Evening Mist cannot figure out her message. He even turns the paper this way and that, hoping to decipher her meaning.

kagiri tote	in the end saying
wasure gataki wo	you will not be the one to forget
wasururu mo	and then forgetting
ko ya yo ni nabiku	doesn't this seem to be the one
kokoro naru ran	who has gone the way of the world?

33

FUJI NO URAHA
WISTERIA LEAVES

Third to Tenth Month of Genji's thirty-ninth year

The First Secretary's Captain decides to repair the situation with the lovelorn Lord Evening Mist while they are attending the funeral of the captain's mother, the Great Princess, who is Lord Evening Mist's grandmother, but a passing shower destroys the moment and opportunity. Later, the First Secretary's Captain invites Lord Evening Mist to his home with the excuse of viewing his fabulous wisteria flowers, but his real intent is to dissolve their differences in poetry and wine. Pretending to be too drunk to go home, Lord Evening Mist asks his good friend, Lord Oak Tree, if he may sleep off the discomfort in his rooms. Lord Oak Tree instead leads Lord Evening Mist to his sister's room, with the father's unspoken approval. At long last the childhood lovers are united.

Genji and Murasaki attend the Kamo Festival together. The occasion reminds Genji of the situation many years ago, how at this same festival Lady Heartvine and Lady of the Sixth Ward competed for a coveted position for their carriages. Genji uses the opportunity to pontificate on his theories and lecture Murasaki on how to be a good person and wife. The end result is that Genji gets his way on a matter close to his heart. Murasaki has always resented the Akashi Lady, which was one of her reasons for wanting to live at a distance from Genji's palace, but she gives in and allows the Akashi Lady to move to the Sixth Ward palace to be near her daughter, who is now a consort of the Emperor.

Lord Evening Mist and Lady Wild Goose in the Clouds take over the Third Avenue mansion, where the two had grown up. The retired Emperor and the reigning Emperor make a visit to Genji's Sixth Ward palace, and there are poems, dancing, and many cups of wine. The coming together of so many men who bear a resemblance to one another only points up how special Genji's good looks are. The chapter ends on a note of reconciliation and peaceful unity between the families reigning supreme.

---

33 - A

fujibana no	one cannot discern
moto no nezashi wa	the origin of the roots of
shira ne domo	wisteria flowers
eda wo kawase ru	the branches have intertwined
shiro to murasaki	the white ones with the purple

---

33 - 1

When the First Secretary's Captain hears rumors that Lord Evening Mist is going to be married off to the daughter of Prince Nakatsu, he begins to regret that he hid from him his daughter Lady Wild Goose in the Clouds. When he meets the lord at the funeral services for the Great Princess, he determines to talk to him seriously, but a sudden rain shower interrupts the conversation as they quickly seek shelter. Later, when the wisteria are at their finest at the villa, the First Secretary's Captain takes the opportunity to invite Lord Evening Mist to see them. He sends his note attached to a magnificent spray of perfect blossoms.

waga yado no	here at my villa
fuji no iro koki	deep colors of wisteria
tasogare ni	in the evening
tazune yawa ko nu	invite you to come before
haru no nagori wo	the last trace of spring departs

33-A. Akiko Yosano's poem, in tracing the tangled growth of the wisteria, also alludes to the contemporary history of the tale, how the Fujiwara Clan rose to supreme importance as its daughters paired with emperors. By virture of its imperial connections through its daughters, the clan acted as a "shadow emperor."

33 - 2

This is the invitation—to come not only as a visitor but perhaps, too, as a son-in-law—for which Lord Evening Mist has waited so long. Still, the young man's answer is very cool.

nakanaka ni	hesitant
ori ya madowan	I wonder if I should break off
fuji no hana	the wisteria flower
tasogaredoki no	I grope my way through
tadotadoshiku ba	gathering shades of dusk

33 - 3

After many cups of wine and scholarly talks, the First Secretary's Captain decides the moment has come to be honest with Lord Evening Mist about, as he names it, "the under leaves of the wisteria." Lord Evening Mist seems not to understand the significance of *urana* (under leaves), which echoes *uratokete* (being honest), so the First Secretary's Captain gives him this verse of his own.

murasaki ni	as just an excuse
kagoto wa kake n	let us use for example purple
fuji no hana	wisteria flowers
matsu yori sugi te	though we realize the pine
ureta kere domo	regrettably is overgrown

33 - 4

To cover his deep emotions, Lord Evening Mist takes a sip of wine before reciting:

ikukaeri	how many the times
tsuyukeki haru wo	because of the tears in spring
sugushi ki te	has it come and gone
hana no himo toku	now the string of flowers opens
ori ni au ran	it is time for us to come together

33-3. The First Secretary's Captain refers to himself as a pine tree; the reference to the pine tree being overgrown alludes to his earlier hasty and presumptive actions, by which the pair were separated.

33-4. *Himo* means "string" or "cord," and *toku* means "undo, untie, thaw, become friendly." *Himo toku,* a metaphor for a man and woman sleeping together, can also mean "to flower" or "open." The phrase is heavily laden with sexual innuendoes, but it is very appropriate under wisteria, which bear strings of clustered flowers.

33 - 5

As Lord Evening Mist pours a cup of wine for him, Lord Oak Tree replies:

taoyame no	a graceful woman's
sode ni magae ru	sleeves can be mistaken for
fuji no hana	wisteria flowers
miru hito kara ya	think of how much lovelier
iro mo masara n	the color is when cared for

33 - 6

Later in the evening, on the pretense of not feeling well because of too much wine, Lord Evening Mist asks Lord Oak Tree to take him to his room to spend the night. Lord Oak Tree instead leads Lord Evening Mist to the rooms of his sister, Lady Wild Goose in the Clouds. She has overheard the bawdy songs her brothers have been singing about "a fence of rushes" and is offended by the reference. Lord Evening Mist assures her he would have liked to have sung about "the stout fence of Kawaguchi," a folk song about the barrier at the river's mouth and the guard who watches there. Lady Wild Goose in the Clouds answers him with her poem.

asaki na wo	a river's mouth
ii nagashi keru	how shallow to gush
kawaguchi wa	about my name
ikaga morashi shi	why did it leak out past
seki no aragaki	a barrier of a stout fence?

33 - 7

Lord Evening Mist finds her anger delightful as he replies:

mori ni keru	for one who guarded
kikuda no seki no	the famous checkpoint
kawaguchi no	at the river's mouth
asaki ni nomi wa	it wasn't mere shallowness
owase zara nan	that caused it to leak

33 - 8

Lord Evening Mist stays as long as possible in Lady Wild Goose in the Cloud's rooms that night but is just able to leave before daylight. Later, when his note arrives, all of her women are laughing and joking. Even her father shows up to see the new husband's poem.

togamu na yo	don't blame me
shinobini shiboru	for secretly wringing out sleeves
te mo tayumi	my hands are too tired
kyō arawaruru	to have to show up today
sode no shizuku wo	to wring out one more drop

33 - 9

At the lustrations before the Kamo Festival, Lord Evening Mist sees Sir Reflected Brilliance's daughter, whom he had visited before and who is now very unhappy to see him married to someone else. Lord Evening Mist sends a note to her through the many people surrounding her.

nanito kaya	how do you call it?
kyō no kazashi yo	this sprig in my hair today
katsu mi tsutsu	on one hand I think
obomeku made mo	it has been so long that
nari ni keru kana	I cannot think of the name

33 - 10

One wonders what the note means to her. She manages to answer, despite the confusion of being assisted into a carriage.

kazashi temo	if put in one's hair
katsu tadora ruru	one should inquire at once
kusa no na wa	the name of the plant
katsura wo ori shi	if one is a laurel-crowned
hito ya shiru ran	scholar he would surely know

33-9. Heartvine, a climber with heart-shaped leaves and hibiscus-like flesh-colored blossoms, was worn in the hair for this springtime festival. Lord Evening Mist wants to forget he had an affair with her now that he is married. In this way, also, he is not like his father, Genji.

33-10. Lord Evening Mist, it will be recalled, spent years studying while many of his contemporaries outpaced him in rank. He is reminded by this poem of those years without rank, a fact that still sits sorely with him.

33 - 11

Lord Evening Mist has never forgotten the nursemaid of Lady Wild Goose in the Clouds who once scorned him for having a mere green-sleeve rank. So one day he hands her a chrysanthemum tinged by frost, with this verse.

asamidori	the pale green
wakaba no kiku wo	of a chrysanthemum petal
tsuyu nite mo	who would have guessed
koki murasaki no	that a spot of dew could deepen
iro to kake ki ya	its color to such a purple?

33 - 12

The nursemaid is both pleased and confused as she replies to Lord Evening Mist:

futaba yori	from infant leaves
nadataru sono no	in such a well-known garden
kiku nare ba	the chrysanthemum
asaki iro waku	appears to rise in color
tsuyu mo nakari ki	without any dew at all

33 - 13

Conditions in the Second Avenue residence of the First Secretary's Captain are somewhat crowded, so Lady Wild Goose in the Clouds and Lord Evening Mist move into the Third Avenue villa, where both had lived as children with their grandmother. Since her death, the garden has become vastly overgrown. Lord Evening Mist has the brook cleared, orders the rooms redecorated, and calls back the women who had worked there previously. One evening, as Lord Evening Mist and Lady Wild Goose in the Clouds sit on the verandah viewing the garden in its autumn glory, he speaks:

nare koso wa	guardian of rocks
iwa moru aruji	you're the master of this house
mishihito no	where has she gone

33-11. When chrysanthemums are frostbitten, the petals become a darker shade of their original hue and then turn brown. The phrase "without any dew at all" refers to his new marriage and the attendant change in his rank.

33-12. She seems to be ridiculing him for not achieving a sexual relationship with her lady earlier.

yukue wa shiru ya	the one whose image was here
yado no mashimizu	reflected in these clear waters?

33 - 14

Lady Wild Goose in the Clouds replies to her husband:

nakihito wa	even the image
kage dani mie zu	of the departed has withdrawn
tsurenaku te	how heartless
kokoro wo yare ru	yet it floats away the gloom
isarai no mizu	water flowing in the garden

33 - 15

On his way home from the court, the First Secretary's Captain happens to stop by the Third Avenue villa because he has heard the garden is now at its autumn best. As he visits with the company there, he notices that someone has written down their poems. He says that he, too, would like to ask the brook their questions, but he doubts they are interested in his senile thoughts.

sonokami no	in the old days
oiki wa ubemo	the honorable and ancient pine
kuchi ni keri	had moldered away
ue shi komatsu mo	the seedling which was planted
koke oi ni keri	is now overgrown with moss

33 - 16

Upon hearing his verse, Lord Evening Mist's old nurse decides to add her sentiments, which amuse him but embarrass Lady Wild Goose in the Clouds.

izure wo mo	I now depend on
kage tozo tanomu	the protective shade of
futaba yori	young leaves

nezashi kawase ru whose roots have been intertwined
matsu no suezue since they were seedling pines

33 - 17

The Reizei Emperor invites the retired Suzaku Emperor to join him in a state visit to Genji's Sixth Ward palace in the autumn. The excursion is so fine, people recall with pleasure how a similar festival was held at the Suzaku residence many years ago. Now it is the son of the First Secretary's Captain who dances to the traditional music, so beautifully that the Emperor takes off his robe to drape it over the boy's narrow shoulders. Genji asks someone to pick for him a chrysanthemum, which he presents to the First Secretary's Captain with his poem.

iro masaru	hues only deepen
magaki no kiku mo	even the chrysanthemum
oriorini	at the brushwood fence
sode uchikake shi	recalls when sleeve splashed sleeve
aki wo kou rashi	that autumn so very long ago

33 - 18

At that moment a sudden autumn shower passes over the party. It is as if the moment was right for the exchange of poems. The First Secretary's Captain responds:

murasaki no	this chrysanthemum
kumo ni magae ru	could be mistaken for
kiku no hana	a purple cloud
nigori naki yo no	such clearness in these times
hoshi ka tozo miru	seems to shine like a star

33-17. In the beginning of chapter 7, Genji and the First Secretary's Captain danced "Waves of the Blue Ocean" together before the ladies of the court. It was this dance that caused the exchange of tanka 7-1 and 7-2 between Genji and Lady of the Wisteria Apartment.

33 - 19

The evening breezes scatter more of the colorful leaves upon the ground; they seem to form a pattern as rich and colorful as the brocades of the people lining the galleries. The Suzaku Emperor speaks:

aki wo he te autumn passes
shigure furi nuru with the showers of early winter
satobito mo even the villagers
kakaru momiji no have never seen in this season
ori wo koso mi ne finer colors of autumn

33 - 20

The Reizei Emperor feels that, though this day is uniquely glorious, it cannot go unchallenged.

yo no tsune no lest we think that these
momiji toya miru colored leaves are ordinary
inishie no a very long time ago
tameshi ni hike ru gardens were the inspiration
niwa no nishiki wo for Japanese brocades

Afterword: *The Tale of Genji* as a Book

Because so many of the questions about how Murasaki Shikibu came to write *The Tale of Genji* are impossible to answer definitively, scholars through out the past millennium have lent their minds to solving the many riddles the work creates. Most of what we believe is conjecture, and there is always another learned expert waiting in the wings who has a different opinion.

It is thought that Murasaki Shikibu probably began writing the story around A.D. 1002 or 1003. It was surely written after the death of her husband and before she entered the service of Empress Shōshi (Akiko), consort of Emperor Ichijō, in 1005–6. There is a reference in *The Sarashina Diary*, written in about 1021, that mentions that the author (another literary woman at the same court) was given the fifty-plus scrolls of the novel, so we know that the series had been completed by then. During the time of her own service to Empress Shōshi, Shikibu also kept a diary *(Murasaki Shikibu Nikki)*, between autumn 1008 and 1010, in which she recorded the events of the imperial scene, but she gives very little information there about her work as a novelist. She does mention that her work *The Tale of Genji* was read to Emperor Ichijō, who then ordered the finest papers, brushes, and inks for additional copies.

It seems that the book was written in chapters, each of which consisted of a scroll. Although at this time, the Japanese were already printing Buddhist texts with carved wooden blocks, novels and diaries continued, up until the nineteenth century, to be copied by hand in calligraphy. A reading of the complete work reveals variations in style and outlook, which have suggested to some authorities that perhaps more than one person contributed to the work.

However, it is usually agreed that the first thirty-three chapters are probably the work of one author and that chapter 33 presents a logical conclusion. It has been argued that Shikibu was male (a theory now put to rest) and that even the thirty-three chapters show a marked split in them, following first one female main character, Murasaki, and then another, Tamakazura (Lady Jeweled Garland). Although the arrangement of the chapters we now follow has been done to make the story as sequential as possible, some of the chapters do overlap, and occasionally events are mentioned or characters referred to before they make their appearance later in the story.

It has been argued that Shikibu meant to end her story with chapter 33, with the Shining Prince at the pinnacle of his success and all the love affairs and dilemmas resolved. Whether Shikibu, after some lapse of time and life, picked up the story again, which is now more subdued with sadness and regrets, to continue another eight scrolls until Genji dies at the end of chapter 41, or someone else wrote the sequel, we cannot know. It has also been proposed that Shikibu's own daughter, Daini no Sammi, continued the story, if not at chapter 33, then perhaps the last thirteen chapters, which are even more disparate in the handling of the altogether different characters and philosophical outlook.

Even fifty-four as the total number of chapters is volatile, since there is reported to have been a chapter titled "Kumogakure" (disappearance in the clouds), which may have described the death and funeral of Genji. Some claim that this chapter existed only as a title, indicating that the grief of describing such sad events was too much to write down. Others claim the chapter has only been lost and not yet found or was suppressed and is thus lost.

The oldest copies of the chapters are those saved from two hundred years after the tale was written down, so much of the original has been lost and is therefore open to speculation.

The one question that has occupied scholars for the longest time is how a woman could write a story that stands like a great mountain above the rolling hills of the known literature of that time. Yes, there were oral tales and romances, some that are available still today. It is possible that there was an oral version of some of *The Tale of Genji,* and there is certainly evidence that a person much like Genji lived about seventy years before Shikibu's birth. However, Shikibu's work is so much more complex, more developed, and bestowed with such a sweeping scope that one can only admit she was surely a genius who built on the available literature to make it soar.[1]

MURASAKI SHIKIBU

Although Shikibu's date of birth cannot be set with certainty, authorities now accept the date of 973, and estimate that her death occurred sometime after 1013—the last time she was mentioned in

[1] An interesting comparison of talents is found by reading Izumi Shikibu's diary (written at about the same time), in which she attempts to write of her affair with a prince as if it was viewed by Murasaki Shikibu; Izumi's style of prose lacks the drive and attention to detail. Being a great poet, Izumi's poems are very powerful, but her prose barely rises above that in the much less esteemed *Tales of Ise.*

another person's writings.[2] It is commonly held that she died at the young age of forty-two. She was the daughter of Fujiwara Tametoki, who early in his career was in the Ministry of Ceremonies (Shikibushō), and the name she took, Shikibu, comes from the name of this office. It was the custom in those times for a woman to take a name from the office held by her father or husband. Murasaki was a nickname taken from the lead female character in her novel for her own name of Tō (for Fujiwara) Shikibu.

Her father was a fourth-generation descendent of Fujiwara no Fuyutsugu, the founder of "the flowering fortune" of the Fujiwara family, while her mother was a fifth-generation descendant of the same man. Murasaki's great-grandfather was one of the leading poets included in the *Gosenshu*, an imperial anthology of *waka* poems. Fujiwara Tametoki was known as a *waka* poet with a special talent for *kanshi* (poetry written in Chinese) and was also a scholar who taught his son Chinese and poetry. In Shikibu's diary, she relates how much faster she learned Chinese, by eavesdropping from behind the curtains, than her brother, which would account for her ease in quoting Chinese poetry and events from the literature.

Donald Keene relates the story that,

> after ten years without office, Tametoki was appointed governor of Awaji, an inferior post. Disappointed, he composed a *kanshi* describing his grief and presented it to Emperor Ichijō. The *kanshi* so impressed the Emperor that he directed Fujiwara no Michinaga, who had already appointed a relative to be governor of Echizen, to cancel this appointment and give the post to Tametoki instead.[3]

From Shikibu's poems we can surmise that she was in love in 996. She had followed her father to his post in Echizen, probably to avoid marrying her second cousin, Fujiwara no Nobutaka. But staying two years in this primitive outpost was so depressing, she returned to the capital and shortly thereafter, in autumn, married the wealthy and prominent Fujiwara no Nobutaka. He was almost twice her age and had several other wives and concubines, as well as a son as old as Shikibu. It is easy to construe the romance between the young Genji and his stepmother, Fujitsubo (Lady of the Wisteria Apartment), as being grounded in Shikibu's real-life experiences with her stepsons.

However, judging from the surviving poems exchanged between husband and wife, their married life was happy. The year after her marriage, she had a daughter, who was later known as Daini no Sammi. In the third year of their marriage, Nobutaka died, perhaps the result of the flulike epidemic that plagued Kyoto. Murasaki was cast adrift in her

[2] Annie Shepley Omori and Kochi Doi, *Diaries of Court Ladies of Old Japan* (Tokyo: Kenkyusha Co., 1935), p. 407.

[3] Donald Keene, *Seeds in the Heart: Japanese Literature from Earliest Times to the Late Sixteenth Century* (New York: Henry Holt, 1993), p. 479.

sorrow, as evidenced in the poems she wrote in those years.

It is suspected that she began to write *The Tale of Genji* during this time of loss. Legend has it that she wrote part of it at Ishiyama Temple, which overlooks Lake Biwa, and tourists are still shown the very room with the inkstone that she used! They conveniently forget that the temple burned to the ground a few years after her supposed stay.

Evidently some of the chapters were already known when she was appointed a lady-in-waiting to Consort Shōshi in 1005 or 1006, as part of the literary circles with which the various women of the court surrounded themselves. Her diary has been listed as written between 1008 and 1010 and covers her years in service to Shōshi, beginning with the birth of Shōshi's first son. After relating the birth event in detail, the diary rapidly becomes vacuous and fragmented—as if, as the author claims, "her desire to write has been extinguished." The exactitude that gives her novel its lasting power was perverted when Shikibu describes in her diary the fashions at court. In addition to her sharp-tongued evaluations of the other ladies of the court, she penned this tableau of herself:

> Pretty and coy, shrinking from sight, unsociable, proud, fond of romance, vain and poetic, looking down upon others with a jealous eye—such is the opinion of those who do not know me, but after seeing me they say, "You are wonderfully gentle to meet with; I cannot identify you with that imagined one." I see that I have been slighted, hated, and looked down upon as an old gossip, and I must bear it, for it is my destiny to be solitary.[4]

Shikibu is credited with two other *monogatari: Yoru no Nezame* (Wakefulness at Night) and *Hamamatsu Chūnagon Monogatari* (The Tale of the Hamamatsu Middle Counselor). These stories, in addition to her diary, and poetry, which was included in several of the imperial anthologies, have contributed to the place she holds in the hearts of her Japanese audiences. There is hardly a person in Japan who has not memorized at least one of her poems, which have been used in education as examples of not only poetry, but also of conduct and sensitivity.

With the current interest in women's issues, there is a new attraction for Shikibu's work, not only for the picture she paints of the lives of the many women portrayed a thousand years ago, but, more importantly, for her insight into the hearts of the women as revealed in her poetry. When all the praise for Shikibu's novel has been laid out in rows, one is still astounded at her ability to recognize emotional states, give them images and actions that carry them accurately across the ages to illuminate issues for today's women and men.

As Donald Keene writes: "*The Tale of Genji* is the central work of Japanese literature. It was read and imitated by genera-

---

4 Omori and Doi, *Diaries,* p. 137.

tions of court writers, and was adapted for use in different forms of drama, not only the aristocratic Noh, but the plebeian Bunraku (puppet) and Kabuki theaters."[5]

VERSIONS OF RE-VERSIONS

It is known that Murasaki Shikibu wrote the original manuscript in *kana,* or *onna de,* a writing method used by women and based on a sound-unit script instead of Chinese characters. This directly facilitated the setting down of the sounds heard in oral transmission, so that reading the manuscript sounded almost like the stories as they had been spoken. At this time, women used this simpler way of writing rather than the male system of Chinese ideograms.

Over the years, as the language changed—often drastically, so that the old versions could no longer be read, even by scholars—Shikibu's story had, again and again, to undergo translation. In this century, another famous woman poet, Akiko Yosano, undertook the enormous job of translating the story into modern Japanese.

Yosano had become a celebrity for her collection of tanka poems entitled *Midaregami* (tangled hair), which rocked the poetry world when it was published on August 5, 1901. The academic tanka poets' groups, as well as the general public, were shocked and delighted by this young girl who was unafraid to write about any thought, any part of her body or soul. The book had "repercussions, not only in poetry, but in all areas of Japanese literature."[6]

After the excitement surrounding her book of poems died down, Akiko Yosano went on to write not only thousands of additional tanka, but an amazing stream of literature. Married to the well-known poet Tekkan Yosano and the mother of eleven children, Yosano wrote in order to support her family. Her literary production included essays, criticism, children's literature, fairy tales, and the complete translations of *Genji Monogatari.* According to one scholar, Yosano read *Genji* over and over as a girl until she was essentially bilingual in classical and modern Japanese.[7] Her first translation, published 1912–13, abridged the earlier chapters, which were familiar to her audience. She later returned to the work to make a full translation. This version was made even more valuable by her addition to each of Shikibu's chapters a tanka of her own reproduced in calligraphy, which acts as an overture. The six volumes of the work were published between 1938 and 1939.

TANKA AS POETRY

Tanka is Japanese for *tan* (short) and *ka*

[5] Keene, *Seeds in the Heart,* p. 508.

[6] Akiko Yosano, *Tangled Hair: Selected Tanka from Midaregami,* trans. Sanford Goldstein and Seishi Shinoda (Rutland, Vt.: Charles E. Tuttle, 1987), p. 18.

[7] Gillian Gaye Rowley, *Yosano Akiko and the Tale of Genji,* Michigan Monograph Series in Japanese Studies 28 (Ann Arbor: Center for Japanese Studies, University of Michigan, 2000), p. 178.

(an alternative of *ku,* for verse), a form of poetry older than the recorded history of Japan. In the *Kojiki (Records of Ancient Matters),* written in A.D. 712, the earliest written account of the country's oral history and oldest surviving Japanese book, many of the stories end with or contain examples of poetry.[8]

Although the form is succinct and compact, its very small size seems to have tremendous elasticity, allowing it to change and grow in content while remaining basically the same in form and technique for more than 1,400 years; a truly amazing phenomenon when one studies the many poetry techniques that have come and gone in other cultures.

In its long history, the tanka has had many roles. First known as *uta* (song), the tanka functioned as a song or incantation, a way of speaking with or about the gods, not unlike what is believed to be the first use of poetry in other cultures. By the time Japanese history was recorded, the earliest employment of the religious song form had already evolved away from its original use.

As with so many things, vestiges of the origin remain in the way tanka are read aloud in imperial ceremonies, still chanted with tone intervals comparable to liturgical intonations as we know them. The preface to the *Kokinshū (Imperial Anthology of Ancient and Modern Poetry),* compiled in 905, states that the tanka was a way to speak with gods and demons.[9] The later adoption and use of tanka in Noh theater was the result of the belief that the sequence of sounds in tanka contained supernatural powers. Noh theater grew out of legendary accounts and replays of humans interacting with gods, ghosts, and spirits intended to keep alive these incidents of mythological history. Noh plays contain both prose and lyrical components, and it is no surprise that the tanka was the poetic form used for the chanted monologues.

At this point a few words regarding the form are in order. A tanka is composed of five phrases containing either five or seven sound units, each represented by a single *kana.* The sound units consist (usually) of a consonant and vowel. From ancient times, the Japanese felt their phrases naturally fell into the length of five or seven sound units. The *uta,* later called the *waka,* and now named tanka, all exhibit a pattern of 5-7-5-7-7, to make thirty-one sound units in all. These units are much shorter than English syllables, thus defeating any attempt to copy this attribute of the genre.

The Japanese recognize exactly when a phrase ends and another one begins, so even when they write the first three phrases in one long vertical line and the two seven sound-unit phrases in one shorter line, the reader knows exactly where each phrase ends and the next begins. In English, we honor this system by inserting a line break, giving our English versions five lines.

No matter which way the poem is

---

[8] Donald L. Philippi, trans., *Kojiki* (Tokyo: University of Tokyo Press, 1968).

[9] Keene, *Seeds in the Heart,* p. 246

written, the inner syntax reveals the original fundamental elements. These come from the fact that the tanka is seen as having two parts: the *kami no ku* (upper stanza), the first three phrases, and the *shimo no ku* (the lower stanza), containing two phrases of equal length.

The use of a pivot word *(kakekotoba)* is a technique that is often found in poetry writing, but in the tanka it achieves its full potential as a means of connecting a facet of nature with a corresponding emotional state. The pivot word often occurs in the third line of a tanka. When this is ignored in translation, the verse usually begins to fall apart.

As one can imagine in a poetry form as old as the tanka, nearly every rule has come into and likewise gone out of fashion. Nevertheless, there are today in Japan several schools of tanka, each believing it alone knows the best way to write a tanka. Most of the controversies center around content, with some believing the tanka should stay centered firmly in nature and its observation. Others, and the more modern poets, believe the tanka should consist of expressions of the author's innermost feelings. Still others believe a mixture is wisest, with emotions played against a matrix of nature, as was dictated by the first manifesto of Ki no Tsurayuki (884–946). Just reading his remarks, which preface the *Kokinshū*, gives one a feeling for the Japanese way with words:

> Japanese poetry has its roots in the human heart and burgeons into the many different kinds of leaves of words. We who live in this world are constantly affected by different experiences, and we express our thoughts in words, in terms of what we have seen and heard. . . . Poetry moves heaven and earth, stirs the invisible gods and demons to pity, makes sweet the ties between men and women, and brings comfort to the fierce heart of the warrior.[10]

In spite of such beautiful and clear instructions, discussions still rage today over the use of foreign words, diction, and such nebulous factors as tone, taste, and spirit. Over the centuries, the placing of the caesura, or line break, has vacillated between the end of the second, the third, or the fourth line.

However, there are certain indications that point to the work as being either a tanka or tanka-like. The most obvious characteristic is the quality of being subjective. This is contrasted to the tradition of the more widely known haiku, which are characterized by objectivity, with any emotion hidden in the images, if it is there at all. However, in this century this aspect is becoming blurred, as some haiku have become more subjective.

The tanka also sports with the Japanese love of punning. Place names offer a wealth of opportunity to join the poem (and the feelings) with a certain place. This aspect can cause one to look anew

[10] Ibid.

at English names of places and even the street on which one lives. It is amazing what thoughts arise when a place name is deeply contemplated: Oxford, Bridgeport, Anchor Bay, Lake Superior, or Land's End.

The tanka furthers this practice with the concept of linkage. Some of our most interesting contemporary poetry exhibits this technique, also. Previously, a connectedness between various images was shown by the use of metaphors and simile in English poetry. Now the relationship is so easily understood that simply juxtaposing two related images causes the modern reader to associate them immediately, as the Japanese have been doing for 1,400 years. It is the study of how this is done, and the ways in which to do it, that brings so many English poets to study the translations of Japanese tanka, whether they write in the form or simply wish to expand their skills with the stretching of a new genre.

In old Japan, the tanka was used as a scale on which to measure one's education, spiritual development, degree of culture, and sensitivity to feelings and nature. Tanka were used as a form of communication between friends and lovers, especially among the educated and members of the imperial court. This aspect is the one most celebrated and is related in history with the idea of two lovers meeting secretly for a night, having to part at dawn when the man leaves, only to carry his thoughts of the tryst to a five-line poem that he sends by courier to the woman's door while she sleeps. Thereafter, she pines away in poem and life, with only her memories. However, it would be wrong to think of the tanka only in this, perhaps more exciting, aspect.

People also turned to writing tanka when they were deeply touched by other emotions. The gamut of feelings could extend from seeing the leaves turn in autumn to the deep grief from the tragic loss of a loved one.

Buddhism also added to the tanka literature, with the poems of solitude, poverty, and religious experiences written by monks, nuns, and priests.

With the mention of nuns, one must add the observation that, though it was the men who made the imperial anthologies, and therefore included a greater number of male-authored poems in them, tanka writing has most often made leaps in style and popularity in the hands of women writers.

Akiko Yosano and Machi Tawara are the examples in the past century. Men ran the "schools" and wrote the rules, but women burst the boundaries with the explosions of their feelings and became famous.

Perhaps one reason for this is the fact that Japanese literature has historically been one of the few avenues open to women, in a strong patriarchy, to advance themselves socially and financially. Earlier, the highest position available to a woman of nonroyal family was to become a concubine of an emperor or some man in his court. For this, one had to be beautiful, educated, and able to write tanka. When the beauty faded and the education was forgotten, the tanka was there for these women to use to express their feelings and thereby gain distance from the vicissitudes of life.

It is possible to chart the changes in the popularity of Japan's various poetry forms and the achievements in the tanka through a study of the imperial anthologies, compiled according to a custom Japan borrowed from China and by which the emperor decreed that certain poets collect anthologies of poetry. The first Japanese anthology was the *Man'yōshū (Ten Thousand Leaves Collection)*, compiled by Otomo no Takamochi in A.D. 759 from poems written after A.D. 670.[11] It contains 4,173 tanka and 324 *chōka* (literally, "long songs").

In the next anthology, the abovementioned *Kokinshū* (A.D. 905), only nine of the included poems were not tanka. There were twenty-one imperial collections made; the last one was compiled in 1439, by Emperor Hanazono. Many of the tanka in each of these anthologies were written by members of the royal family or their surrounding courts.

The fact that the emperor was not only a protector of the form but was also expected to be proficient in tanka writing continues in an unbroken line down to the present Emperor Akihito and Empress Michiko, who, when they were crown prince and princess, created a collection of their *waka* entitled *Tomoshibi.* The collection has been translated into English as *Light* by Marie Philomène and Masako Saito.[12]

Each year, shortly after New Year's Day, all the members of the royal family write a tanka on a subject chosen by the emperor. In an elaborate and ritualistic ceremony, the poems are chanted before a select group of government officials and guests. Commoners can participate in this ceremony only if their tanka have been selected by court-appointed judges to be included with the 10 chosen from the 40,000 entries. On this special day, each person whose tanka has been selected stands while his or her poem is intoned by a man on a team of professional readers. The poem is then recited in a liturgical manner, sounding much like a Gregorian chant, and finally it is sung as a melody. The event is a high state ceremony, a reporting to the gods of Japan, as it were, the innermost feelings of the peoples' hearts.

In Japan today there are over 1,000 active tanka clubs. Most of them have a periodical that publishes members' work and serves as a means of recruiting new members to their method and style of writing, as exemplified by their teacher-leader. Hatsue Kawamura is the editor of *The Tanka Journal,* the only one of these publications in English and Japanese. The schools fall into three main lineages that trace back to Realism (Masaoka Shiki), Romanticism (Akiko Yosano), and the Reizei School, which goes back to the Reizei Emperor, Genji's son.

In 1988, Machi Tawara, who had just

[11] Ian Hideo Levy, *The Ten Thousand Leaves: A Translation of the Man'yōshū, Japan's Premier Anthology of Classical Poetry* (Princeton: Princeton University Press, 1981).

[12] Emperor Akihito and Empress Michiko, *Tomoshibi: Light,* trans. Marie Philomène and Masako Saito (New York: Weatherhill, 1991).

begun to teach school after completing her college studies, had a book of her tanka published as *Sarada Kinenbi (Salad Anniversary)*. Tawara's fresh use of language (instead of reusing acceptable "classical poetical phrases" of the beauties of nature and confessions of emotion), her ability to speak directly and yet shyly of her own "swayings of the heart," rocketed this first book to fame, with sales of over eight million copies in Japanese alone. Two versions exist in English translation.[13]

Tawara's success has reawakened interest in writing tanka in Japan and propelled this interest around the world. Renewed interest in the poetry written by another woman, Murasaki Shikibu, in her famous masterpiece *The Tale of Genji*, encourages, a millennium after its composition, new English readers to explore the tanka in this great Japanese classic.

[13] Machi Tawara, *Salad Anniversary*, trans. Juliet Winters Carpenter (Tokyo: Kodansha International, 1990) and trans. Jack Stamm (Tokyo: Kawade Bunko, 1990). Of the two versions, only Stamm treats the poems as tanka.

HUNT

OTHER TITLES IN THE ROCK SPRING COLLECTION OF JAPANESE LITERATURE

Hojoki: Visions of a Torn World by Kamo-no-Chomei

Basho's Narrow Road: Spring and Autumn Passages by Matsuo Basho

Milky Way Railroad by Kenji Miyazawa

The Name of the Flower by Kuniko Mukoda

Life in the Cul-de-Sac by Senji Kuroi

Evening Clouds by Junzo Shono

Still Life and Other Stories by Junzo Shono

Ravine and Other Stories by Yoshikichi Furui

Naked by Shuntaro Tanikawa

The Cape and Other Stories from the Japanese Ghetto by Kenji Nakagami

Death March on Mount Hakkoda by Jiro Nitta

Wind and Stone by Masaaki Tachihara

Right under the big sky, I don't wear a hat by Hosai Ozaki

CONTEMPORARY JAPANESE WOMEN'S POETRY
A Long Rainy Season: Haiku and Tanka
Other Side River: Free Verse
edited by Leza Lowitz, Miyuki Aoyama, and Akemi Tomioka

STONE BRIDGE PRESS, P.O. BOX 8208, BERKELEY, CA 94707
To comment on this book or to receive a free catalogue of other books about Japan and Japanese culture, contact Stone Bridge Press at sbp@stonebridge.com / 1-800-947-7271 / www.stonebridge.com.